The Schools
and Socialization

W9-BSZ-791

"Critical Issues in Education"
Under the Advisory Editorship of Louis Fisher

The Schools and Socialization

Audrey James Schwartz

University of Southern California

BRIAR CLIFF COLLEGE
LIBRARY
SIOUX CITY, IOWA

Harper & Row, Publishers
New York, Evanston, San Francisco, London

Sponsoring Editor: Michael E. Brown
Project Editor: Eleanor Castellano
Designer: June Negrycz
Production Supervisor: Will C. Jomarrón

THE SCHOOLS AND SOCIALIZATION
Copyright © 1975 **by Audrey James Schwartz**

Printed in the United States of America.
All rights reserved. No part of this book
may be used or reproduced in any manner
whatsoever without written permission
except in the case of brief quotations
embodied in critical articles and reviews.
For information address Harper & Row,
Publishers, Inc., 10 East 53rd Street,
New York, N.Y. 10022.

Library of Congress
Cataloging in Publication Data
Schwartz, Audrey James.
    The schools and socialization.

    (Critical issues in education)
    Bibliography: p.
    Includes index.
    1. Educational sociology.   I. Title.
LC191.S28   301.5'6   74-14104
ISBN 0-06-045823-2

LC
191
.S28

To Sylvia James

76590

Contents

Editor's introduction

In a diverse, pluralistic culture the institutions, policies, and practices of education will be influenced by the major disagreements of the times. Education in America, a diverse nation searching to define its brand of pluralism, most certainly reflects the major conflicts of the culture.

The dominant tradition of our past attempted to keep the public schools above or away from the controversies of the times and attempted to transmit a common core of learnings. Those tranquil days are gone, perhaps forever. Today, consistent with John Gardner's phrase that "education is the servant of all our purposes," various interest groups attempt to influence and even control public education. Such groups represent political and economic diversities; racial, ethnic, and religious preferences; business interests, conservationists, internationalists, isolationists; proponents of women's liberation, sex education, and sensitivity training, to name but the best-known voices. In addition to these influences from the culture at large, developments more indigenous to schooling must also be considered. Among these are the various forces urging innovation, accountability, professionalism for teachers, and community control. They are also concerned with combating institutional racism and sexism, violence in the schools, and the civil rights of teachers and students.

Teachers must become informed about these issues and

conflicts if they are to function as professionals. Toward this end, a beginning must be made in teacher education programs and continued into a teacher's maturing years. The titles in this series were conceived with such a goal in mind. Each volume can stand on its own, yet the several volumes are easily relatable. This arrangement maximizes flexibility for professors who may select one or more volumes, while the student's budget is also respected.

The authors were selected on the basis of their competence as well as their ability to write for an audience of nonspecialists, be they teachers, or others interested in the dominant issues in our culture that influence the schools.

Louis Fischer
Amherst, Massachusetts

Preface

In recent years Americans have become sensitized to discrepancies in the kind of socialization that is available to school children—even to those enrolled in the same school. Many people view these differences as a denial of equal educational opportunity. At the same time, Americans have taken increased notice of differences in the socialization that children receive at home and of the fact that some families continue to cling to norms and values of their foreign-born forebears. Awareness of the persistence of family culture has brought the once accepted melting-pot model of cultural homogeneity into question and is responsible for a growing acceptance of the notion of cultural pluralism that gives legitimacy to cultural diversity. Contemporary issues such as these are best understood in light of what it is that American schools are trying to do, what they in fact do, and the relationship between children's in-school behavior and their nonschool socialization.

This book provides an introduction to the functions of schooling and deals extensively with questions about the socialization of children in schools, families, and elsewhere. It attempts to increase the reader's knowledge of social processes that are critical to molding children into adults so that topics, such as equal educational opportunity and cultural pluralism, can be examined from a sociological perspective. No assumptions have been made about the reader's prior training or experience in either sociology or education. This book will be useful to many audiences, including students in social science and professional courses and wherever a general knowledge of what schools do is required.

Like all authors who wish to acknowledge the influence of others, I can only scratch the surface. Louis Fischer of the University of Massachusetts, Amherst, conceived the idea of the Critical Issues in Education series and invited me to participate in it. I am grateful for his confidence, encouragement, and patience. I owe a large, intellectual debt to my teacher, C. Wayne Gordon of the University of California, Los Angeles, who introduced me to many complexities of social life. I owe a similar debt to Robert Wenkert of the University of California, Berkeley, who undertook the arduous task of reading an early draft of this book and whose thoughtful criticisms brought substantial improvements. Finally, to my husband, Murray L. Schwartz, my thanks. Without his judicious blend of positive and negative reinforcements this project might yet to be completed.

Audrey James Schwartz

Introduction

Historically, American schools have served two separate but interdependent functions. One has been to provide continuity between generations by preparing children to carry out the social roles that are traditionally performed by adults. The other has been to furnish for at least some children the opportunity to participate in the larger society in rewarding ways. These functions are obviously interrelated. The development of individuals who can perform personally significant social roles with competence correspondingly provides society with the human resources it must have in order to endure. The quality of any society—the extent to which it deals constructively with the challenges that face it and the kinds of social bonds that hold it together—is, in essence, determined largely by the preparation it provides its children for adult life.

Formal responsibility for this preparation rests primarily with schools, even though deliberate educational programs are but a part of what goes into total social development. More important than formal curricula are the schools' informal or "hidden" curricula that emerge out of the social interaction of the people who inhabit them. Of greater importance than either of these are children's experiences at home; within their families they acquire perspectives about themselves and the world around them which influence in some way most of what they do in later years.

A major, contemporary concern in the United States is to provide formal education that will give all children, regardless of their family background, equal access to meaningful and rewarding social roles. In spite of the American folklore that desirable positions are equally available to everyone, most people still end up in a relative social position close to that of their parents. The fact that there is not total equality of opportunity in American society is due to a number of complex factors. Among the most significant are the differential access that children have to high-quality education, the varying experiences that family life provides, and the prejudicial treatment often received by people from low-income and racial or ethnic minority groups. These factors intertwine and, in combination, enhance or inhibit children's subsequent opportunities. Even if, contrary to current practice, every adult social position were to be filled solely on the basis of a person's capacity to carry out its obligations, some people would have advantages originating in childhood experiences that give them more "life chances" than others.

This book treats the social antecedents of adult life. Concerned primarily with the socialization of children, it examines how children acquire the social patterns of the groups to which they belong and what the content of these patterns actually is. It is hoped that this material will help the reader come to grips with some pressing educational issues that must be faced if equal opportunity is to be more than social and political ideology. Although educational policies in the United States are increasingly informed by the ethic of social mobility, these policies must be embedded in theoretical and empirical knowledge if they are to be effective. Specifically, it is necessary to know:

1. what socialization most adults must have in common in order to maintain a society.
2. what socialization gives each person maximum opportunity to participate in and contribute to that society, and
3. how such socialization can be accomplished in a way that insures that individual and group differences will be respected and developed.

In the first chapter socialization is approached from the perspective of the larger American society. The part that this process plays in maintaining social order and preparing individuals to fill existing social positions is described, and some of the values and behaviors that must be transmitted if the society is to continue along its present course are discussed. Schools and families jointly socialize children to adult roles. Schools are most concerned with roles relating to work and public life. Families and other nonschool groups are concerned with family and friendship roles. While in an ideal situation school socialization would build upon initial and concurrent experiences provided by the home, these experiences are in reality often at variance in actual life. Some of the most intractable educational problems originate in disaccord between the expectations of home and school. For example, educational objectives that seem easily attainable for most middle-class white children often are never accomplished by children from low-income and racial-minority groups.

In the second chapter, socialization is treated from the perspective of the individual. This section stresses the fact that people can neither develop as social beings nor participate effectively in a society unless they are socialized to do so. Without socialization, many distinctly human characteristics, including a concept of self, a capacity for human empathy, and the acquisition of a culture never emerge. Although much has been written about inherent conflicts between individuals and society, these conflicts are not inevitable. Most people whose socialization is consistent with generally accepted patterns comply voluntarily with the demands their society makes upon them. The socialization process is also described from the theoretical perspective of symbolic interactionism. This assumes that people's reactions toward all things are based on the meanings that these things have for them. It also assumes that these meanings are derived from social experience.

The family, which is the most significant group for almost every person in the determination of social meaning, is discussed in Chapter 3. Family patterns provide the content to which children are initially socialized and, in addition, they restrict and direct later socialization. Although each person is unique in many respects, knowledge of early life often yields useful insights into personal behavior. Of the many differences found among American families, those deriving from socioeconomic status go a long way in accounting for the behavior of children in school. For example, many youngsters who grow up in a so-called culture of poverty have not been prepared to meet their teachers' expectations and, as a consequence, do not attain educational goals as readily as do their classmates. Racial and ethnic background are also related to school socialization because variant language and cultural patterns often hinder in-school participation and because children from minority groups are frequently treated differently from other children.

Popular attitudes toward those whose culture differs from the dominant American culture have undergone considerable change during this century. Initially it was anticipated that people would relinquish their ancestral heritage and become Americanized by adopting widespread Anglo-Saxon patterns. Common school practices were expected to foster assimilation. This orientation was replaced in the public mind by the notion of a melting pot which holds that variant cultures would eventually fuse into one homogeneous culture reflecting the best of each. However, neither of these expectations have been totally realized, as can be seen by growing racial and ethnic pride among many separate groups. At present, a third orientation, that of cultural pluralism, is rapidly gaining acceptance. Cultural pluralism implies that people can retain their unique cultural patterns if they so desire as long as these patterns are not socially divisive. Accordingly, efforts are now underway to introduce multi-cultural educational programs into public schools so that children will learn to respect differences among the various groups that make up the American society. As cultural pluralism becomes more widely accepted, prejudice against those who are different should be reduced, thereby extending opportunities to many minority people who have historically suffered from discrimination.

The remaining chapters essentially deal with schools and with the people who work and occasionally play in them. American public schools are usually structured as bureaucracies: they have an established set of formal positions and a series of formal rules prescribing how the people who occupy these positions are expected to behave. This formal structure creates only a part of a school's educational environment, however, because individuals are vastly different and often interpret and implement rules in dissimilar ways. Each school, therefore, has a unique social system created out of the blend of pupils, educators, and supporting staff who happen to be assigned to it. The educational environment created by this social system can support, neutralize, or even subvert educational objectives and goals.

The prime, formal socializing agents within schools are teachers, since they are the only personnel in continuous contact with pupils. Teachers are given responsibility for transmitting to their pupils knowledge of the dominant culture and for developing literacy and computational skills. In addition, they are expected to stimulate their students' intellectual curiosity and sense of aesthetics and to foster both their capacity to solve problems creatively and their ability for self-socialization. One cannot assume that all pupils are both competent and motivated to acquire these skills, knowledge, and attitudes: some children have not been able to overcome initial, educational handicaps and others just do not like school. Laws compelling compulsory attendance have, in fact, kept many children in school long after they have left it psychologically.

Classmates also have an impact on the socialization of individual pupils. Their influence is felt as early as first grade and expands as children become increasingly independent of adults. By secondary school, classmates and other friends often rival parents and teachers in importance. Peers are especially significant during adolescence when they provide the social norms and valued emotional support that help clarify the ambiguities that arise out of the transition from child to adult status. Adults sometimes complain that peer norms limit the extent to which adolescents comply with their expectations; nevertheless, peer groups are functional to the extent that they protect pupils against the harmful effects of excessive competition and assist them in developing autonomy from parental control.

Peer groups become so personally meaningful to many adolescents that they conform to most peer-group expectations merely so that they can belong. Intergenerational conflict between parents and children, and occasionally between teachers and pupils, is frequently attributable to fear of rejection by one's peers. Even though the drive for independence by teenage children presents obvious sources of family strain, much overt disagreement is explained by the fact that children are less certain of peer than of parental support. In case of competing demands, they often bow to peer pressures because they know that in the final analysis they can count on their parents.

The kind of socialization provided by peer groups differs, depending upon the special subculture that develops out of the background, interests, and abilities of its members. Some subcultures are antithetical to the attainment of educational goals and consequently incompatible with widely accepted adult patterns, whereas others support school achievement and subsequent success in the larger society. To the extent that peer-group norms are conducive to academic achievement, the school performance of below-average pupils usually increases. Indeed, the potentially positive influence of high-achieving classmates on the academic performance of their peers provides a major argument for socioeconomic and racial-ethnic school integration and against segregation of pupils according to their academic performance.

Universal, free education has been established and is supported in the United States for what is believed to be the collective good.

Schools have, in the main, prepared generations of children to participate in adult social life and to meet voluntarily many of the expectations that adult members of society have of them. In addition, schools have provided one of the few ways to prepare children to move up the occupational ladder and for some to ultimately pass the socioeconomic status of their parents. But schools have also served to lock other children into the relative social position of their birth. In the past, even though social origins have largely determined the chances one has as an adult, school socialization provides a transition between home and the larger society and consequently has the potential to mitigate many initial disadvantages.

That schools have not done more to equalize opportunities is due in large part to the fact that the quality of available schooling is often related to the pupils' home background: children from low-income families attend schools that provide them with fewer educational resources than do those attended by children from moderate-income families. As a result, their initial handicaps are compounded. It has been clearly demonstrated that quality schooling, quite apart from pupil background, can increase or decrease the opportunities that pupils will have eventually. School factors that are most related to school success and therefore to subsequent opportunity include who one's classmates happen to be, what tangible and intangible resources have been allocated to education (this includes the quality of the teaching staff), and the educational goals and objectives set for local schools.

The campaign for equality of opportunity through education has made considerable gains since the close of World War II. In 1954 the Supreme Court declared that deliberate segregation of children in school because of racial-ethnic origins is unconstitutional. Since then other courts have declared that some school segregation resulting from segregated living patterns is unconstitutional as well. Beginning with the Elementary and Secondary Educational Act of 1965, Congress has provided financial support for school programs designed to compensate children for educational disadvantages that derive from nonschool factors, such as home language. Litigation is also under way to ensure that the resources expended by public schools in each state will be allocated without regard to the wealth or poverty of local school districts. In addition, many colleges and universities now admit freshmen who do not meet their traditional scholastic entrance requirements and, when necessary, they provide these students with tutorials and financial aid.

Obviously, many more changes will have to take place in school and elsewhere before total equality of opportunity is reached. Nevertheless, the tenor of the times seems to indicate that people who are in a position to bring about change are increasingly willing to try. Given the diversity of the American population, the best way to accomplish equality remains an open question. However, it is clear that part of the solution lies in the kind of socialization that children receive for becoming adults.

1
Socialization and society

INSTITUTIONS FOR THE SOCIALIZATION OF THE YOUNG

This book is about the socialization of young Americans. It is concerned with how they acquire the ways of the social groups in which they now participate or will participate in the future, and with the content of what they acquire. Some socialization is deliberate: the mission of public schools, for instance, is to transmit formally to younger generations many of the dominant behavior and value patterns of the larger American society. Families also engage in deliberate socialization, albeit less formally than schools, when they instruct children in their own patterns. Parents, teachers, and other socializing agents purposely select the behaviors and values they assume are desirable and present them to members of the younger generation in order to shape the kind of people they will become and, in effect, to shape the kind of society they will maintain. Most socialization, however, is neither formal nor intentional: as people go about their usual activities within social groups, for the most part, socialization just happens. Through repeated contact with others in families, schools, neighborhoods, and elsewhere, children acquire and come to value many of the recurring behaviors they observe.

The content of socialization—whether formal or informal,

intentional or incidental—usually derives from the behaviors and values that are commonly expected of those who hold similar social positions. For example, the expectations of pupils in traditional public schools typically include prompt arrival to class, deference toward teachers, completion of assigned work, and the like. The expectations of parents include, among other things, giving children care, emotional support, and instruction in acceptable behavior. Socialization to social positions such as pupil and parent normally encompasses the behaviors and values that one must have in order to satisfy these common expectations.

Socialization, then, produces social patterns in that it provides both a body of expectations and ways to meet them that are more or less shared by other members of a social group. Shared expectations make it possible for people to predict within limits how others will behave and how others expect them to behave in return. From the point of view of individuals, socialization helps them to cope with the demands of their social groups by giving them the capacity to meet these demands. From the point of view of a group, socialization contributes to its stability and continued existence by transmitting established behavior and value patterns to its members.

Socialization begins shortly after birth, first within the family and then within increasingly complex social systems. It is a lifelong process: each group to which a person belongs and each social position a person holds provides some socialization. The emphasis in this book is on families and schools for several important reasons. First, socialization in childhood and adolescence significantly influences all subsequent socialization. Second, socialization is a prime function of both of these institutions. And third, most Americans spend a relatively large portion of their preadult years under their direct influence.

Schools are less significant in preindustrial societies where children learn from their parents and other relatives most of the things they need to know to participate in the adult social world.[1] Even occupational skills are often acquired through actual participation or apprenticeship to family members. In contrast, postindustrial societies, utilize new and specialized knowledge, have less homogeneous membership, and employ complex systems of social relations which are usually very different from those of families. Family socialization alone is seldom adequate in modern societies. Therefore they establish a separate social institution—the school—to prepare children for many aspects of adult life.

Basic school curricula contain the knowledge assumed to be needed by all members of a social group or society such as language skills, computational skills, and an understanding and appreciation of its culture. In addition, curricula include the special things individuals are supposed to know in order to carry out successfully the adult roles for which they appear to be destined.[2] As knowledge requirements for participation in a society become more complex, so do the curricula of its schools until, as in the United States, formal education often begins before age 6 and extends through 12 years of elementary and secondary schools, 4 years of college, and occasionally into years of graduate study.

The major responsibility for socialization in the United States rests first with families, then with families and schools together, and, at advanced educational levels, with schools alone. Ideally schools build upon initial and concurrent experiences in the home by reinforcing and extending them until children attain some expected level of competence. In reality, this ideal relationship is more the case for middle-class children than for others, inasmuch as the dominant culture of American public schools is largely received from the middle classes. A chronic concern of public schools has been how to both socialize all children to some universal patterns while, at the same time, respecting subcultural differences and providing curricula that interest and motivate the entire student body.

The content of family and school socialization is partly what the adults in these institutions intend to transmit and partly something quite different. Much socialization comes about from the unintended or *latent* consequences of deliberate socialization activities and of other activities which occur within the boundaries of socializing institutions. For example, small informal groups such as teenage cliques or pairs of siblings typically develop within schools and families, each with some distinctive values and behaviors that become potent sources of socialization in themselves. Stated otherwise, both formal and informal processes for deliberately transmitting social patterns have unexpected socialization effects. In fact many social changes that have not been planned come about in large part as by-products of intentional socialization.

The principal theme of this chapter is the *content* of socialization —both intentional and unintentional—that occurs within the social institutions of the family and the school.

THE NEEDS OF A SOCIETY

Although this discussion is largely concerned with the United States, there are basic similarities in the problems that all societies and social groups encounter in ensuring their survival. Each society, for example, must adapt to external social and nonsocial environments, such as foreign powers and natural elements. It must allocate existing manpower to its work force and allot other scarce resources, such as food and clothing, to its various members. It must integrate social behavior so that work is coordinated and destructive conflict is prevented by cooperative effort. Finally, it must provide for its own continuation by transmitting established cultural and social patterns.[3] Above all other concerns, each society must deal with the fact that all humans are mortal: unless provision is made for the preparation of children to assume the social positions of their elders, the society and its culture will not endure beyond its present generation of adults.

Thus every ongoing society socializes younger generations to its cultural heritage. The content and method of socialization differ depending upon the knowledge available to a society, the values its members hold and the behaviors they expect, and the will of those who have the greatest social influence. The emphasis that is placed on intact transmission of culture relative to that placed on provisions for social change also differs. However, regardless of the unique characteristics of a society, its degree of modernization, and its rate of social change, the basic socialization problem is always the same—to assure its preservation.

The transmission of general social values

A persistent problem in social theory relates to the phenomenon of *social order*. Why is it that since earliest times men and women have been reported to behave in regular, expected ways—working, mating, rearing children, and respecting authority?[4] This is the so-called Hobbesian question after Thomas Hobbes, the English philosopher, who asked what it was that prevented humans from engaging in a "war of all against all."[5] The question searches for an explanation of how social order is possible.

The earliest explanations of social order had to do with divine creation and the relationship between man and supernatural forces. The Old Testament, for instance, contains laws governing interpersonal relations that presumably have the force of God behind them. More recent explanations emphasize the relationships among men. They usually include one or more of the following social phenomena:

1. Power is used by stronger members of the group to force weaker members to comply with their preferences.
2. A social contract is voluntarily entered into by most members of the group, each of whom willingly relinquishes some personal freedom out of enlightened self-interest and promise of personal reward.
3. A core of values is held in common by most members of the group which guide and control their behaviors.

The last explanation, involving value consensus, points up the relationship between socialization to the patterns of a group and the maintenance of its social order. When people voluntarily engage in expected behaviors not because of rewards and punishments but because they feel that these behaviors are intrinsically good, social order is easily accomplished.

The value consensus theory of social order. This theory holds that every group has a core of relatively stable values on which there is general correspondence. This does not mean that all members hold identical values, but that there is tacit agreement on basic premises. According to the consensus explanation, people assume that others will judge events by the same criteria that they do and that all group members will mold their behavior to be consistent with these criteria. People then shape their own actions to conform with the actions they expect of others. In this way, shared expectations develop which support the fundamental patterns of the group.

Because consensus provides some predictability about social behavior, it substantially reduces the need for constant communication concerning what people should or should not do. It also lessens the need for other forms of social control. Even if the value consensus answer to the Hobbesian question is only partly tenable, every group has some collectively agreed upon, or "institutionalized," values and most group members assume that people shape their behavior to be consistent with them.[6] Further, when either coercion or enlightened self-interest are the chief mechanisms for maintaining social order, there is usually a residue of compliance brought about because people value the behaviors in which they engage.

A distinction should be made between knowing the content of social values and *internalizing* them. To know a value is a purely intellectual process: it is the cognition or knowledge of what the family, society, or some other group holds desirable. To internalize a value is both a cognitive and an emotional, or "affective," process: it is the development of the personal conviction that these standards are inherently good, or are at least to be taken for granted so that they form the basis of one's own behavior. This distinction can usually be illustrated by the behavior of students during an unproctored traditional examination: although all students know the value "honesty," only those who have not internalized it will take practical advantage of the opportunity to refer back to books and notes.

The notion of value consensus does not require that social values be internalized by everyone in a group, only that these values guide the behavior of a substantial number. The extent to which the maintenance of social order depends on the internalization rather than the mere knowledge of values depends on the availability of other forms of social control. In rural areas and small towns, for example, where there is usually a cadre of friends, neighbors, and family to stand guard, it is not as necessary for every individual to value correct behavior as it would be in large urban areas where people are relatively isolated from close interpersonal relationships.

Most groups tolerate behaviors from some of their members which deviate from institutionalized values. Consider, for instance, those who are physically ill, very young or very old, or who are experiencing personal misfortune or bereavement: none are held responsible for social transgressions unless they inflict grave harm on others. Variations by entire groups are also permitted under certain circumstances such as holidays like Mardi Gras, and at times of extreme physical danger such as earthquake, fire, and flood. General social order is not possible, however, unless a large portion of the population customarily behaves in predictable ways.

A major socialization task, then, is to transmit group values and to build personal commitments to them. Socialization in schools, at least in their formal aspects, is concerned primarily with transmitting values upon which there is broad consensus, while socialization in the home is concerned more with transmitting important family values. Family values, such as preferred modes of expression and interpersonal relations, are learned through direct contact with other family members who have internalized them and whose behavior is consistent with them. The home provides optimum conditions for socialization in that family members interact with great frequency and have many opportunities to observe and influence one another. Also, the strong emotional component in family relationships gives potent sanctioning power to the responses of each to the other. In spite of the occasional family black sheep whose values differ radically from other relatives, in the main, home socialization is highly effective; most of the personal values held by adults derive from their early experiences within family settings.

Transmission of societal values is often an expressed objective of schools. For instance the Educational Policies Commission of the National Education Association specified in 1918 that one of the goals of public education is to help students "develop an appreciation of the ethical values which should undergird all life in a democracy."[7] Similarly, the White House Conference on Education in 1955 concluded that schools should develop in the student "appreciation for our democratic heritage" and "ethical behavior based on a sense of moral and spiritual values."[8] For this reason many Americans advocate that *all* children, regardless of family background and culture, attend common public schools and share in common socialization experiences. In this connection Katz has recently argued that the overarching concern of many people who pushed for the expansion of public education was to gain control of the behavior of poor and immigrant children through socialization. They saw schools as leading rather than reflecting the general will and basically hoped for an increased "standardization of institutions, practices, and culture in American society."[9] In the United States, as in other nations, pressure for the universal socialization of children increases as the society becomes more heterogeneous.

Given that schools are expected to transmit generally held values, the problem of the content of value socialization remains, for values cannot be deliberately transmitted unless they are known to socializing agents. What are the consensual values that should be passed to rising generations of Americans? What is it that schools should attempt to teach? School curricula usually incorporate those values that have been made *explicit* in official documents, creeds, and public expressions of principles. "Democracy," "equality," and "government of laws, not men" are examples of agreed-upon premises and, as such, they appear repeatedly in history and civics courses.

Some of these values are reflected in texts: one well-regarded American history book, for example, conveys traditional American values when it describes the typical mid-nineteenth century person as one who admired people who were inventive, ingenious, and practical; who believed in progress and in the obligation of mankind to be humanitarian; and who was convinced that his nation stood out among all the other nations of the earth and had the responsibility to be an example to the world.[10] Values are also structured into school activities so that pupils experience them in operation: the value, "government of laws," for example, is sometimes incorporated into student-body government where the first order of business is to decide upon rules of procedure.

There are other collectively held values that have not been made explicit and are not, therefore, formally stated in school curricula. Nonetheless they are held by many members of society and are transmitted without special tutoring. Unarticulated values are manifested, for example, through favorable attitudes shown toward children who conform to the traditionally expected behaviors of their sex. Additional social rewards are given to people with physical beauty, athletic prowess, sex appeal, and economic success. These values seem to be caught more than taught.

The values that have been made explicit are those about which high levels of agreement are assumed. Indeed part of the value consensus in American society is to avoid ideological controversy. Rather than articulate disputed—and potentially disruptive—values that could become rallying points for dissent, these values remain implicit. A prime concern of the "new left" student movement in the late 1960s', for instance, was the apparent contradictions among common social values, particularly those relating to constitutionally protected civil rights. The young people's awareness that explicit value premises, such as "government of laws, not men," are not always honored stimulated overt conflict directed at bringing official behavior into line with values that are deliberately taught. As a result of efforts to reduce discrepancies of this kind by force, many universities suffered serious tangible and other damage. Whether these conflicts led to changes in governance is questionable, at best.

Conflict per se is not necessarily bad and need not be destructive. However, from the standpoint of an ongoing society, conflict must in some way be limited through public forums and the like if the underlying causes of conflict are to be communicated and destruction is to be avoided. From that standpoint, conflict can be useful for identifying and clarifying incongruities in basic values and in recognizing accepted behaviors which are inconsistent with them. Social groups often make provision for controlled expression of disagreement, since stifled discontent leads to unrestrained hostility and is potentially disruptive.[11]

Fundamental values of American society. There have been many attempts to identify the fundamental values of American society. Perhaps because it is assumed that foreign spectators can be the most objective, their observations are often cited. Of these, de Tocqueville in the nineteenth century and Myrdal in the twentieth are probably the most authoritative.[12] Domestic observers include journalists, philosophers, social scientists, and others too numerous to list, with methods ranging from armchair speculation to rigorous empirical study. However, despite the large number of commentators on American values, there is noticeable agreement among them. Basic values are usually thought to include: rationalism, impersonal justice, universal ethics, achievement, democracy, equality, freedom, respect for the individual, wealth, power, work, and efficiency.[13]

Some observers report that American society has undergone value changes in recent years which entail a gradual shift from emphasis on personal achievement to emphasis on interpersonal relations. Riesman's formulation of *inner-directed* and *other-directed* orientations describe this notion. According to Riesman, inner-directed people are driven to continually test their own ability through "experiments in self-mastery," whereas other-directed people believe that "making good becomes almost equivalent to making friends."[14]

If Riesman's assumption that there has been a notable increase in other-directedness is correct, this change may reflect a mode of interpersonal relations that is appropriate to postindustrial society, rather than a basic modification in underlying social values. Characteristically, technological societies emphasize social and geographic mobility at the expense of immediate and extended families: their interpersonal orientations are therefore often those that are conducive to the ready development of new friends. Moreover, high levels of interpersonal skills are sometimes necessary to help people balance the many relationships that modernization forces upon them.

Preparing individuals to fill adult social roles

The building blocks of every social group are its sets of statuses and roles. While closely related, the terms *status* and *role* have somewhat different meanings: status properly signifies a social position without reference to the behavior it entails; role, on the other hand, refers to the dynamic aspects of status, to the behavioral expectations that all persons who hold similar social positions are expected to meet. The social positions of parent, teacher, and pupil are examples of social statuses; what the people who hold these statuses do are their social roles. A status automatically conveys certain rights, privileges, and rewards to the people who hold it. Thus, one sometimes refers to higher or lower social status. A role assigns to people of a given status the obligation to behave in a particular way.

In addition to assigning obligations, a role prohibits some behaviors and allows for, but does not demand, others. Many of the
variations in the behaviors of people who hold the same status arise
because some activities are permitted but not required. A role, then,
is a collection of *prescribed*, *proscribed*, and *permitted* behaviors associated with a social position or status. The status of school principal, for example, contains the expectations that, among other things,
principals take administrative responsibility for their schools, refrain
from criticizing their faculties publicly, and have the option of assist-
ing teachers with specific educational problems within the classroom.

Each person holds statuses in different social groups and is, therefore, required to learn the content of many social roles. The more
complex the society, the more roles people usually have to know, and
consequently, the more elaborate their socialization. Some common
statuses like friend, relative, and citizen, are held by almost all members of a society. Others, like infant, adolescent, and senior citizen,
are assigned to all people of a particular age group. Still others, like
daughter-wife-mother and son-husband-father, are held by most people of a given sex sometime during their lives. Socialization to common roles is usually informal and often takes place while people are
holding these social positions.

Occupational roles. There are also less commonly held statuses
that are assigned to people because of what they have already accomplished or what it is assumed they will be able to accomplish in
the future. High-ranking statuses relating to work, for example, are
often available only to those who have had some special training or
who demonstrate particular abilities. This is especially so in tech-
nologically advanced societies that have extensive divisions of labor
and require highly developed skills to perform many of their occupations.

Equality, achievement, and universalism, noted earlier as some
collectively held American values, imply that the qualifications for
gaining high-level occupations are related to a person's ability to
behave in the manner that these positions require and, further, that
people can attain a desired available vocational status if they have
the capacity and commitment to carry out its duties. There are miti-
gating social factors that limit occupational opportunity, to be sure,
particularly those related to discrimination in employment and access
to education. Nonetheless, allocation to occupations in the United
States, as in other postindustrial societies, tends to be more on the
basis of ability to perform than on extraneous social characteristics.

Wealth, social contacts, and high social prestige are often assets in matching a person with a desired occupation. However, without some academic preparation, accident of birth is not usually a sufficient qualification for high-level employment.

Formal educational institutions are largely responsible for the initial preparation of the semiskilled and skilled American labor force. Along with technical job training, schools ideally provide some systematic socialization, such as knowledge of widely held values, acceptable interpersonal behaviors, and adequate communication skills. They also provide additional socialization to those who will hold more demanding statuses. The assumption that education is necessary for a skilled labor force did as much for the adoption of compulsory school attendance laws and the expansion of secondary education as did the assumption that immigrants must be Americanized. Many of the early twentieth century advocates of increased education argued that compulsory schooling was needed to supply the labor for growing industrialization.

The amount and kind of education people receive is closely related to their future occupations. Those who have had prolonged and difficult schooling usually attain elite statuses that are highly rewarded in terms of wealth and social prestige; those who drop out are often stigmatized and disadvantaged in obtaining a job. Occupants of elite statuses sometimes carry much of the responsibility for the well-being of other people. For example, graduates of professional schools are usually allocated to positions in which they make critical decisions relating to some of society's most basic problems; medical doctors treat problems of individual and group health, lawyers are concerned with the management of social conflict, and educators determine how best to prepare young people to become social replacements. Many occupations are currently experiencing educational upgrading and some positions, most notably those in scientific research, require equivalent or even greater educational preparation than traditional professions. It is probably accurate to say that few influential occupations, whether or not they are viewed as professions, are available to people who have not had lengthy training.

The United States has in fact developed a *credentialed society* in which many occupations are open only to those who are formally certified by educational institutions to have completed some specific course of study—this despite the fact that certification sometimes refers more to the length of exposure in a particular educational institution than to the demonstration of competence. Credentialism implies that completion of a specified amount of schooling is relevant to subsequent work performance. Employers often require their workers, except those at the lowest levels, to hold at least a high school diploma even if workers are taught essential skills on the job. This suggests that completion of secondary school in itself is viewed by many as an indication of some level of motivation and of a particular kind of social and intellectual exposure.

Credentialism also has its critics who take exception to many of the educational requirements that have been built into hiring practices. They argue that credentials are often unrelated to subsequent work and that demand for certificated employees creates an artificial barrier between people with less education and the jobs they are competent to perform. Some critics have pointed out that since the amount and kind of education people receive are often related to the social status of their parents, seemingly unrelated employment requirements have been used to select workers from a particular social background without giving the appearance of prejudicial hiring.[15]

The claim that secondary schools do not socialize youngsters directly to occupational roles appears to be supported by commonly stated educational objectives. However, when one takes into account incidental learning within the broad school social environment, the part schools play in preparing people for occupational roles becomes clearer. The most important factor to consider is the opportunity that informal relationships among students provide for learning values and behaviors that are widely accepted throughout the society. Regardless of whether or not these patterns are internalized, interaction with peers whose behavior conforms with them gives pupils the opportunity to know their content. It is not the formal curriculum alone, then, that gives meaning to the high school diploma. Rather it is the combined formal and informal socialization experiences of school. Some employers assume that high school completion indicates knowledge of generally accepted patterns, a factor which they believe is related to a person's ability to perform certain kinds of jobs.

Similarly, baccalaureate degrees from predominantly upper-middle-class and upper-class colleges often signify that people are "cultivated" more than that they are experts—that they know the value and behavior patterns of the elite. For example, the graduates of Ivy League schools, regardless of their social origins, are somewhat familiar with the styles of dress, manners, speech, and recreation associated with the upper classes. Knowledge of these patterns is sometimes believed to be as important to the performance of occupational roles as the information and skills contained in formal role definitions. Entrance into prestigious institutions is granted in greater proportion to children from higher-status families than to those from families with lower status, but those from poorer homes who do gain admission have substantially increased life chances. When it comes to subsequent employment opportunities, a baccalaureate from these institutions often neutralizes the disadvantages as well as advantages stemming from home background.

Acquisition of norms and values that govern social roles. The prescribed, proscribed, and permitted behaviors of social roles constitute the *norms* of a society. Norms are social rules or principles of conduct that regulate behavior and provide socially approved ways for people to satisfy their own social and biological needs. Norms and values both refer to standards, but they are not the same: values are general conceptions of what is desirable, whereas norms are standardized ways of acting. They are related because values supply legitimacy to the behaviors contained in norms and are the criteria by which norms are judged.[16] One widely accepted norm in American society is that every normal child past age six or seven attends school. A common social value that often underlies this norm is that equality of educational opportunity is inherently good.

Norms, like values, introduce order into social life. Without some commonly agreed upon norms there would be widespread confusion and conflict over appropriate behavior. For example, norms tell how one ought to behave in church, in school, in the public library, in the courtroom, at family gatherings, and so on. As people learn the norms of their own social roles, they learn many of the norms which govern the social roles with which they come into contact. In this way, they can anticipate what others expect of them and know how they are expected to behave in return.

Because of this reciprocal relationship between roles, they are usually learned in pairs, and people often know the content of some of their future roles long before they occupy them. For instance, during the period that children learn the role of child within the family setting, they also learn the roles of other family members, such as spouse and parent that they themselves will probably fill at a later time. In fact, childhood socialization within the family is one of the few sources of socialization to these adult family roles. Socialization to a role before a person is ready to occupy it is called *anticipatory socialization*.[17] People will usually modify their early understandings of roles once they fill them, but anticipatory socialization provides them with their initial expectations.

A person's first knowledge of the norms and values of many non-family roles is often obtained in school, since, in postindustrial societies many roles relating to work and public life can seldom be learned within the family. The norms and values governing these roles are not only different from those governing family life, many actually conflict with them. Even if this were not so, children do not always hold the same cluster of adult roles as do their parents, and the pace of social change makes much of what their parents teach them obsolete by the time they are mature.

Just as families provide socialization to the role of child in the family and anticipatory socialization to the roles of adult family members, schools provide socialization to the role of pupil and anticipatory socialization to many nonfamily adult roles. Socialization in early school years is directed chiefly at the acquisition of the pupil role, whereas socialization in secondary and higher levels is geared toward the acquisition of adult roles. Indeed, many young people become impatient with the extent to which schools provide anticipatory socialization, an impatience that is sometimes reflected in cries for curriculum "relevance." Rather than have schools focus on things they will need to know to meet future expectations, pupils often prefer to learn that which will help them carry out currently meaningful roles.

Without regard to the content of courses, the formal arrangements of schools facilitate the acquisition of the norms and values of adult roles. Rules regulating attendance, authority relationships, and a system of sanctions and rewards based on achievement transmit behavioral expectations that are often involved in occupational and other public roles. Equally important is the social interaction among pupils, since school situations present, usually for the first time, large cohorts of peers of roughly the same age and grade level. Peer groups provide the opportunity for individuals of relatively equal status to learn to develop patterns for mutual cooperation and for the control of conflict that might arise among them.[18]

Schools are often the only institution in which children systematically learn about the negative consequences of behaviors which deviate from social expectations. By the time they complete primary grades, they have been exposed to most of the norms incorporated in the pupil role and have usually acquired these norms as part of their own behaviors. Schools typically have little tolerance for deviancy in the performance of the pupil role, probably because that role contains norms that are assumed to facilitate learning and to be the best way to manage large numbers of pupils. Elementary schools often stress proper role performance above all else, including the acquisition of information and skills.[19] Teachers and other school adults carefully note and usually punish behavioral transgressions. In this way pupils learn both the norms governing their role and their obligations to conform with them. They also learn how and when they can get around these norms without being caught or punished.

Children learn something about adult roles in the school in the same manner that they learn about adult family roles in the home. As they acquire the behavior of pupil, they become familiar with the reciprocal roles of teacher, principal, custodian, school nurse, and so on. The fact that so many teachers tend to teach as they were taught can often be traced to the anticipatory socialization they received while interacting with their own teachers. Norms learned in childhood about teacher behavior are sometimes difficult to modify, even when teachers know of more effective techniques. Anticipatory socialization to traditional educational practices is one major reason why school organizations resist large-scale changes. Perhaps the reason that many teachers are uncomfortable in team-teaching situations or in classrooms where they are expected to "individualize" instruction is that they find these expectations contrary to their early notion of teacher.

It was previously stated that a major concern of every society is the maintenance of its social order. Schools contribute to order by supplying children with the behaviors required in many established social roles. They do this by providing them with an arena in which to develop the ability to move easily from one role to another, learning in the process how to minimize personal strain and balance conflicting obligations. They also teach children that they are responsible for meeting the expectations of their social roles, even when the expectations contained in these roles conflict with one another. Nevertheless, many children do not conform to the behaviors of the established pupil role. When this is due to the fact that they are not aware of all its expectations or do not know which behaviors will meet these expectations, additional experience with the role or contact with others who know the role more thoroughly usually brings about the desired conformity.

Of greater concern are pupils who do not meet these expectations because they do not like the pupil role or because they like other conflicting roles better. Consensus is usually assumed to be the ideal way for bringing about expected school behavior, but when consensus is absent, school officials emphasize rewards and punishments.

Punishment orientations are so common in some schools that they take on the characteristics of "total institutions" such as prisons: pupils are locked in behind closed gates, they require passes to walk in hallways during class time, they are forcibly detained after school, and are occasionally paddled for infractions of rules. How to get all pupils to value the pupil role sufficiently so that they will conform to its expectations is clearly an unresolved educational problem.

Political socialization. Political socialization is the acquisition of values, norms, knowledge, and skills needed for the competent performance of political roles. Although these roles are part of the general complex of public roles, they deserve special attention because of their salience to a democratic form of government. Democracy implies first, that there is shared agreement on the type of political structure that is used to maintain social control, and second, that there is shared participation in arriving at political decisions. The importance of an educated electorate to the operation and preservation of democratic government has also been a common justification for universal, free education. Cremin notes that "to study the literature of the Progressive era is to be overwhelmed by the extent to which political reform is conceived essentially in educational terms."[20]

As early as 1779, Thomas Jefferson saw the necessity for developing an enlightened citizenry and political leadership through education. He proposed for his state of Virginia both a remarkably modern public school system which would rake the best geniuses "from the rubbish [sic]" and a university to train "a natural aristocracy" of talent regardless of social origins.[21] When the right to vote was extended to all white men during the Age of Jackson, opportunities for schooling were extended as well. Following the Civil War, when the vote was given to all men regardless of race and color, educational facilities in the South expanded to include newly enfranchised Negroes.

Contemporary pressures to provide equal educational opportunity from preschool to graduate school seem to parallel the removal of most of the remaining formal barriers to political participation. It should be noted, however, that current extensions of education are more often justified in terms of individual preparation for economic activity than of group preparation for political participation. According to Welter, a historian who has traced popular attitudes toward public education, Americans continue to place great faith in the power of schools to overcome the defects of their society, but they now view schools more as a means of providing individualistic educational competition than as a means for groups to obtain the rewards that economic competition used to provide. "To this extent, at least, they continue to identify democracy with education, and equal rights to education with social and economic democracy."[22]

Democratic societies require that their underlying philosophies be contained in the values and norms on which there is general agreement, and they typically rely upon public schools to transmit them. Since the more powerful cannot repeatedly force their will on the less powerful without developing alienation or estrangement, an important objective of political socialization in schools is to develop and preserve this consensus. Alienation, at best, is manifested in apathy and withdrawal from political participation; in its more virulent forms it leads to behavior that can destroy the political system. Recall, for example, the consequences of extreme alienation in the violent activities of the "Weathermen" faction of the Students for a Democratic Society, where young people engaged in the manufacture of bombs and other weapons of war in an effort to change the political process by force.

Certain values are commonly thought to be basic—although not unique—to the American political system. Some of these values are:

1. Patriotism. The society is good in its own right and should therefore be protected from internal and external conflict that could destroy it.
2. Belief in legitimacy of existing government. The government has exclusive authority to regulate the use of political force.
3. Democratic ideology. Most appropriate for the society are: (a) a political structure that provides opportunities for widespread adult participation and, (b) an opportunity structure that gives each person a fair and equal chance to compete for desirable social positions.
4. Belief in the legitimate authority of government employees. Officials earn positions through rational-legal processes and personal achievement, and citizens are expected to comply with their decisions.
5. Toleration of minority views. Individuals have the right to dissent from the general consensus of opinion.
6. Participation. Adults are expected to be psychologically involved and to take part in the political decision process.

Political socialization, like all socialization, takes place both in family and school settings. Basic values that underlie political goals seem to be learned primarily within the family, whereas norms, knowledge, and skills to pursue these goals tend to be acquired elsewhere. It has been found, for example, that political party affiliation is usually that of one's parents,[23] yet the amount of political participation is closely related to the extent to which a person participated in the activities of school and other nonfamily groups.[24] Whether people are politically conservative or radical and whether they tend toward authoritarian or democratic government have been traced to family socialization where children first encounter authority and decision-making structures and acquire general orientations toward man, society, and politics.[25]

Because young children learn so much within the family, it was once thought that early socialization was the only salient source of political orientation. However, more recent studies show that family influence wanes if individuals become members of other personally significant groups, such as friendship cliques and the families of spouses, which have values that conflict with those of their parents.[26] In general, the relative influence of the family on political values diminishes as other people and groups take on more significance. Political values emerge, then, from the cumulative experiences—both political and nonpolitical, spontaneous and formally structured—of early childhood, adolescence, and adulthood.

Except to the extent that children observe their parents in political activities, they do not usually learn political norms within the home. As with the norms in many other nonfamily roles, some are first encountered when children begin school. Political norms are usually incorporated into formal curricula in courses such as civics, social problems, and history. For example, a study of political socialization provided by elementary schools in eight representative American cities documents the fact that, not only do curricula contain political values such as the importance of elections in democratic societies, they also contain political norms such as the rules of morality that surround elections and the obligation to express solidarity behind winning candidates. Hess and Torney, who conducted this study, report that by the end of the eighth grade most pupils have developed "a sense of the need for consensus and majority rule in democratic processes," although they do not usually recognize the "role of debate, disagreement and conflict."[27]

In addition to providing anticipatory political socialization, schools often encourage the use of political norms in controlling relationships within student organizations and between student organization and the school, as, for example, in student government. Peer social systems sometimes provide opportunity for pupils to gain experience in the exercise of political skills, especially when democratic governance and parliamentary procedures are encouraged. Within this framework, pupils of roughly the same age and grade have a chance to choose among viable alternatives and to express opinions about their choices in an attempt to influence others. For a smaller number of pupils, there is also the opportunity to gain and exercise leadership.

The objective of political socialization is often held to be the creation of "political men," that is, the development of people who are psychologically involved in governmental decisions. According to some political scientists, the attributes of political men are that they:

1. have an interest in the political process.
2. have a concern for the outcomes of this process.
3. have sufficient knowledge and information to make wise political decisions.
4. actively participate in political decision-making.[28]

It is doubtful that American public schools can ever provide all of the experiences necessary to create political men. For one thing, introduction and discussion of controversial issues are inhibited by the schools' dependence on local citizens for support, and many of these citizens disagree among themselves about political issues. For another, the free exercise by pupils of political decisions pertaining to school affairs runs counter to traditional notions of school authority in which adults are responsible for the activities of the school and act *in loco parentis,* that is, in place of parents. Schools, nevertheless, provide some political socialization, both in the formal curricula they present and in the opportunities they afford pupils for participation in both political and nonpolitical groups.

FAMILIES AND FRIENDS CONTRASTED WITH OTHER SOCIAL GROUPS

It should now be clear that throughout life every individual has many social statuses and is expected to carry out a variety of role responsibilities required by each. As adults, for example, people usually need to know how to perform several roles within family and friendship groups and a number of other roles that revolve around work and public life. Fortunately the values and norms required by social roles are seldom unique. Otherwise it would be extremely difficult for people to become socialized sufficiently to meet most of the duties and obligations of the roles they occupy. Since there is only a limited number of basic ways that people can behave, new roles are usually acquired, at least in part, by the reorganization of value-normative patterns that people have already learned from other roles.

Gemeinschaft and *gesellschaft* groups

The patterns involved in family and friendship roles are closer to each other than they are to the patterns of other, more formal roles. Family and friendship units are sometimes referred to as *gemeinschaft* groups, from the German word meaning "community" or "fellowship." Typically, the relationships among *gemeinschaft* group members are informal, spontaneous, highly personal, and they carry broad mutual obligations. *Gemeinschaft* groups can be contrasted with dissimilar social units termed *gesellschaft* groups. *Gesellschaft* is also a German word and it means "organization" or "society." Role relationships within *gesellschaft* groups are comparatively formal, rational, impersonal, and they carry limited mutual obligations.

Gemeinschaft patterns are learned initially within families and play groups, while *gesellschaft* patterns are often learned first in schools. The patterns employed by schools in the early grades are closer to those of the family, but, in later grades, they become more and more similar to those of nonfamily and nonfriendship units. Schools, therefore, help children to make a transition from the *gemeinschaft* roles of early childhood to *gesellschaft* roles of adulthood by providing them with opportunities to try out some of the adult behaviors they have previously observed, and by exposing them to entirely new behaviors.

Pattern-variable analysis

A fruitful way to examine differences between *gemeinschaft* and *gesellschaft* roles is by pattern-variable analysis, a technique developed by the American sociologist Talcott Parsons.[29] Pattern-variable analysis begins with the assumption that there are at least four basic value-normative patterns contained in every social role and that these patterns are critical in carrying out its expectations. The significant components of social roles include:

1. the extent of the obligations that the role occupant has toward people who occupy reciprocal roles, whether wide or limited in scope.
2. the source of these obligations, whether obligations arise out of their personal significance to the role occupant or are determined by general criteria that are uniformly applied to all occupants of reciprocal roles.
3. the extent to which the role occupant is expected to express or conceal personal feelings.
4. how the role occupant initially acquires the role and the extent to which role performance is emphasized as compared to the emphasis given to the personal qualities of the role occupant.

When people learn social roles, they learn the expectations that relate to these value-normative components. The expectations that are germane to each are one or another of a pair of alternative patterns which Parsons terms pattern variables. The four sets of pattern-variable alternatives developed by Parsons for describing values and norms in each of these role components are discussed below.

Diffuseness-specificity. Diffuseness-specificity is the pattern-variable set of alternatives that describes the scope of the obligations that role occupants have toward those who occupy reciprocal roles. A role relationship is *diffuse* when there are deep emotional bonds and wide-ranging duties toward others. It is *specific* when obligations are limited to some particular purpose or task.

The nuclear family provides excellent examples of diffuse obligations, especially the responsibilities of mothers or mother-surrogates toward young children, and those between husbands and wives. Relationships between close friends also carry diffuse obligations. The recipients of diffuse obligations have deep personal significance to the role occupant and are viewed more as ends in themselves than as means for attaining some further end.

Diffuse obligations are limited only by some deeper involvement and sense of responsibility toward another. Since all roles have a hierarchy of obligations built into them, some relationships take precedence: a mother's obligation toward her infant, for example, has greater priority than her obligations toward older, more self-sufficient children. In addition, people give higher priority to some roles than to others because these roles have more personal significance. A man is often limited in his role of friend because he values his roles of husband and father more, and women teachers are sometimes limited in their relationship with pupils because of their more personally meaningful roles of wife or mother.

Examples of specific role obligations are numerous in work and other public-role relationships, especially in postindustrial societies where specialization and division of labor are extensive. Specific role relationships are those such as doctor-patient, lawyer-client, professor-student, plumber-homeowner, shopkeeper-customer, and the like. Responsibilities in each of these relationships are restricted to some particular purpose which is often made explicit in laws, contracts, or professional codes.

In American society, the difference between the diffuse orientation of most families and the specific orientation of many occupations is often extreme. On the other hand, schools are a blend of the two and provide many children with an opportunity to practice the diffuse orientations they acquired at home at the same time that they acquire the specific orientations they will need to know later on. At lower-grade levels, expected school behaviors are similar to many of those of home; at higher-grade levels, they approach the specificity of many adult occupations. When pupils enter school, they are obligated to only one teacher with whom they employ some of the behaviors they use in their relationships with parents. To cite an instance, how many young children inadvertently call their teachers mommy? The diffuse orientations of young pupils are supported initially by the orientation of primary schools toward the whole child and the fact that children are typically assigned to one teacher for an entire school year. Later on, pupils' orientations toward teachers become more diffuse. This change is fostered by corresponding changes in school practices. A shift in emphasis in secondary schools from the development of the whole child to the development of competence in subject matter areas, and the provision of several teachers instead of one both encourage diffuse orientations in young students.

Particularism-universalism. This is the pattern-variable set that refers to the source of obligations that role occupants have toward those who hold reciprocal roles. *Particularism* implies that role obligations depend on whether the other person is a member of a special group or has personal emotional significance to the role occupant. In contrast, *universalism* implies that these obligations are determined by some general criteria which are applied in the same manner to all people who hold similar reciprocal roles. This difference is illustrated by comparing ways in which a school faculty might select the pupil who is to give a high school commencement address. If they employ universalistic patterns, criteria involving school grades, service to the school, public-speaking ability, and the like are developed, and the pupil who best meets these criteria is chosen. If they employ particularistic patterns, the faculty might appoint a pupil it personally likes or one who is related to some staff member, friend, or influential person in the community.

The personnel policies of public agencies such as schools are often guided by universalistic norms, especially if they come under civil service regulations and have explicit rules to guard against particularism. School nepotism rules, for example, often prevent children from enrolling in their parents' classes or prevent husbands and wives from teaching in the same departments for fear that family members will treat each other differently from nonfamily members of similar status. Other sources of particularism arise when a role occupant gives favorable treatment to members of certain groups, such as a fraternity, church, or social class.

Particularistic treatment is not always favorable: prejudicial treatment of members of social, religious, and political minorities are common forms of particularism. In recent years, the nepotism policy of many schools has come under attack as still another kind of particularism. Although that policy was initiated to prevent particularistic practices that favor family members, many women have pointed out that refusal by institutions to employ qualified women because their husbands have faculty appointments is more often an arbitrary form of particularistic discrimination than a form of universalism.

The ideology of democratic government contains assumptions of universalism. Common interests of the entire society are expected to take priority over the personal interests of individual members and government officials are expected to treat all citizens equally. The example, "government of laws, not men," carries with it the notion of universalism: all laws are applied uniformly without consideration of a person's social roles or group memberships. The obligations of the judge to a defendant, the policeman to a criminal suspect, and the public assessor to a property owner are the same, regardless of who fills these social statuses.

Families are highly particularistic in that family members are treated as they are precisely because they are part of the same social group. However, just as particularism enters into the relationships of predominantly *gesellschaft* groups, universalism enters into family relationships. For example, parents in large families often classify their children for some purposes into universalistic categories based on sex and age: sons typically help fathers with yard work, whereas daughters help mothers with housework, and children who attend secondary school usually receive larger allowances than those received by children in elementary school.

Formal relationships within schools often provide pupils with the opportunity to learn some of the values and norms of universalism since each child is part of a cohort of peers in which particularistic ties are frequently irrelevant. Pupils usually learn in early elementary school that for educational purposes, they must give up some of their uniqueness and acknowledge the right of others to treat them as members of a group.[30] Opportunities for learning patterns of universalism expand as pupils reach secondary school and meet with many teachers who instruct them in different subjects. They then discover that pupils of roughly equal academic competence tend to be treated alike over a wide range of activities and that relatively uniform demands for performance are applied to all.[31]

Affectivity-neutrality. These are the pattern variables that describe the extent to which a social role permits its occupant to express personal feelings. Roles that are characterized by *affectivity* allow for the external manifestation of affect, such as the expression of positive emotions in laughter and negative emotions in anger or tears. Roles characterized by neutrality, in contrast, require emotional self-control and permit expressions of affect only under specified circumstances.

The alternatives in this set of pattern variables are not absolute in that they describe the behaviors that a role tends to emphasize. Some self-control is necessary in almost every social situation, with the possible exception of the role of infant which allows for total impulse indulgence. People are encouraged from early childhood to control their behaviors and by the time they become adults they have usually learned to recognize the circumstances under which expressions of affect are permitted.

Family and friendship roles tend to employ high affect, whereas occupational roles which require rational, intellectual behavior are characterized by neutrality. Professional roles involving decisions with far-reaching consequences afford relatively little opportunity for spontaneous emotional expression. Physicians do not normally treat members of their immediate families for fear that affective involvement will impede their judgment, and it is commonly said that a lawyer who defends himself has a fool for a client. Although some teachers do become affectively involved with their pupils, research findings suggest that those who are predominantly rational and hold their own emotions in check bring about greater academic growth in their pupils than do those who are highly affective.[32]

Schools help children to learn neutrality in role performance. The formal roles of schools, like the roles of work, tend to be affectively neutral and permit expressions of emotion only at designated times. Increasing amounts of self-control are demanded by pupils as they move through grade levels, and by the time they enter secondary school they have usually learned that public expressions of affect are to be put aside until the tasks at hand are completed.

Ascription-achievement. These pattern-variable alternatives refer both to how a role is acquired and to the aspects of the role that are emphasized. This pattern-variable set answers two questions:

1. Is the role ascribed to individuals on the basis of characteristics such as age, sex, and family membership, or is it given to those who can perform its duties and obligations?
2. Is the role more concerned with who the role occupant is or with what the person does in carrying out the role?

In *ascribed* roles, performance is taken for granted. All male youngsters in a family occupy the role of son, regardless of their behavior. While there can be both good sons and bad sons, performance doesn't alter the fact that young boys occupy this role. The role of pupil is also commonly ascribed to normal children when they attain the age of compulsory schooling regardless of their school performance.

Achieved roles stress role performance more than the characteristics of role occupants; they are concerned primarily with how role occupants carry out role expectations. Although most children between the ages of about 13 and 18 are ascribed the roles of adolescent and pupil, only those who excel in school take on additional roles like honor student and class valedictorian. It should be noted that achieved roles are not necessarily obtained through competence as this word is generally understood; they are obtained because the role occupant has the competence to carry out role expectations. Roles such as idiot, mental retardate, and patient, for example, are acquired because of some inability rather than some ability which allows people to perform as expected.

Children begin to differentiate between achievement and ascription in their early years, as parents and other family members reinforce their performances. However, the reactions of family members to the behavior of their children are partly influenced by their particularistic relationships, and often it is not until children enter school that they experience situations in which achievement criteria predominate. When school marks and other scholastic rewards are given on the basis of academic mastery and proper behavior, pupils observe the universalistic implementation of performance criteria. School children also have an opportunity to observe performance

TABLE 1.1.   *Gemeinschaft* **and** *Gesellschaft* **Groups Described by the Pattern Variables**

"Pattern-variable" alternatives	*Gemeinschaft* groups	*Gesellschaft* groups
Diffuseness-Specificity The extent role occupant has obligations to occupants of reciprocal roles.	*Diffuse* Wide-ranging obligations. Deep emotional bonds.	*Specific* Narrow obligations limited to a particular purpose.
Particularism-Universalism Source of role occupant's obligations to occupants of reciprocal roles.	*Particularistic* Obligations arise from membership in a special group or from the personal significance of the occupants of reciprocal roles.	*Universalistic* Obligations are determined by general criteria uniformly applied to all occupants of reciprocal roles.
Affectivity-Neutrality Extent to which role occupant is expected to express or conceal feelings.	*Affective* Emotional feelings are expressed.	*Neutral* Emotions are held in check. Rationality predominates.
Ascription-Achievement How the role is acquired and the extent to which role performance is stressed.	*Ascriptive* Roles are assigned on the basis of personal characteristics. Performance is taken for granted.	*Achievement* Roles are given on the basis of ability to meet role expectations. Performance is stressed.

criteria in the athletic arena where individual and group achievement are the criteria for success. The fruits of athletic performances have been so valued in American culture that many people willingly compete to attain them, even against those with whom they have diffuse and particularistic ties.

Since only some can win, pupils also have experiences in losing. Schools not only provide an opportunity for pupils to observe and experience the application of performance criteria, but to gain experiences in managing their consequences. The social effects of success are different from those of failure and pupils often learn the skills of coping with either of them or both. In addition, schools usually stress the widely accepted value that achievement criteria are inherently good in many situations and that people should accept their consequences, regardless of whether or not they are favorable. This lesson is often justified as anticipatory socialization for adult competition.

The essential differences between *gemeinschaft* roles such as those within family and friendship groups, on the one hand, and *gesellschaft* roles, on the other, are summarized in Table 1.1. The distinctions between the pattern-variable alternatives that are used to describe these two types of social groups have been exaggerated for didactic purposes; they are seldom found in the pure form presented here. However, families do tend to employ one set of alternative value-normative patterns, and many adult roles, the other. Schools are the social institution in which opposing pattern variables are blended.

NOTES

[1] *Society* as used here refers to people with their own culture living together in a more or less self-sufficient manner. Some authors define society as the largest collectivity with which one associates as, for example, a nation. According to this definition, all of the people in the United States constitute a society, and smaller groupings within are subsocieties. *Group* and *social system* are more general terms that refer to people engaging in cooperative activity regardless of their number or length of association. People on a chartered bus, a teenage clique, a family, and the PTA are all examples of a social system.

[2] This conservative, "functional" view of education is expressed in the influential work of Emile Durkheim, an early twentieth century French philosopher, sociologist, and educator:

Education is the influence exercised by adult generations on those that are not yet ready for social life. Its object is to arouse and to develop in the child a certain number of physical, intellectual and moral states which are demanded of him by both the political society as a whole and the special milieu for which he is specifically destined.

Emile Durkheim, *Education and Sociology*, trans. Sherwood D. Fox, New York, Free Press, 1956, p. 71. First published 1922.

[3] That all societies have four basic problems is a common theme in the functional tradition of modern social science. These problems—often referred to as the "functional prerequisites" of a society because they must be met in order for it to survive—were originally described as follows:

1. *adaptation* to the nonsocial and social environment (sexual reproduction of members, recruitment of new members, procurement of resources, security from external threat).
2. *goal attainment* (setting goals, allocation of resources and manpower to attain them).
3. *pattern maintenance* and *tension management* (learning shared cultural patterns, regulation of expressive behavior that might disrupt society).
4. *integration* (coordination and control of social behavior, maintenance of morale and solidarity).

See Talcott Parsons and Robert F. Bales, "Theoretical Statement of the Functional Prerequisites of a Social System," *Working Papers in the Theory of Action*, New York, Free Press, 1953.

[4] Jessie Bernard, *American Community Behavior*, rev. ed., New York, Holt, Rinehart & Winston, 1965, p. 42.

[5] Thomas Hobbes, *Leviathan*, New York, Dutton (New American edition), 1950. First published 1651.

[6] *Value* as used here refers to an abstract conception of what is desirable. Values are standards around which social groups and individuals organize activity. They are the criteria by which some behavior is chosen over others. Thus values determine the goals toward which groups and individuals seem to strive and they determine what means can legitimately be used in pursuing goals. See Talcott Parsons, *Social Structure and Personality*, New York, Free Press, 1964, pp. 194–195.

[7] Commission on the Reorganization of Secondary Education, *Cardinal Principles of Secondary Education*, Washington, D.C., National Education Association, 1918.

[8] *U.S. President's Committee for the White House Conference on Education: A Report to the President*, New York, Greenwood, 1969.

[9] Michael B. Katz, "From Voluntarism to Bureaucracy in American Education," *Sociology of Education*, 44, no. 3 (Summer 1971), 327.

[10] John W. Caughey, John Hope Franklin, and Ernest R. May, *Land of the Free: A History of the United States*, New York, Benziger, 1966, p. 270.

[11] For a comprehensive analysis of social conflict see Lewis Coser, *The Functions of Social Conflict*, New York, Free Press, 1956.

[12] Alexis de Tocqueville, *Democracy in America: The Republic of the United States of America and Its Political Institutions*, trans. Henry

Reeves, New York, Schocken, 1961. First American publication 1863. Gunnar Myrdal, *An American Dilemma*, New York, Harper & Row, 1944.

[13] For a discussion of these values see Robin M. Williams, Jr., *American Society: A Sociological Interpretation*, 3rd ed., New York, Knopf, 1970, chap. 11.

[14] David Riesman, Nathan Glazer, and Roul Denney, *The Lonely Crowd*, New Haven, Yale University Press, 1950, p. 66.

[15] See, for example, Randall Collins, "Functional and Conflict Theories of Educational Stratification," *American Sociological Review*, 36, no. 6 (December 1971), 1002–1019.

[16] Robin M. Williams, Jr., "Individual and Group Values," *The Annals of the American Academy of Political and Social Science*, 371 (May 1967), 20–37.

[17] Robert K. Merton, *Social Theory and Social Structure*, rev. ed., New York, Free Press, 1957.

[18] These ideas are fully developed by Robert Dreeben, *On What Is Learned in School*, Reading, Mass., Addison-Wesley, 1968.

[19] Talcott Parsons, "The School Class as a Social System: Some of Its Functions in American Society," *Harvard Educational Review*, 29, no. 4 (Fall 1959), 297–318.

[20] Lawrence A. Cremin, *The Genius of American Education*, New York, Random House, 1965, p. 10. But see Katz, *op. cit.*, who sees social control rather than political socialization as the major impetus to public schools.

[21] Thomas Jefferson, *Crusade Against Ignorance*, Gordon C. Lee, ed., New York, Teachers College Press, Columbia University, 1961, p. 94, *passim*.

[22] Rush Welter, *Popular Education and Democratic Thought in America*, New York, Columbia University Press, 1962, p. 329. The relationship between equal rights to education and economic democracy has recently come under attack. Jencks, for one, concludes from estimates of earned income that efforts to keep everyone in school longer make little economic sense. Christopher Jencks, *et al.*, *Inequality: A Reassessment of the Effects of Family and Schooling in America*, New York, Basic Books, 1972, p. 224.

[23] Herbert Hyman, *Political Socialization: A Study in the Psychology of Political Behavior*, New York, Free Press, 1959, p. 56.

[24] Gabriel A. Almond and Sidney Verba, *The Civic Culture: Political Attitudes and Democracy in Five Nations*, Boston, Little, Brown, 1965, pp. 284–306. First published 1963.

[25] Hyman, *op. cit.*, pp. 52–55.

[26] *Ibid.*, pp. 79–84.

[27] Robert D. Hess and Judith V. Torney, *The Development of Political Attitudes in Children*, Garden City, N.Y., Doubleday (Anchor), 1967, pp. 91 and 246.

[28] Robert A. Dahl, *Modern Political Analysis*, Englewood Cliffs, N.J., Prentice-Hall, 1963, pp. 56–57. But, as Banks points out, the influence of education upon political attitudes is very complex and, although it may

be correct to assume that a high level of education is necessary for participation in democratic government, there is no guarantee that education and democratic attitudes are necessarily related. Germany and Japan are examples of nations that had both high literacy rates and totalitarian forms of government. Olive Banks, *The Sociology of Education*, New York, Schocken Books, 1968, p. 210.

[29] Talcott Parsons, *The Social System*, New York, Free Press, 1951, pp. 58–67. For a restatement, see Harry M. Johnson, *Sociology: A Systematic Introduction*, New York, Harcourt Brace Jovanovich, 1960, pp. 132–142.

[30] Robert Dreeben, "The Contribution of Schooling to the Learning of Norms," *Harvard Educational Review*, 37, no. 2 (Spring 1967), 229. Evidence suggests that people must experience membership in homogeneous, equalitarian systems such as the school class in order to learn patterns of universalism. Studies of game playing, for example, indicate that children do not understand the notion of rules until they have been part of such a group. Until that time, they view all rules as a form of particularism in which more powerful people impose their wishes on the less powerful. See Jean Piaget, *The Moral Judgment of the Child*, trans. Marjorie Gabin, New York, Free Press, 1948. First published in English 1932.

[31] Dreeben, *op. cit.* "The Contribution of Schooling," p. 232.

[32] C. Wayne Gordon and Leta McKinney Adler, *Dimensions of Teacher Leadership in Classroom Social Systems: Pupil Effects on Productivity Morale, and Compliance*, Los Angeles, University of California, Department of Educaion, 1963. Affective involvement of teachers with pupils should not be confused with expressions of the teacher's personality. Teachers who appear warm and supportive to pupils can, in fact, be affectively neutral toward them.

2

Socialization and the individual

In the preceding chapter, some of the consequences of socialization—including the relationship between the socialization of young Americans and their subsequent ability to occupy existing adult social roles—were discussed primarily from the perspective of a society at large. In this chapter, the consequences of socialization are again discussed, but the predominant perspective will be that of the individual.

SOCIETY VIS-À-VIS THE INDIVIDUAL

What effect does socialization have on those who are being socialized? Does it, as many Freudian psychoanalysts contend, curtail their natural instincts and constrain them to behave in ways which are inconsistent with their biological endowment? Or does it, as many sociologists believe, provide the only means by which they can develop their essentially human characteristics? This debate has recurred as least since the time of Aristotle. Although more is continually learned about human beings, it is not likely that the issue will be totally resolved.

That there is at least some basic conflict between the biological person and the external social order has long been assumed. One pioneer American sociologist, W. I. Thomas, explained it this way:

There is therefore always a rivalry between the spontaneous definitions of the situation made by the member of an organized society and the definitions which his society has provided for him. The individual tends to a hedonistic selection of activity, pleasure first; and society to a utilitarian selection, safety first. Society wishes its member to be laborious, dependable, regular, sober, orderly, self-sacrificing; while the individual wishes less of this and more of new experience. And organized society seeks also to regulate the conflict and competition inevitable between its members in the pursuit of their wishes.[1]

The assumption of conflict between man and society is carried further in the writings of psychoanalytic theorists who hold that many *essential* human qualities are not dependent upon a social environment for their development.[2] In their view, society is in opposition to the biological person and social learning is largely the imposition of restrictions upon natural impulses. Sigmund Freud, the intellectual father of psychoanalytical theory, wrote that the processes of individual development and cultural or social development "must stand in hostile opposition to each other." Further, the urges toward personal happiness and toward union with other human beings "must struggle with each other in every individual."[3]

In keeping with Freud's position, many contemporary psychoanalysts view the heart of the socialization process as little more than child-rearing practices in which individuals are taught by other members of society to control their physiological urges. Furthermore, to a great extent they view professional psychoanalysis as an attempt to deal with the frustrations and anxieties that result from practices such as toilet training and weaning, which accentuate the inherent conflict between the individual and society.[4]

More recently, A. S. Neill, a psychologist and founder of Summerhill, a well-known progressive English boarding school, wrote that the child is "innately wise and realistic. If left to himself without adult suggestion of any kind, he will develop as far as he is capable of developing."[5] Neill believed that children must be allowed freedom to live their own lives: "to impose anything by authority is wrong. The child should not do anything until he comes to the opinion—his own opinion—that it should be done."[6] Neill concluded that, although the elaborate schools built by most societies educate the young child, they do nothing to surmount "the emotional damage and the social evils bred by the pressure on him from his parents, his school teachers, and the pressure of the coercive quality of our civilization."[7] According to Neill, only schools that, by renouncing all discipline and direction, allow children freedom to be themselves, can be successful.

Many romantic and humanistic philosophers also hold that there is fundamental discord between the spontaneous person and society. For example, the great eighteenth-century philosopher, Jean Jacques Rousseau, championed the individual against the repressions of society. Although he saw education as necessary for human survival, he took the position that infants at birth are totally good and it is only as they are educated that they become bad:

> A child cries as soon as born, and his first years are spent in tears. At one time we trot and caress him to pacify him, and at another we threaten and beat him to keep him quiet. We either do what pleases him, or we exact of him what pleases us; we either subject ourselves to his whims, or subject him to ours. There is no middle ground; he must either give orders or receive them. And so his first ideas are those of domination and servitude. . . . It is thus that, at an early hour, we pour into his young heart the passions that we straightway impute to nature; and that, after having taken the trouble to make him bad, we complain of finding him such.[8]

In contrast with these views, most contemporary sociologists assume that man *qua* man cannot exist without the socialization provided by society. Newborn infants have no distinctly human characteristics: they have no personality, no consciousness of self, no capacity for empathy, and no concepts to guide their perceptions of reality. These develop from interaction with other people, not from biological inheritance alone.

Although people are born with the potential to behave in a number of different ways, their potential is realized only through contact with a society that transmits to them its "designs for living."[9] All people share physiological needs such as food and shelter and all people have similar capacities for meeting them, but the manner in which they solve such basic human problems is learned in great part from the other people with whom they live. Thus, for example, the life styles of most Australian aborigines are radically different from those of people born in New York, yet a healthy aborigine infant who is adopted into the home of an average Brooklyn couple would be culturally similar to most of his classmates by the time he entered school.

This sociological view is in sharp contradiction to the Freudian-romantic view of "man against society." It holds that basic conflicts between the two are impossible in that the individual and society are both created out of the interaction of human beings: one cannot exist without the other.[10] It also holds that the notion that society is contrary to the freedom of the individual is false: freedom exists only in and through society. "The social order is antithetical to freedom only insofar as it is a bad one."[11]

These contrasting orientations toward the relationship between the individual and society are shown by two common metaphors about the human developmental process. The first is the growth metaphor which compares the child to a growing plant that has within it all elements necessary for maturity. By supplying optimum conditions for the operation of the laws of nature, human attention can assist in its development, but it is not essential. The second is the art metaphor in which some raw material, such as clay, stone, or wood, must be fashioned by an artist if it is to reach the desired specifications.[12] The growth metaphor fits the Freudian-romantic view because it points out that although society can assist human development, it can also restrain it by pushing people into directions that are inconsistent with their inherent qualities. In like manner, the art metaphor corresponds with the sociological view, since it takes the position that people cannot develop at all without the external forces provided by society.

The far-reaching implications of these two orientations for formal socialization are illustrated by some of the perennial questions relating to the selection of socialization goals. Should schools, as the growth metaphor suggests, stress the unique, the creative, and the spontaneous in each individual? Or should they, as implied by the art metaphor, stress the acquisition of knowledge and behavior that are thought necessary for the adjustment of individuals to society, and for the maintenance of society itself? These views have implications for the practice of education as well: for example, should the prime task of the classroom teacher be to provide a secure environment in which children are encouraged in those activities that they themselves seek, or should the teacher present a formalized curriculum and make demands upon children which will help them meet the expectations of other members of their society?[13]

Patently, the growth versus art controversy has implications that extend beyond academic discussion, but, because infants are initially incapable of caring for themselves, it is unlikely that one can ever know what people would be like without long periods of dependency on others. There has been, nonetheless, much speculation about people who have had little or no contact with socialized humans and the folklore of many societies contain reports of "feral," or wild, children who were raised by animals or foraged for themselves. Subsequent investigations into these reports, however, have invariably cast doubt on their accuracy. There is no sound evidence to date to show that people can exist if they are initially isolated from other humans.

The sociological view that the individual as a person is a social creation is presented more fully in the following pages.[14] The position is taken that, while children are neither social nor antisocial at birth, they have the capacity for social development. Because children depend on others for survival, the socialization process begins immediately, since they are necessarily in contact with their caretakers. Through this process, they acquire many distinctly human characteristics including the self, the capacity for human empathy, and the culture of their families.

THE DEVELOPMENT OF SELF

At birth human infants have no sense of self as either a biological or a social entity. When they move their hands to their mouths, for example, they do not realize that the object touching their lips belongs to them or even that they can control its movements. They experience their bodies and their environment as a "more or less amorphous continuous body-field matrix."[15] By age six months, however, they are somewhat aware of boundaries between what is and what is not their own bodies. As the ability to discriminate between themselves and the environment continues to develop, they acquire concepts to define what is uniquely their own.

The organization of these concepts about one's own person is structured into what has come to be called the *self*. The self is those qualities that people attribute to themselves. Although it is not possible for them to point to the self as they can point, for example, to the heart or the brain, the self is ordinarily the most real object in the experience of each individual.[16] Because of the existence of self, people can interact with themselves: they can interpret their own psychological and physical states and they can plan and guide their own conduct. These abilities are uniquely human.

Defining the self is a lifelong activity that continually takes into account observations people make of the opinions that others have about them. Charles H. Cooley, an early twentieth century American sociologist, referred to the self as the "looking-glass self," since it mirrors the evaluations of others. In Cooley's words:

Each to each a looking-glass
Reflects the other that doth pass.[17]

He points out that the self is not identical to the views of other people but is one's own perception of these views. The self, according to Cooley, is created through a process of "reciprocal imagining" which includes: first, the imagination of one's appearance to the other person; second, the imagination of the other person's judgment of that appearance; and, third, some sort of "self-feeling" such as "pride" or "mortification."

The concept of looking-glass self provides an explanation of why socializing agents such as parents and teachers have strong influence on the formulation of a child's self. Adult behaviors which children interpret as expressing approval support their positive sense of self, whereas behaviors they see as disparaging foster a negative self. Self-feelings that arise from adult-child interaction often have profound effects on the lives of children. Feelings of self-confidence, for example, have been shown repeatedly to be related to achievement in school and elsewhere.[18] One wonders whether socializing adults are aware that frequent negative evaluations and criticisms often impede a healthy sense of self in children and undermine the very social and intellectual development they are attempting to accomplish.

Cooley summarizes the process through which the self develops in this picturesque passage:

I imagine your mind and especially what your mind thinks about my mind, and what your mind thinks about what my mind thinks about your mind. I dress my mind before yours and expect that you will dress yours before mine.[19]

Implicit in Cooley's theory of development is the ability of individuals to react to their own bodies, thoughts, and feelings in the way they anticipate that others will react to them. As young children acquire a sense of self they are able to play the roles of others and respond to themselves as they imagine the responses of others. Observations of children playing house reveal the extent to which they have learned their parents' roles and the expectations that their parents have of them. Observations of children playing school reveal a similar knowledge about their teachers. Young children often praise, chastise, and instruct themselves in play in a manner that can only be their conceptions of these adult roles.

Much human behavior can be understood as efforts to promote the self in one's own eyes and in the eyes of others.[20] The approval of some people, of course, is more important to the individual than that of others. Those who are most influential in the development of a person's self and in molding a person's behavior are, in the terminology of social psychologist George Herbert Mead, *"significant others."*[21]

The first significant others are usually parents or nurturing surrogates. Young children continually modify their behavior to meet with their approval and in this way learn their early social roles. As they are assigned more social roles, they acquire additional significant others, first from among family members, and then from among teachers, peers, and so on. To some children the influence of the father may be most salient, to others it may be the influence of the mother. Older brothers or sisters also become significant others; it is not uncommon to find children organizing their behavior to gain the approval of older siblings. Teachers who become significant others to their pupils have wide-ranging influence over their development, and playmates with whom children spend many hours can also affect their behavior. Not only do people alter their behavior to build a positive image in the eyes of a circle of significant others, they learn the criteria by which significant others evaluate them, and these become part of their own value systems.

Significant others are not always those whom they want to impress favorably; they can include any others who figure prominently in molding behavior. People sometimes participate in activity designed to harm or destroy significant others, as, for example, the enemy during war time. Or they sometimes engage in behavior which will never affect the significant other, as in the hero worship of some distant, historical or fictional figure. In short, significant others are people living or dead, real or imaginary, present or absent, whose perspectives are taken into account and who are to some degree responsible for the behaviors and values of an individual.

With growing maturity, children participate in other social groups and learn the orientations of many people besides significant others. They organize all of these orientations into what Mead has called a *"generalized other."*[22] Once a generalized other develops, individuals are able to view themselves from the vantage of all those they have come to know. Only after this level of personality organization has occurred can children engage in games which require that they put themselves in the place of all of the players.

Mead used the example of the baseball team to illustrate the concept of generalized other, since all players must know the behaviors of all other players in order to formulate their own behavior. The baseball team is a generalized other to each of its players. Every position does not have to be present in the consciousness of every player at all times, but

> . . . at some moments he has to have three or four individuals present in his own attitude, such as who is going to throw the ball, the one who is going to catch it, and so on. These responses must be, in some degree, present in his own make-up.[23]

The concept of generalized other is, in essence, the individual's view of society. It is created out of all the groups one has encountered and is a composite of one's perceptions of many social roles. According to Mead, it is in the form of the generalized other that "social process or community enter as a determining factor into the individual's thinking."[24] That is to say, it is because of the generalized other that individuals are able and willing to participate in their ongoing society. Consequently, society exercises control over its members in the form of the generalized other.

This early description of the development of self laid the foundation for a contemporary orientation in social psychology known as *symbolic interactionism*, an orientation compatible with much sociological theory and heavily relied upon in this chapter. The two central theses of symbolic interactionism are: first, that human beings act toward all things on the basis of the meanings these things have for them; and, equally important, that these meanings are socially derived. From the viewpoint of symbolic interactionism, the self develops *after* the individual had had human contact.

Herbert Blumer, who coined the term symbolic interactionism, agrees with Cooley in many important respects. For example, in summarizing the social interaction process he writes:

> Human beings in interacting with one another have to take account of what each other is doing or is about to do; they are forced to direct their own conduct or handle their situations in terms of what they take into account.[25]

Other important tenets of symbolic interaction follow:

1. Valid principles of human social behavior are developed only from the study of humans, since they are qualitatively different in many respects from other forms of animals.
2. The most fruitful way to study human social behavior is through the analysis of society; the basic unit of observation is the inter-action of individuals because society and individuals are both derived from this activity.
3. The human infant is an active rather than a passive organism which is asocial at birth but has the potential for social development.
4. Humans do not merely respond to all stimuli outside themselves, but select and interpret those which constitute their own environments.[26]

Another way of explaining self is simply that it is the integration of all of the social roles a person has acquired. This definition stresses the dynamic aspect of self and points out that it is in continual flux as new roles are learned and existing roles are modified or eliminated. Human infants are ascribed some social roles from birth, as, for example, baby, son, and brother. Members of their families soon expect them to behave according to their own understandings of such roles, and as infants become aware of these expectations they begin to acquire a definition of self which incorporates them. Their self definitions will be modified as they learn new role expectations, but these early conceptions significantly influence later views because they supply the framework within which new expectations are interpreted.

In the United States, adolescents and young adults are usually required to learn a large number of roles within a few years' time, a social demand that may be an important contributor to the high incidence in this age group of so-called identity problems. As an example, consider the series of roles a girl undergraduate preparing for a career in education may hold within a short period of time. It can include college student, cadet teacher, graduate student, probationary teacher, and tenured teacher. During the same period she can also move successively through the roles of date, betrothed, spouse, and—perhaps—divorcee. As each new role is undertaken, the self works to adjust to its new expectations and to integrate them with roles previously acquired.

CAPACITY FOR EMPATHY

Another human quality that is not found in animals is the ability to react both to oneself as others do and to others, as if one were they. This characteristic of placing oneself in the position of another is sometimes known as *empathy*. Empathy is the capacity to imaginatively transpose oneself into the thinking, feeling, and action of another, and so structure the world as he does.[27] In simpler words, empathy is the ability of one person to take the role of another.

Cooley heavily stressed this quality in making his distinction between human nature and the nature of lower forms of animals: Human nature, according to Cooley, involves those sentiments and impulses that

> . . . *belong to mankind at large, and not to any particular race or time. It means, particularly, sympathy and the innumerable sentiments into which sympathy enters, such as love, resentment, ambition, vanity, hero-worship, and the feeling of social right and wrong.*[28]

The capacity for empathy, then, is the ability to respond affectively to the affective states in others and to impute to others some underlying motives for their action. Empathy is responsible for the *shared* nature of human behavior because it enables one person to understand and often to predict the behavior of others. The concepts of looking-glass self, significant other, and generalized other are all acquired because the individual has empathy for other people. Empathy enables the social patterns of behavior and values to enter the individual. Because of this, it is responsible for social order.

The ability to empathize has long been of interest to students of human behavior and there is wide agreement on its significance to the social interaction process. Nonetheless, the study of empathy is a relatively undeveloped area of inquiry and views about it are largely speculative.[29] It does seem clear, however, that very young children do not have the ability to put themselves in the place of others. The Swiss psychologist, Jean Piaget, who intensively studied the development of children over many years, describes the behavior of early childhood as predominantly *egocentric* in contrast to the behavior of later childhood, which he describes as *sociocentric*. According to Piaget, the activities and responses of young children radiate from themselves; they take only their own view into account.

Because young children are incapable of simultaneously considering both the points of view of others and their own, they center on their own perspective. However, as they mature in a social environment, they develop the ability to consider varied orientations and only then can they engage in sociocentric behavior, in which empathy figures significantly.[30]

In order for children to accept and act upon the views of other people, they must first have the ability to perceive them accurately. The capacity for empathy is potential in all individuals but its development is contingent on socialization. The quality and number of role relationships a person has experienced, for example, is often related to this capacity. Those whose social interaction has been limited or who lack normal development of their senses or other mental processes are handicapped in their ability to perceive how others view them and their common social milieu. As a consequence they often have unrealistic concepts of themselves and of society. Severe defects in the ability to empathize can lead to a mental condition commonly called schizophrenia, a disorder of orientation in which the individual has an oversimple and rigid conception of reality. Recent research suggests that this form of mental illness is related to how children perceive, assess, and deal with reality, and with the patterns of interaction and communications that exist within their families.[31]

CULTURE

A third quality that is presumed unique to humans is culture. Culture, according to anthropologist Ralph Linton, is "the configuration of learned behavior and results of behavior whose component elements are shared and transmitted by the members of a particular society."[32] Sociologist Robin Williams looks at the concept of culture as the patterns of behaviors and values of the total set of social roles in a particular society. He defines culture as the "relatively standardized prescriptions as to what must be done, ought to be done, should be done, may be done, and must not be done."[33]

In both definitions, culture is viewed as a society's total way of life. The prime difference between the two is the extent to which material objects such as tools, pottery, and clothing are considered to be part of culture. Anthropologists, as a rule, follow Linton and extend the definition of culture to include the tangible products of a society; sociologists usually take a narrower view and include ideas about these objects and the social behaviors and values that relate to them, but not the objects themselves. In keeping with the socio-logical perspective, the concept of culture employed here is limited to abstract patterns for living.

The notion of socialization assumes that culture is antecedent to the individual and is acquired by the individual through interaction with other members of the group. While it goes without saying that culture is modified to some degree as it passes from one generation to another—depending on physical and social conditions and upon individual differences among societal members—the patterned ways of a society are usually transmitted sufficiently to ensure that it survive beyond the lifespan of its members.

Many societies contain subsocieties or smaller groups of people who share patterns of behaviors and values that are somewhat dif-ferent from those of the general culture. These variations are usually referred to as *subcultures* because they are not sufficiently differenti-ated to constitute a distinct culture. Subcultures are common within age groups such as adolescents, college students, and senior citizens. The so-called generation gap is often more attributable to subcultural differences than to lasting social change. Subcultures also develop among members of occupational groups who have had similar train-ing and who perform similar tasks in their work; for example, teachers, physicians, and lawyers. Professional preparation for many occupations often includes the acquisition of work-related subcultural characteristics, such as a professional demeanor, unique jargon, and mode of dress.

The subcultures of families within a society also differ, depending upon such factors as the family's position in its social-stratification system and the religion, race, national origin, and education of family members. By the time they enter school, children have learned many significant subcultural patterns which occur in their families, yet they may be relatively naive about the culture of the dominant society. One of the perceived missions of the public school is to socialize children to the dominant American culture so that they can interact effectively with people who do not share their own subcultures.

A useful distinction is sometimes made between the socialization processes of *enculturation* and *acculturation,* both of which refer to the acquisition of cultural patterns.[34] Enculturation takes place when people learn the culture of their own society; for example, the sub-culture that is acquired within the family. Acculturation takes place when they learn the patterns of a society that is different from their own. Formal socialization within public schools entails both of these processes. When the content of home and school socialization draw from the same culture, as is usually the case for children from middle-class homes, schools are engaged in enculturation. When cultural continuity between home and school is lacking, school socialization is more nearly acculturation. Needless to say, acculturation is the more complicated of the two processes, inasmuch as children must learn patterns which are totally new to them and often contradictory to the norms and values they have accepted as their own. Navajo children, for example, who spend their early years within the traditional tribal culture have been encultured to Navajo ways; in later years at Bureau of Indian Affairs schools they are acculturated to other patterns.

For many years formal school policy did not reflect the extent to which public education was a process of acculturation for large numbers of pupils. In addition to Navajo and other American–Indian children, pupils from many Spanish-speaking families of the Southwest, French-speaking families of the Northeast, and children from recent immigrant families, among others, experience school as an institution for acculturation. The notion of biculturalism is, however, gaining currency; i.e. both the culture of the pupil's family and of the larger society are drawn upon and advanced in curriculum and instructional practices. Increasing numbers of children now receive instruction in both their home language and in English and many aspects of their family cultures are becoming serious subjects for academic study.

In addition to the above definitions, culture may be analyzed into the knowledge and beliefs, the values and norms, and the symbols common to a social group which give direction to the behavior of its members.

Knowledge and beliefs

Knowledge and beliefs are cognitive components of culture which pertain to what actually does exist or is supposed to exist, and represent the understandings of reality that are widely shared within a group. Individuals acquire the cognitive elements of their culture as they interact with other people and these provide them with the concepts through which they interpret the world around them and their own place within it. To the extent that people differ in their knowledge and beliefs, they also differ in their perceptions of the environment and in the meanings they attribute to these perceptions.

Despite many individual variations in cognition, however, there is usually enough agreement to provide a community of understanding or consensus among the members of a group.

In Western cultures *knowledge* most often refers to cognition that has been gained through the empirical or scientific method: a method that so far seems to be the most fruitful way to describe and predict relations among physical and social phenomena. The scientific method requires: first, that observations be made through the human senses such as sight and taste, or the extension of these senses in the form of instruments; and second that other investigators using the same techniques under the same conditions come up with identical observations. An example of knowledge that is easily verified through the scientific method is the phenomenon that at sea level water boils when it reaches a temperature of 100 degrees centigrade. This occurs regardless of who conducts the experiment, the kind of vessel in which the water is contained, and the kind of fuel that is used to heat it. It is a publicly verifiable event.

Belief, on the other hand, refers to cognition that has not yet been scientifically verified or is outside the domain of empirical observation. It is impossible to make observations of some physical and social phenomena under controlled conditions because of factors such as man's limited understanding; the complexity of these phenomena; or, as in the social sciences, moral proscriptions against measuring and controlling important elements relating to humans. Beliefs also emanate from nonobjective observations such as private revelations and dreams. By definition, these exclude other observers who can verify them empirically.

Values and norms

As noted in Chapter 1, values and norms are the shared standards of a group that serve as the organizing principles of social life. Cultural *values* represent what is worthwhile to most members of a group; they orient individuals toward common goals and behaviors. *Norms* are based upon cultural values in that they define the behaviors expected of people who perform specific roles. The values and norms contained in a culture can be distinguished from its cognitive elements by the words used to express them: knowledge and beliefs are stated in terms such as "is" and "is not"; values are manifested in affective terms such as "good" and "bad"; and norms, in prescriptive terms such as "ought" and "ought not."

The norms of a group are enforced to different degrees, depending upon the strength of the values that underlie them. Both folkways and mores are norms, but behavior that is contrary to folkways is ignored or quickly forgotten, whereas behavior that is contrary to norms is severely punished. Little attention is paid to the man who does not remove his hat in a public elevator, for example, while the person who is convicted of murder receives the group's severest sanctions, often life imprisonment or capital punishment. The avoidance of destructive conflict among members of a society is a commonly found value in all societies. The norms associated with this value range from folkways pertaining to manners, such as shaking hands, to mores against assault, theft, and murder.

Values and norms develop as people interact with one another on a repetitive basis. Through the process of empathy, they formulate expectations of one another and acquire mutual values which give cohesion to their society. When these mutual expectations are met, social interaction is predictable and destructive conflict is avoided or reduced. Knowledge of the values and norms of a group, from the point of view of individuals, enables them to cope with the demands made upon them by others.

Since each person is a product of unique experiences, there are both individual and subcultural differences in values and in interpretations of social norms. An example of such differences is the extent to which success in the form of material acquisitions or high scholastic attainment is valued. Within the American society these kinds of success are important to some people and to some subgroups and not important to others. Also, although norms relating to the attainment of success proscribe practices considered to be forms of cheating, the norms of some subcultures define cheating differently from the norms of others. Cheating in school examinations, for instance, may be viewed by the majority of pupils of one school as a contest between individuals and school authority, whereas cheating in another school may be considered an affront to one's peers. Pupils who move from the first to the second school can incur the disfavor of many of their new classmates if they unwittingly violate norms against cheating before they have the opportunity to learn the local subculture.

Values and norms are to some extent modified as they are transmitted so that every group or society undergoes a continuous process of cultural change. Nevertheless, many values and norms persist even if they have outlived their usefulness. This condition, known as *cultural lag,* is especially noticeable in societies experiencing rapid social change, wherein the circumstances that fostered the values and norms in the first place have disappeared, and altered circumstances have stimulated new and perhaps conflicting values and norms.

There are many examples of cultural lag in the United States; among the most glaring are those that relate to sexual conduct. The advent of the automobile combined with advances in contraception have given rise within two or three generations to some radically changed norms and values pertaining to premarital sex. Even so, adults often oppose the introduction of materials relating to sex in the school curricula because they deal with behaviors that are contrary to the standards they themselves were taught. Consequently, if estimates of veneral disease, teenage pregnancies, and nontraditional living arrangements are valid indicators, a large number of schools formally ignore one of the most serious social concerns of their pupils and of society as a whole. This view is occasionally carried to an extreme by districts that prohibit married pupils from attending regular classes because of the possible effects on fellow pupils. At the same time that schools censor materials which treat matters of sex, many youngsters obtain vicarious and explicit sexual experience through television, films, and nonschool books, and a few, reportedly, have their first realistic sexual encounters within the physical confines of the school.

Symbols

Symbols are the vehicle in which individual and group experiences are stored and through which they are communicated. The most significant form of symbols from the point of view of socialization is verbal language, or speech. The knowledge, beliefs, values, and norms of a group are transmitted primarily, although not exclusively, through spoken and written verbal symbols. All social groups employ speech; even the most primitive are believed to have fully developed linguistic structures.

The capacity to convey abstract ideas through language is uniquely human.[35] Although some animals can be taught to talk, this is not the same as human language. The utterances of myna birds and parrots may appear similar to the babbling of a young child, but there are two crucial differences: first, young children have the potential ability to decipher the word patterns of others so that they can comprehend the thoughts behind them; and second, children can rearrange these symbols into new combinations so that they can express thoughts of their own. Neither of these abilities has been demonstrated by lower animals.

Many species have some form of communication, but it is based on signs rather than symbols. A sign is a proxy for an object with which it is paired, and the presence of one of the pair elicits the other in the mind of the observer.[36] The "language" of the bees, for example, is a series of signs that inform other bees of the existence of nectar-giving flowers, and the courting dance of the male bird informs the female bird of his readiness to mate. The ability of one animal to interpret the signs of another is the basis of so-called animal intelligence.

Humans also possess animal intelligence, though their interpretation of signs is complicated by the influence of culture. Since a sign can stand for a number of things, its meaning to a particular individual is derived from the social context which produces it. Susanne Langer lists some of the possible cultural meanings of a familiar sign, the sound of a bell:

> *As for bells, the world is mad with their messages. Somebody at the front door, the back door, the side door, the telephone—toast is ready—typewriter line is ended—school begins, work begins, church begins, church is over—street car starts—cashbox registers—knife grinder passes—time for dinner, time to get up—fire in town![37]*

How people react to this sign is related to their previous experiences with its announcements.

The uniqueness of human language lies not with responses to signs, however, but with the capacity to conceptualize through the use of symbols. Because of the human ability to express ideas through symbols, the experiences of one person are added to the experiences of others and, in this manner, culture is created and transmitted. There is no longer need, for example, for fishermen to fear falling off the horizon, since the knowledge that the world is not flat has been verbally communicated from one man to another.

Language. Language is an integral part of culture as well as the vehicle by which culture is transmitted. Some theorists believe that language is the key determinant of all thought and behavior. They maintain that the concepts contained in language and the way in which these concepts are structured determine how people perceive, interpret, and organize events in their physical and social environments: without language there can be no development of self, no acquisition of the cognitive and evaluative elements of the culture, and no patterns of thought.

This view was stated in extreme by Edward Sapir who wrote, "We see and hear and otherwise experience very largely as we do because the language habits of our community predispose certain choices of interpretation."[38] His student, Benjamin Whorf, expanded this thesis and concluded that because language patterns are always associated with distinctive cultures, we are

> . . . introduced to a new principle of relativity which holds that all observers are not led by the same physical evidence to the same picture of the universe, unless their linguistic backgrounds are similar, or can in some way be calibrated.[39]

In support of his principle of linguistic relativity, Whorf provides examples of concepts contained in the speech of some cultures and not in others. He makes the assumption that the existence of linguistic concepts allows speakers of the language to make certain observations and to hold certain ideas that speakers of other languages cannot. English-speaking people, for example, have one all-inclusive word for snow and, according to Whorf, are thereby limited in the observations they make about it. Eskimos, on the other hand, have separate words to refer to falling snow, fallen snow, hard-packed snow, slushy snow, and wind-driven flying snow. For the Eskimo, each of these words indicates something which is "sensuously and operationally different."[40]

The notion that language precedes thought has become known as the *Whorfian Hypothesis*. Contemporary spokesmen for this view no longer take as extreme a position as did Sapir and Whorf with respect to the total influence of language on culture, but many continue to maintain that language is necessary for the development of mental processes. For instance Basil Bernstein, a contemporary British sociolinguist, claims his view differs from that of Whorf primarily because of his belief that new distinctive linguistic forms can develop within a common language which then "induce in their speakers different ways of relating to objects and persons." These variant forms come about as a result of social interaction and are, therefore, products of past behavior as well as causes of subsequent behavior. According to Bernstein, his own thesis "leaves open the question whether there are features of the common culture shared by all members of a society that are determined by the specific nature of the . . . language."[41]

Other theorists take a different position. They believe that thought can and does occur before the acquisition of language, although language makes communication among people possible. That thought takes place prior to the acquisition of language is supported by Piaget's studies of young children. Piaget concludes that the child has the ability to create mental symbols of the objects he has previously encountered and to think about them, even though he has no notion of their verbal symbols. The acquisition of language, according to Piaget, is the *result* of the child's mental ability, rather than its cause. And even after language is acquired and thought processes are aided and constrained by its concepts, a child's thoughts can still be independent of it. In Piaget's view, children impose their own meanings on the language of their culture. Contrary to the Whorfian Hypothesis that thought is dependent on language, he holds that language is probably more dependent on thought.[42]

In this connection it is interesting to speculate about reports that the great physicist, Albert Einstein, was unable to speak until age three. Some have attributed his achievements in the development of nonverbal, abstract concepts of space, time, and energy to his early freedom from the cultural restrictions of language.

An intermediate view maintains that the role of language in the acquisition of culture has been grossly exaggerated because all known languages have the potential to express the thoughts of which humans are capable. In this view, children are born with principles of grammatical structures, some of which are activated when they hear the speech of their own particular culture. Language acquisition is not entirely dependent upon culture, however, for although culture stimulates inborn grammatical structures and provides the semantic component of speech, it does not affect the age at which speech is acquired.[43]

The chief issue among contemporary theorists revolves around the question of the amount rather than the necessity of language for the acquisition of thought. All of them agree that language is essential for communication among humans and there is little doubt that the acquisition of language is the most important single feature of human development. Language is a person's most important tool in dealing with others and with self.

Nonverbal communication. This subject has received increased scholarly attention in recent years. Although it is not as seminal as language for the transmission of culture, hand gestures, facial expressions, and the general positioning and movement of the body often convey conceptional meaning. Consider, for example, the raised eyebrow of a teacher who has observed pupils exchanging messages during a time set aside for study. This simple gesture might communicate chaffing, questioning, mocking, or derision; in addition, it can command pupils to return to the task at hand.

Nonverbal symbols, like their verbal counterparts, are usually learned from other members of the social group and must, therefore, be interpreted within the context of a culture. Professor Birdwhistell, a student of body-motion communication, reports that although he has been searching for many years he has been unable to find a gesture or body motion that has the same meaning in all societies. In fact, he has not found a single facial expression—not even a smile—that conveys a universal meaning.[44]

Some forms of nonverbal communication are learned even before the acquisition of speech. The preverbal infant can effectively communicate desire for social interaction and physical discomfort through a conversation of gestures. But acquisition of speech stimulates, rather than extinguishes, nonverbal communication in that it provides a greater opportunity for social interaction, thereby expanding the nonverbal repertoire. Nonverbal symbols sometimes appear alone; at other times, they supplement verbal communication. A discerning viewer can often perceive inconsistencies between verbal and nonverbal messages which are simultaneously communicated, and the reader no doubt can testify that written correspondence and telephone conversations are seldom as communicative as face-to-face interaction.

The discussion thus far in this chapter has been concerned with the part socialization plays in developing individuals and preparing them to cope with the demands that other members of the social group make upon them. There are three major points to make in summary:

1. Through the process of socialization, people define their own self or social identity, which is similar in some respects and different in others from every other person in their social group.
2. People develop the capacity for empathy, which is needed to learn social roles that allow them to satisfy basic drives.
3. People acquire a shared culture, which provides them with the knowledge, beliefs, values, norms, and symbols that enable them to participate in group life and to contribute to the quality of their own existence.

In sum, individuals can neither develop as social beings nor effectively participate in society without social learning. When their socially acquired needs and their learned ways of meeting them are consistent with the general expectations of most members of their group, group expectations fall lightly upon them and they can easily comply with most social demands.

HUMAN INTELLIGENCE AND THE NATURE-NURTURE CONTROVERSY

Unlike earlier social theorists who used to engage in extensive debate over the relative importance of inborn characteristics as compared with social and physical environmental factors in the development of intelligence, contemporary sociologists do not usually consider mental functioning separately from the individual's history of socialization. This so-called nature-nurture controversy had been dormant within the social sciences for many years. It was recently revived, however, by the educational research of the 1960s which showed large differences in academic achievement among pupils from different racial and ethnic backgrounds.[45] A few writers now assert that the relatively low levels of school success of some groups of pupils are the consequence of inherited differences in their intellectual capacities.

A leading spokesman for the position that differences in measured intelligence between white and black pupils are genetically based is psychologist Arthur Jensen, whose presentation in the *Harvard Educational Review* in 1969 drew fire from fellow social scientists, civil rights leaders, and others.[46] As Jensen had hoped, one of the consequences of his work was to reopen discussion about the part played by genetic factors in human behavior. However, two major unintended consequences of his work were, first, to stimulate school districts to reevaluate the desirability of testing for intelligence because of the controversy he initiated over the interpretation of test results, and, second, to encourage both school districts and parents to reevaluate the desirability of racial integration in public schools in light of his conclusions that the educational needs of white and black pupils are not the same.

Intelligence as genetically determined

It is Jensen's thesis that about 80 percent of intellectual functioning is fixed from the moment of conception. Although he believes that

environment also plays a part in the development of intelligence,
Jensen takes social scientists to task for their belief in the "almost
infinite plasticity of intellect" and their "ostrich-like denial of biological factors in individual differences."[47] To ignore the role of
genetics in the study of intelligence, according to Jensen, "can only
hinder investigation and understanding of the conditions, processes,
and limits through which the social environment influences human
behavior."[48] He goes on to explain that differences in intelligence
among races must necessarily derive from inheritance since:

> . . . Any groups which have been geographically or socially isolated
> from one another for many generations are practically certain to dif-
> fer in their gene pools. . . . There seems to be little question that
> racial differences in genetically conditioned behavioral characteristics,
> such as mental abilities, should exist, just as physical differences.[49]

Intelligence as environmentally determined

Many social scientists take the position that the nature-nurture controversy revolves around a pseudoquestion because environmental influences are so intertwined with genetic endowment that it is impossible empirically to unscramble the two. They hold that research
efforts should more properly be directed toward understanding *how*
environment and genetic endowment interact to create a mature human being, rather than determining the relative influence of one or
the other. Jensen's critics, in general, believe first, that environmental
factors come into play from the moment children are conceived
through their mothers' physical and emotional states and that these
states largely determine conditions surrounding their birth and im-
pinge upon their development throughout life; and, second, that
although genetics may set the maximum and minimum of a person's
ultimate development, environmental factors account for most ability
within the normal range. One psychologist makes the point that
while genetics may predict proficiency in extremely difficult and creative areas, such as mathematics or music, the competencies demanded in school are well within the ability of all children who do
not have serious brain damage.[50]

Other critics have emphasized that social environment is composed of sentient beings who note genetic differences among people,
such as skin color and facial features, and consequently act to differentiate them further.[51] They refer to the sociological concept of
the *self-fulfilling prophecy* in which the perception a person has of

a situation—whether correct or not—sets processes in motion that turn this perception into a reality.[52] Educationally disadvantaged children often have negative self-fulfilling prophecies about their academic potential which are created by the reaction of teachers and others to their biological and social heritage. The self-fulfilling effect of teachers' perceptions of pupils' academic abilities on their school performance has, in fact, been experimentally shown.[53]

Sociologist Alan Wilson attempted to identify the factors that most contribute to a child's I.Q. test score. In addition to race and socioeconomic background, he took into consideration the advantages to children of their relationships to family and peer groups, to school, and to society as a whole, as well as the kind of social bonds that attach them to each. Through the use of analysis of variance, a statistical method that permits one to determine the unique influence of each of these factors, Wilson shows that race per se has little effect on the measurement of intelligence.

The factors most related to intelligence test scores of Wilson's sample of seventh grade pupils are: the academic quality of the elementary school, teachers' expectations of pupils, pupils' commitment to their parents' goals, and pupils' feeling of control over their own destinies. Those most related to the scores of the sample of tenth grade pupils are father's education, teachers' expectations, and pupils' educational aspirations.[54] Wilson admits that these data are not conclusive, but they present sufficient support for the influence of environment in the development of intelligence to shift the burden of proof in the nature-nurture controversy to those who would argue that I.Q. distinctions are "based upon assortative mating within differentiated genetic pools."[55]

Jensen was also criticized by psychologists who take issue with his use of intelligence tests as measures that are supposed to be without cultural connotations. They claim that it is impossible on the basis of intelligence-test scores to differentiate between what children have learned and what they might learn because tests are culture-bound and constructed within a certain kind of culture.[56] Even if culture-free tests could be devised, which is improbable since the very idea that one should engage in tests of this kind is itself culture-bound, they cannot measure inborn ability because children's language and motivations during the testing situation have also been learned. Many of Jensen's critics further point out that differences between the scores of black and white children from similar home background are smaller than differences between children from different socioeconomic strata within the same race.

Finally, Jensen has been criticized by some anthropologists because of his concept of race. In response to Jensen's article, Anderson writes that 'race' as used by Jensen is not a genetic but a social term. Contrary to general opinion, blacks and whites in the United States do not represent different biological populations since they have interbred in the past and continue to do so today. Anderson believes that if I.Q. scores are to be used for studies of heritability, it is more appropriate to compare one geographic region within which there has been considerable interbreeding, than to compare two "pseudo-populations" that have been defined socially rather than genetically.[57]

THE INTERACTION OF SOCIALIZATION AND MATURATION

If one takes the view that human intelligence is fashioned more from physical and social environments than from genetic inheritance, there are still certain biological factors that must be taken into account in the explanation of intelligence or, indeed, of any behavior. First, there is the obvious assumption of normality; children must be free from neurophysiological defects that prevent them from behaving within a range of commonly expected behaviors. They cannot learn to behave in certain ways if their bodies lack the potential capacity to do so.

Second is the factor of maturation; children must have realized some of their biological potential for neurophysical development in order to acquire competence in a specific behavior. Young children, for example, cannot learn to use the eating utensils of their culture if the muscles and nerves controlling their hands are not sufficiently mature; nor can they learn to talk until the muscles and nerves controlling the organs of speech have been adequately developed.

Third, there are optimum periods during maturation in which children will most profit from environmental experience. For example, it is generally thought that a first language must be learned before the onset of puberty if a child is to speak at all, and foreign languages are totally mastered only if they are presented in early childhood.[58] The larger portion of a person's total capacity for intellectual functioning is also thought to develop early. From a review of research in this area, Benjamin Bloom reports that 50 percent of one's ultimate intellectual ability is attained by age 4, 80 percent by age 8, and 99 percent by age 20. He also notes that changes in intellectual behavior are most common during periods of rapid physical growth such as early childhood and early adolescence.[59] That there are optimum periods in which children acquire certain knowledge and skills should have far-reaching implication for school curricula. If, for example, it is more efficient and effective to introduce a second language before adolescence, then the common American practice of delaying foreign language instruction until secondary school would be difficult to justify.

Just as maturation limits socialization, socialization can limit one's capacity for maturation when things that are already learned interfere with future development. Consider once more the example of speech. The muscles that are developed when people learn their first language may so hinder the development of the muscles involved in speaking that they will never speak in the newer language without some telltale accent of the first. Socialization also curtails maturation if it inhibits a person from having certain kinds of experience. Fear learned by children who have had a close brush with death by drowning, for instance, may constrain their aquatic activities to the point that they are never able to develop their potential ability to swim.

Socialization also gives direction to maturation by supplying individuals with the knowledge, skills, and values of their culture which motivate them to pursue activities leading to certain kinds of physiological and intellectual development at the expense of other kinds. To take a familiar example, children who grow up in communities in which participation in athletic events is stressed and incorporated as a school objective are, as a rule, better coordinated physically and have greater muscular development than children who grow up in communities that do not give priority to these considerations.

Human development, then, is the interaction of maturation and socialization. Maturation accounts for development which is genetically programmed; for the maximum and minimum amounts possible for a person to learn, and for the optimum stage of development for certain kinds of learning to take place. Socialization accounts for all that is learned, including those things which encourage or inhibit further physical and intellectual development.

NOTES

[1] William I. Thomas, *The Unadjusted Girl*, Boston, Little, Brown, 1927, pp. 42–43.

[2] This is not to say that *all* psychoanalysts hold this position. Sullivan,

for example, viewed the development of man in a manner similar to that of Cooley, Mead, and other symbolic interactionists and was a leader in the interpersonal movement of American psychiatry. See Harry Stack Sullivan, *Conceptions of Modern Psychiatry*, New York, Norton, 1953.

[3] Sigmund Freud, *Civilization and its Discontents*, trans. James Starchey, New York, Norton, 1962, p. 88.

[4] Research in socialization had been dominated until recently by the Freudian psychoanalytical approach. Critical reviews of this research often conclude that the effect of child-rearing practices on personality development which is their primary concern, has not been demonstrated. William Sewell, "Some Recent Developments in Socialization Theory and Research," *The Annals of the American Academy of Political and Social Science*, 349 (September 1963), 165.

[5] A. S. Neill, *Summerhill: A Radical Aproach to Child Rearing*, New York, Hart, 1964, p. 4. First published 1960.

[6] *Ibid.*, p. 114.

[7] *Ibid.*, p. 28.

[8] Jean Jacques Rousseau, *Émile*, trans. William H. Payne, New York, Appleton, 1918, pp. 14–15.

[9] Ralph Linton, *The Cultural Background of Personality*, New York, Appleton, 1945.

[10] The notion that man is only man because he lives in a society goes back at least as far as Aristotle. It was further developed by John Locke in his conception of *tabula rasa* and was the view held by French sociologist Emile Durkheim who sparked the functional orientation to the analysis of social life. This notion also underlies the symbolic interaction school of social psychology. Early proponents of this position in the United States include Cooley, Dewey, and Mead, among others. See Charles Horton Cooley, *Human Nature and the Social Order*, rev. ed., New York, Scribner, 1922; John Dewey, *Human Nature and Conduct*, New York, Holt, Rinehart & Winston, 1935; George Herbert Mead, *On Social Psychology*, Anselm Strauss, ed., Chicago, University of Chicago Press, 1964. First published 1956 under title *The Social Psychology of George Herbert Mead*.

[11] Cooley, *op. cit.*, p. 47.

[12] These metaphors are described by Israel Scheffler, *The Language of Education*, Springfield, Ill., C. C. Thomas, 1966, pp. 49–53.

[13] For an interesting discussion of the implication of these metaphors plus the implications of a third view which incorporates the developmental views of Dewey and Piaget, see Lawrence Kohlberg and Richelle Mayer, "Development as the Aim of Education," *Harvard Educational Review*, 42, no. 4 (November 1972), 449–496.

[14] Although the socialization process may, as the Freudians assert, frustrate some of the individual's basic desires, these desires are themselves products of social learning. For example, the gratification of hunger, bodily discomfort, and sex differ greatly according to the manner in which

people have been taught to define their need level. See Ralph H. Turner, *Family Interaction*, New York, Wiley, 1970, p. 173.

[15] Herman A. Witkin, "Social Influence in the Development of Cognitive Style," in David A. Goslin, ed., *Handbook of Socialization Theory and Research*, Skokie, Ill., Rand McNally, 1969, p. 689.

[16] Turner, *op. cit.*, p. 29.

[17] Charles Horton Cooley, *Social Organization: A Study of the Larger Mind*, New York, Schocken Books, 1962, p. xv. First published 1909.

[18] Some of these studies are listed below. See Chapter 6, note 20.

[19] Cooley, *Social Organization*, p. 184.

[20] Because humans mold their behavior so that they will create a favorable impression, man has sometimes been characterized as an "acceptance seeker." Nevertheless Wrong holds that there are natural forces within man that resist total socialization: "The view that man is invariably pushed by internalized norms or pulled by the lure of self-validation by others ignores—to speak archaically for a moment—both the highest and the lowest, both the beast and angel, in his nature." Dennis Wrong, "The Oversocialized Conception of Man in Modern Sociology," *American Sociological Review*, 26, no. 2 (April 1961), 183–193.

[21] Mead, *op. cit.*, Part VI.

[22] *Ibid.*, p. 218.

[23] *Ibid.*, pp. 215–216.

[24] *Ibid.*, pp. 219–221.

[25] Herbert Blumer, *Symbolic Interactionism: Perspective and Method*, Englewood Cliffs, N.J., Prentice-Hall, 1969, p. 8.

[26] Sheldon Stryker, "Symbolic Interaction as an Approach to Family Research," *Marriage and Family Living*, 21, no. 2 (May 1959), 111–119.

[27] Roslind F. Dymond, "A Scale for the Measurement of Empathic Ability," *Journal of Consulting Psychology*, 13 (April 1949), 127–133.

[28] Cooley, *Social Organization*, p. 28.

[29] Leonard S. Cottrell, Jr., "Interpersonal Interaction and the Development of the Self," in David A. Goslin, ed., *op. cit.*, p. 552, footnote.

[30] Herbert Ginsburg and Sylvia Opper, *Piaget's Theory of Intellectual Development: An Introduction*, Englewood Cliffs, N.J., Prentice-Hall, 1969, p. 115. The social learning theory of Jean Piaget is developed in his early works. See *The Language and Thought of the Child*, trans. Marjorie Gabin, London, Routledge & Kegan Paul, 1926; *The Moral Judgment of the Child*, trans. Marjorie Gabin, New York, Free Press, 1948. First published in English, 1932.

[31] Melvin L. Kohn, *Class and Conformity: A Study in Values*, Homewood, Ill., Dorsey Press, 1969, pp. 198–200; Jay Haley, "The Family of the Schizophrenic: A Model System," in Gerald Handel, ed., *The Psychosocial Interior of the Family*, Chicago, Aldine, 1967.

[32] Ralph Linton, *The Cultural Background of Personality*, New York, Appleton, 1945, p. 32.

[33] Robin M. Williams, Jr., *American Society: A Sociological Interpretation*, 3rd ed., New York, Knopf, 1970, p. 26.

[34] For example, see Margaret Mead, "Socialization and Enculturation," *Current Anthropology*, 4, no. 2 (April 1963), 184–187.

[35] The dolphin may prove the exception to this generalization. It has been discovered that these mammals make a variety of vocal sounds which seem to have the characteristics of a functional language.

[36] Susanne K. Langer, *Philosophy in a New Key: A Study in the Symbolism of Reason, Rite, and Art*, 3rd ed., Cambridge, Harvard University Press, 1969, p. 59. First published 1942.

[37] *Ibid.*, p. 61.

[38] Edward Sapir, "The Status of Linguistics as a Science," *Language*, 5 (1929), 207–214.

[39] Benjamin Lee Whorf, *Language, Thought and Reality: Selected Writings of Benjamin Lee Whorf*, John B. Carroll, ed., Cambridge, MIT Press, 1956, p. 214.

[40] *Ibid.*, p. 216.

[41] Basil Bernstein, "The Role of Speech in the Development and Transmission of Culture," in Gordon J. Klopf and William A. Hohman, eds., *Perspectives on Learning*, New York, Banks Street College of Education, 1967, p. 17.

[42] Ginsburg and Opper, *op. cit.*, pp. 72–74; Jean Piaget, *The Origins of Intelligence in Children*, trans. Margaret Cook, New York, International University Press, 1952. Investigations into the intellectual process of children who have been deaf from birth and, consequently, never acquire the verbal language of their culture has led to the conclusion that "the internal organization of intelligence is not dependent on the language system; on the contrary, comprehension and use of the ready-made language is dependent on the structure of intelligence." See Hans G. Furth, *Thinking Without Language: Psychological Implications of Deafness*, New York, Free Press, 1966, p. 228.

[43] Noam Chomsky, *Aspects of the Theory of Syntax*, Cambridge, MIT Press, 1964; John Lyons, *Noam Chomsky*, New York, Viking Press (Modern Masters Series), 1970.

[44] Ray L. Birdwhistell, *Kinesics and Context: Essays on Body Motion Communication*, Philadelphia, University of Pennsylvania Press, 1970, p. 81.

[45] The best known of this research is James S. Coleman, *et al.*, *Equality of Educational Opportunity*, Washington, D.C., U.S. Office of Education, 1966.

[46] Arthur R. Jensen, "How Much Can We Boost IQ and Scholastic Achievement?" *Harvard Educational Review*, 39, no. 1 (Winter 1969), 1–123.

[47] *Ibid.*, p. 29.

[48] *Ibid.*, p. 29.

[49] *Ibid.*, p. 80.

[50] Jerome S. Kagan, "Inadequate Evidence and Illogical Conclusions," *Harvard Educational Review*, 39, no. 2 (Spring 1969), 277.

[51] Richard J. Light and Paul V. Smith, "Social Allocation Models of Intelligence: A Methodological Inquiry," *Harvard Educational Review*, 39, no. 3 (Summer 1969), 510.

[52] The notion, self-fulfilling prophecy, was introduced by the early sociologist, W. I. Thomas, as the "definition of the situation." He wrote: "If men define situations as real they are real in their consequences." This notion was further developed by Merton as the self-fulfilling prophecy. Robert K. Merton, *Social Theory and Social Structure*, rev. ed., New York, Free Press, 1957, pp. 421–436.

[53] Robert Rosenthal and Lenore Jacobson, *Pygmalian in the Classroom: Teacher Expectations and Pupils' Intellectual Development*, New York, Holt, Rinehart & Winston, 1968. This study is discussed in Chapter 7.

[54] Alan B. Wilson, "Sociological Perspectives on the Development of Academic Competence in Urban Areas," in A. Harry Passow, ed., *Urban Education in the 1970's: Reflections and a Look Ahead*, New York, Teachers College Press, Columbia University, 1971, pp. 135–137.

[55] *Ibid.*, p. 138.

[56] Martin Deutsch, "Happenings on the Way Back to the Forum: Social Science, IQ, and Race Differences Revisited," *Harvard Educational Review*, 39, no. 3 (Summer 1969), 581–585.

[57] E. N. Anderson, Jr., "Correspondence: Political, Technical, and Theoretical Comments," *Harvard Educational Review*, 39, no. 3 (Summer 1969), 581–585.

[58] Eric H. Lennenberg, "Capacity for Language Acquisition," in Jerry A Fodor and Jerrold J. Katz, *Structure of Language: Readings in the Philosophy of Language*, Englewood Cliffs, N.J., Prentice–Hall, 1964, pp. 579–603.

[59] Benjamin Bloom, *Stability and Change in Human Characteristics*, New York, Wiley, 1964.

3
The family

KINSHIP PATTERNS

At birth children have no sense of self, no ability to empathize
with others, and none of the cultural elements of the groups into
which they are born. These fundamental human characteristics
are acquired only by association with others. What is more,
newborn children are totally incapable of caring for themselves.
Their physical development, like their human development, is
accomplished by social interaction. Most societies provide for the
care of their young—and their initial socialization—through family
units made up of one or both biological parents and often other
blood relatives as well. This most universal of all social institutions, the family, is sometimes classified into two general types,
the nuclear family and the extended family, depending upon the
closeness of the blood relationships of its members.

Nuclear families

Nuclear families consist of husband, wife, and children living
in comparative isolation from other kin.[1] This plan of organization
is of relatively recent origin: it is most associated with modern
industrial societies in which workers are often geographically and
socially mobile and must, therefore, be independent from many of

their other relatives. The newly married couple of the nuclear family typically establishes a household separate from that of their parents and assumes major responsibility for each other's welfare and behavior and for that of the children born into the marriage. The marital partners make important decisions relating to family planning, child-rearing practices, financial affairs, occupational careers, place of residence, and the like—with or without consultation with others. And as responsibilities for the new family grow, obligations which husband and wife may once have had toward their parents and other relatives become attenuated.[2]

Extended families

Extended families are based on common lineage rather than on sexual partnership, and are composed of many blood relatives and marital partners of either the husband or wife.[3] Though the nuclear-family pattern seems to be gaining as urbanization and industrialization spread, the extended family is still a common form of family organization, even within the United States. It is often found where family members are clustered geographically or are part of a self-sufficient economic organization such as a family farm or business. It is also found frequently among members of some ethnic and religious groups who retain the family organization associated with their traditional cultures. The extended family is also common among the American upper classes in which older generations attempt to maintain the family's preferred social position by means of controlling the socialization of young children as well as over property which is jointly owned.

Of the two types of family patterns, the nuclear pattern is more closely associated with social change. Aside from the fact that it is stimulated by industrial development which comes at a time when other social patterns are also changing, its relative isolation prompts nuclear-family members to break with traditional socialization practices. For example, major responsibilities for child rearing are usually placed on neophyte parents who are insufficiently socialized to the parental role and who, if they are without assistance and advice from older generations, either innovate or rely on nonfamily sources of opinion. The availability in the United States of "expert" information on child rearing has both encouraged changes in traditional practices and served to homogenize them. Shifts in patterns of infant care during the twentieth century correspond strikingly to changes in practices advocated in successive editions of U. S. Children's Bureau bulletins and similar sources of expert opinion and show a marked coming together of attitudes and techniques.[4]

Kinship, nevertheless, is an important factor in the lives of most Americans, even though they may live within a nuclear unit. It now seems that early observers of modernization had underestimated the strength of the extended family's influence over that of the nuclear family.[5] They overestimated both the extent to which friendship ties replace kinship ties, especially within the middle classes, and the extent to which children are reared in two-parent homes. In addition, evidence is gathering to suggest that although social relations among children within nuclear families are often curtailed during late adolescence and early adulthood, they tend to be reestablished in later years when pressures for developing occupational and parental roles are reduced.[6]

It is also worth noting that nuclear families are less isolated in societies that have been industrialized for some time since many of the changes accompanying industrialization work to join, rather than separate extended-family members. For example, improved communication and transportation reduce geographic distances among them, and improved living standards and opportunities for education reduce social-class symbols that create barriers between those who are more and those who are less successful.[7] There may come a point in the modernization process when related nuclear families will federate into extended family organizations with each nuclear family retaining a substantial amount of independence, yet drawing cultural and emotional support from the larger unit.

Whether children acquire the major portion of their early learning from the relatively few people in their immediate families or from the many members of their extended families, the family is more salient to total social development than any other social institution. Within its boundaries the individual acquires a sense of self, a human nature, and a cultural heritage.

THE FAMILY AS A PRIMARY GROUP

The family is the first *primary group* in which a person participates. The concept of primary group, like looking-glass self, was developed by Charles Cooley:

By primary groups I mean those characterized by intimate face-to-face association and cooperation. They are primary in several senses, but chiefly in that they are fundamental in forming the social nature and ideals of the individual . . . it involves the sort of sympathy and mutual identification for which "we" is the natural expression.[8]

In contrast, relationships in *secondary groups* are impersonal and conventional, and communication is relatively superficial. The discussion of pattern-variable analysis presented in Chapter 1 is directly related to these essential differences. Interpersonal relations within primary groups tend to be dominated by the *gemeinschaft* norms of diffuseness, particularism, affectivity, and ascription; whereas interpersonal relations in secondary groups are characterized by the *gesellschaft* norms of specificity, universalism, affective-neutrality, and achievement.[9]

During the period of a lifetime people are members of a number of primary groups in addition to the family into which they are born. A sampling might include a neighborhood play group, school chums, a teenage clique, a street-corner gang, a pair of lovers, and a new family of procreation. Although interaction within each of these groups can usually be described by similar *gemeinschaft* norms, the *family of origin*, that is, the family in which one grows up, differs from other primary groups in several important respects. First, membership is always ascribed; children enter an ongoing social system and have no control over the extent of their initial participation. Second, the culture of the family is already set by the previous history of other family members and by the patterns of the larger society; it does not emerge as it would in friendship groups, for example. Third, the family has an existing structure with lines of authority drawn in such a way that older members control the behavior of younger members; as children mature, family authority systems may approach, but probably do not attain, equality as is common in many peer groups. And, fourth, the extent to which members are tied to one another through affection and intimacy varies among families and between individual family members; relationships in some families are characterized by high affectivity and in others by neutrality. Affective bonds among members of other primary groups are usually strong and highly positive.

Although every primary group is a source of some socialization, the family is the most significant in shaping the social identity of the overwhelming majority of people. Family life presents optimum conditions for socialization: it is the group to which children belong during their most formative period, and it supplies the people with whom they have the most frequent and enduring interpersonal relationships. The first culture children acquire is the culture of their families, and, because family members share a common culture, they usually relate to one another with relative ease and develop mutual dependency and loyalty. More often than not, family members become mutual significant others and value one another's approval to a greater extent than they do that of nonfamily members.

THE SOCIALIZATION PROCESS

Although there has long been interest in how people acquire the culture of their society, internal psychological processes of socialization are still largely conjecture. Explanations tend to vary depending upon the orientation of the person asking the question. Some theorists explain all learning as *conditioning* in which learners acquire responses to stimuli because they are rewarded for making them. Although at first learners may respond in a way that only resembles what is expected of them, as they are rewarded for increasing precision, they continue until their responses become exact and specific.[10]

Other theorists view learning more as a result of *modeling*, or identification with someone the individual perceives as receiving social rewards such as affection, prestige, and power. Learners identify with people whom they for some reason value and then model or imitate their behavior.[11]

Most sociologists believe that socialization is brought about by a number of different and complex processes. To the extent that there is debate among them, it centers around which of the processes are most influential. There is general agreement, however, that all socialization results from some combination of external and internal reinforcements which people associate with what they have learned.

Although healthy newborns have the ability to breathe, ingest and digest food, eliminate body wastes, and sleep, they are not capable of supplying their own bodies with food or protecting them from harsh environmental elements. Mature members of society attend to these and other physical needs, and, as they do, newborns begin the lifelong process of socialization. At first, learning centers around the satisfactions derived from life-maintaining requirements. Not unlike learning in lower animals, early learning in humans is a form of conditioning in which infants associate the elimination of physical discomfort and accompanying feelings of well-being with the surrounding circumstances, including their own behavior.[12] They learn, for example, that reduction of hunger is in some way related to a nipple and to their own sucking activity; even very young infants often exhibit excitement and begin to suck at its presentation.

The concern here, however, is not with the internal processes of need-reduction, but with the fact that the gratification and frustration of physiological needs are important reinforcements in the process of socialization, especially in the early months of life. As the perceptual field of infants widens beyond immediate sources of physiological satisfaction such as breast or bottle, they increasingly associate repeated cycles of discomfort, need-reduction, and gratification with their nurturing figures. And as they develop the ability to generalize from past experiences to future events, they come to expect their nurturing figures to continue to satisfy their needs. Often the mere presence of the nurturing figure can elicit the gratification infants connect with nurturing behavior.

For these reasons, the initial nurturing figure—usually but not always the biological mother—most often becomes the first significant other, and probably one of the most influential people in the development of the infant's personality. Responses by significant others like food and physical comfort have reinforcement power and lie at the heart of the socialization process. The saliency of the first signficant other derives from the primacy and the intensity of the infant's emotional involvement with her, and from her initial ability to control many reinforcements.

The strong emotional bonds between infant and mother are not altogether positive, however, as some overly romantic views of motherhood would have it. They contain a substantial negative component as well. For example, in typical nuclear families mothers also have duties and obligations toward other household members and cannot or will not meet all demands made by self-centered infants. The orientations of infants, by contrast, are primarily toward the mother if she is the dispenser of gratifications; but since they have not yet learned to tolerate frustration, their feelings toward the mother will be intensely negative when she fails to satisfy their needs. The indignant cry of rage that is common to the repertoire of most healthy babies is an expression of such negative feelings.

Starting from infanthood, then, the family provides an arena in which positive and negative emotional feelings are created and in which irresolvable conflicts are translated into love-hate relationships that often endure throughout life. Part of early childhood socialization includes learning to cope with the frustrations that develop from interaction with other people and things that appear to have wills of their own. The patterns for dealing with the interplay of love and hate that are developed in these early years usually set the mode of social interaction in later life.

Importance of human contact

Research in child development indicates that infants benefit from the body warmth provided by a nurturing figure, the rocking and petting, the sound of voices, and the visual stimuli created by movement in their environment, and by being moved themselves. After about the age of six months, when children are able to discriminate among the faces of different people, they become affectively tied to a single person. Even in situations where several nurturing figures are available, children are attracted to one special significant other with whom they seek social interaction.[13]

A comparison by René Spitz between babies who had been institutionalized in a prison nursery and in a foundling home dramatizes the importance of this early interaction.[14] The babies in the prison nursery were born to imprisoned pregnant girls, each of whom nursed, fed, and cared for her own infant. The babies in the foundling home were mostly from socially adjusted urban girls who were financially unable to support their children. Aside from an occasional wet nurse, the foundling home infants had no contact with their mothers or with mother surrogates. Spitz observed that the foundling babies were much less physically and socially developed than the babies in the prison nursery. They were extremely susceptible to infection and disease, and even at ages two or three were unable to speak, to feed themselves, to acquire habits of cleanliness, or to walk.

> . . . In contrast, prison nursery children ran lustily around on the floor; some of them dressed and undressed themselves; fed themselves with a spoon; nearly all spoke a few words; they understood commands and obeyed them; and the older ones showed certain consciousness of toilet requirements. All of them played lively social games with each other and with observers.[15]

From this and other investigations of institutionalized children, Spitz concluded that the damage inflicted by deprivation of maternal care, stimulation, and love is irreparable.

Internalization of culture

By age six months, infants are usually able to discriminate between what is and is not themselves, between their human and nonhuman environments, and between nurturing figures and all other people. They have developed emotional attachments to their significant others and imagine how significant others perceive them. They begin to take notice of the expectations that significant others have of them and sometimes shape their own actions so as to gain their approval. Further, they have developed wills of their own and have learned how to get other people and sometimes things to do what they would like.

To the extent that they can, they repeat behavior that has been favorably received, and if it is continually reinforced, they infuse it with value. Eventually, they *internalize* this behavior; that is, they organize it into their concepts of self and suffer emotional discomfort when they cannot conform with it. In this manner, the values, norms, language, and other elements of the culture of significant others become part of the individual and are no longer totally dependent on external reinforcements.

In like manner, older children and adults internalize parts of the culture of subsequent significant others. Cultural properties which are similar to what they have already internalized are easily learned and integrated into the self system, whereas radically different cultural properties create culture conflict and lead to confusion about which patterns are appropriate in given situations. For this reason, people tend to be more comfortable with others who share similar socialization experiences and form friendships with those with whom they have most in common. Even in schools where many different subcultures are represented among the student body, pupils usually interact most frequently with those of like background, thereby selecting significant others who reinforce the culture they have already internalized.

Identification or modeling

Large segments of behaviors are internalized through the process of *identification* or *modeling*. People identify with other people if they so value the others (or the rewards that others receive) that they empathize with them, want to be like them, and imitate their behavior. Patterns thus acquired are reinforced by the pleasure individuals gain from knowing that they are like those whom they value, as well as by the other tangible or social rewards they may receive. Children first identify with their nurturing figures and then develop behavior which reflects their perceptions of what they do. Their behavioral repertoire is enlarged toward the end of the first year as they identify with others as well.

Many of the expectations associated with sex roles are acquired through identification with the parent of the same sex. For instance, ambivalence toward the male role on the part of some men, is traced sometimes to a lack of opportunity for intimate association with male models from whom boys can acquire culturally defined characteristics of maleness. This does not mean that socialization to sex roles comes about *only* through identification. Most boys who grow up in families without fathers or father surrogates can and do learn the cultural expectations of their sex, in part through the reinforcement of that behavior by significant others. Nonetheless, the opportunity to model one's behavior on someone else facilitates learning because it provides examples of what is expected and encourages the internalization of entire patterns in place of the acquisition of isolated behaviors.

Emphasis has recently been given to the importance of placing men teachers in urban elementary schools where many heads-of-household are mothers, so that boys will have opportunities to identify with adult males. It should be added, however, that male role models are important to all boys; it cannot be assumed that because a boy comes from a two-parent home, his father is a likely model. For example, young fathers of middle-class boys are often so occupied with the development of their own occupational careers that they are unavailable to their sons during the period in which sex-role identification usually occurs. Given high divorce rates in the United States, the isolation of nuclear families when children are little, and external demands made on fathers, boys often find role models outside the home from among relatives, elementary school teachers, "big brothers," athletic coaches, and the like.

Girls do not typically experience the same difficulties in locating appropriate sex-role models since the first significant others are usually women. Family tasks have traditionally been divided so that mothers remain in the home, available to deliver and nurse babies born into the family, and fathers assume responsibilities for the family's survival in the larger environment. However, with medical advances in maternity care, family planning, and prepared infant diets, the need for the nurturant figure to be the biological mother is considerably reduced. More and more couples now elect to share or even to reverse formerly sex-linked role responsibilities. One might speculate about the effect of the contemporary sexual revolution, which downgrades differences between male and female roles, on the acquisition of sex-roles in both boys and girls. It is likely that children reared in atypical families will never fully identify with the models of masculinity and feminity that were once traditional in the American society.

Reference group identification

When people identify with a particular person, they not only learn the values and norms that guide the other person's behavior, they tend to be guided by the same criteria. In like manner, people identify with entire groups which also become sources of values and norms as well as *reference groups* against which all other groups are evaluated. The family is usually the first group with which a person identifies. At the time young children realize that there are other families with patterns that are different from their own, they have already internalized its culture. By contrasting their own families with those of their friends and neighbors, they become aware of these variations as well as of the fact that some groups are more personally significant than others.

Even though people participate in many groups during their lives, only the ones with which they identify are reference groups. They can also select reference groups from among those in which they hold no membership, for one need not participate in a group in order to value it and be influenced by it. Children often identify with fictional groups they have come to know through mass media and books. Reported instances of children whose behavior has been molded by their acquaintance with fairy tales and television adventure stories are numerous. Even very young children may assign themselves to certain groups and then model their behavior and form criteria of what is desirable from their perceptions of the group's culture.

The concept of reference groups is useful in accounting for some behavior which might otherwise be difficult to interpret. For example, orientation toward specific reference groups sometimes explains gross variations in the actions of members of the same family, or why some people seem to be satisfied with little achievement whereas others in similar circumstances are constantly striving. *Ethnocentrism,* or prejudicial attitudes toward members of culturally different groups, can also be explained at times by the fact that the criteria for evaluating them are related to the extent to which they resemble or differ from a person's reference groups. Knowledge of one's frame of reference, then, helps in the understanding of behavior. Even so, it is sometimes very difficult to associate individuals with their salient groups, since people do not always actively participate in their reference groups and many times these groups are figments of the imagination.

STRUCTURAL DIFFERENCES AMONG FAMILIES

The study of socialization deals with the regular or persistent patterns of norms and values common to people who are part of the same social group. It should again be emphasized, however, that although people are similar in many respects to others in their groups, each person has some qualities that are unique. Individual differences are the consequence of the interaction of the biological organism and a combination of personal experiences. Because variations are infinite, it is never possible to predict the behavior of any one individual with total accuracy. It *is* possible, however, to describe within limits some of the general patterns shared by people with similar experiences and background. For instance, knowledge of the structure of a person's early family and of its culture usually supplies gross outlines of customary behavior.

From a synthesis of the findings of many studies concerning the effects of family organization and cultural variations, social scientists have come to know a considerable amount about which factors are germane to socialization. It is clear, for example, that the culture of the family into which one is born has an extreme impact on social development. Family culture determines the content to which the child is socialized and at the same time, restricts and directs later socialization. It is also clear that the structure of the family (how it is organized) modifies family culture, influences the extent to which the culture is transmitted, and makes an independent contribution to the child's social development.

The components of family structure that are most important for the socialization of children include: the number of adults living in the home; its division of labor; the kinds of authority relationships that exist; and the number, birth order, and sex of children.

Parents

The number of adults with whom children interact independently influences both the process and the content of their socialization.

It has already been noted that two-parent families with a discernable division of labor facilitate children's acquisition of culturally defined roles appropriate to their sex, and the availability of more than one adult with whom they can identify aids them in formulating their concepts of self and of generalized other. Whether the family is nuclear or extended also affects socialization by determining the number of role relationships children must develop and the scope and intensity of each.

Children in extended families interact with many adult relatives and the influence of any one person is usually less salient than in nuclear families where relationships are limited to one or two parents. Further, children in extended families often depend on several relatives for daily care, whereas children in nuclear families depend primarily on one person, usually the mother. The mother in the typical nuclear family, therefore, is often a more powerful socializing agent than the mother in the extended family.[16]

Some of the same factors arising out of industrialization that fostered the growth of the nuclear family and the saliency of the mother's role have encouraged women to work outside the home. Mothers of school-age children have joined the ranks of paid and unpaid labor because of increased opportunities for financial remuneration and self-expression, and because of the overall downgrading of the position of housewife. Small families, the elimination of the family's productive economic activities, and the introduction of labor-saving devices into the home have taken away many of the functions and intrinsic rewards of homemaking. Employment rates for women have risen dramatically throughout this century and can be expected to continue as efforts are made to provide women with employment opportunities equal to those of men.[17]

The result has been that although many children in contemporary families are more dependent upon their mothers than were children in traditional families, today's children actually receive less maternal attention. The effects on children left without a substitute for maternal guidance and emotional support are not yet clear. Much of the literature that treats this issue has pointed to the negative consequences of long periods of isolation and lack of supervision. It is speculated, however, that extended absences by the mother can have positive as well as the more commonly discussed negative effects, particularly as children enter the adolescent period. An unfulfilled mother's excessive reliance on children for social reinforcement can stimulate either their greater dependence or their rebellion against her.[18] On the other hand, the mother's acquisition of an occupational role can offer some of the missing elements in her life and thereby reduce the intensity of her relationship with her children. It would seem that this situation might facilitate a wholesome severance of the "golden cord."

Recognition of sex differences

To the extent that there is a division of labor by sex between the adults of a group, there are also differences by sex in child-rearing practices and in cultural expectations for boys and girls. A review of ethnographic data collected from 110 cultures throughout the world, indicates that over 85 percent of them expect girls to demonstrate greater nurturant behavior and to be more responsible.[19] The largest sex differences in child-rearing practices were found among hunting and nomadic societies, which are particularly dependent for survival on physical strength and motor skills. The smallest differences were found in societies in which isolated nuclear-family patterns dominate and both husband and wife must occasionally carry out parts of each other's role.[20] In American society, the differentiation of adults by sex and the resultant differentiation in the socialization of children by sex, are minimal when compared with other cultures.

There are, nevertheless, patterned variations in the content and process of socialization provided to American boys and girls. A number of women's rights groups have correctly pointed out that these differences are prejudicial because they do not allow children of either sex full opportunity to choose many childhood and adult roles. For example, by teaching that the roles of wife and mother are the most appropriate ones for women, the potential educational and occupational opportunities for girls are greatly restricted and boys are discouraged from becoming a nurturant figure to their own children. Without denying the merits of this argument, one must recognize with Freud that to some extent "anatomy is destiny" in that the biological reproductive function of women is not shared. To ensure sexual reproduction, societies provide social norms that give women protection during times, such as late pregnancy and the early postpartum period, when they may be physically vulnerable. Thus biological differences will probably always limit the extent to which the exact same socialization is provided to boys and girls.

Sex differences are socially ascribed at birth and parents typically treat their infants in accordance with the sex-role stereotypes of their own subculture. In the United States, boys are generally expected to be more independent, task-oriented, and aggressive than girls; and girls are expected to be more dependent, obedient, responsive, and affective. Also, girls are usually given more supervision than boys: their development is more closely scrutinized and their opportunities for experimentation are fewer. As a result, girls typically have more frequent and intense interaction with adults and, compared to boys, tend to be more sensitive to adult approval and considerably more verbal.

The sex of children affects cognition in areas other than acquisition of culturally defined sex roles. Studies of scholastic achievement of elementary school children indicate that there are noticeable differences between the overall academic performances of boys and girls.[21] The greater verbal ability of girls is reflected in their more developed reading and spelling skills, and greater concern with correct detail is shown in their higher computative skills. Boys tend to excel in areas that relate to autonomy; for example, they are considerably more adept in higher-level mathematics, which requires speculation, analysis, and abstraction.[22]

Sex-related differences in academic performance have often been ascribed to innate biological differences and differences in rates of maturation, but evidence increasingly points to the independent effect of socialization on school achievement. A study by Wilson of eighth-grade pupils in a northern California community shows that girls, in general, outperform boys in the traditional school curriculum and are more concerned with "correct" form, "right" response, and with approval from adults. Boys, on the other hand, are more concerned with understanding how and why certain events occur and are not as conscious of adult reactions to their behavior. Of special interest is Wilson's observation that boys who are as concerned as girls with adult approval have higher scholastic achievement than boys who are not. Further, the greater proportion of concerned boys come from the middle class, rather than the working classes where child-rearing practices show more variation by sex.[23]

Family authority structure

In the first months of life, parents have almost total control over the tangible and social reinforcements of their children and, thereby, have sizable influences over their behavior. The period of almost exclusive control lasts only until children are mature enough to find their own reinforcements or receive them from people other than parents. Thereafter parents often rely heavily on deliberate socialization practices to encourage children to conform with their expectations. The extent to which parents attempt to control the behavior of their children, the methods they use to obtain compliance, and whether control is by one or both parents is the *structure of authority* within the family. The kind of family authority that exists and the specific uses that are made of it are themselves potent sources of socialization which have implications for how children will cope with the authority structures of groups in which they will later participate.

All parent-child authority relationships are initially asymmetrical in that adults control the behavior of children. In comparison with other cultures of the world, however, the authority structure of the typical American family gives children wide latitude for independent action. So much is this the case that some observers have characterized the American family as having a "collateral" authority structure, implying that decisions are *shared* between parents and children. This mode of socialization to authority within the family has sometimes been related to the ability of adults to participate competently in democratic forms of government.[24]

However, active participation in family decisions by American children may reflect more the way authority is commonly implemented in the United States than a greater willingness by parents to share decision making with their children. The concepts of *direct* and *indirect* authority are germane to this difference. In direct authority, parents or other socializing agents present children with prescriptions for behavior which have positive or negative reinforcements associated with them, and children comply because of fear of punishment or promise of reward. In indirect authority, children are presented with a set of alternative behaviors along with the reasons why one alternative should be preferred over the other. While it may appear that children are making independent choices, in reality they are being manipulated to choose preferred behavior.

Both modes of authority are usually found within a single family, but the American middle class more often than other social classes tends to employ indirect control. Direct authority is not usually assumed to be as effective as indirect authority because it focuses more on correct behavior than on the underlying reasons for it. Also, direct authority often requires the use of punishments which can produce alienation and thereby impede socialization.[25] Indirect authority, on the other hand, is assumed to lead to more effective socialization because it presents rational principles than can be used to evaluate broad classes of behavior in the future.[26]

Birth order and family size

Position in the family and the number of other children also affect what is learned. Firstborn children, like girls, are often more closely supervised by their parents than children who are born after them. As a result, they tend to acquire the adult culture at an earlier age and seem to be less imaginative than their siblings. In the United States, firstborn children have been found to be early talkers, more sensitive to adult approval, and more driving and ambitious. Later children usually receive proportionately less attention from socializing adults and the quality of adult-child interaction is noticeably different. Since parents have already been socialized to the parental role, their relationships with subsequent children are characterized by less strain, anxiety, and inconsistency. Later children tend to be more independent and exhibit fewer emotional disorders than do the firstborn.[27] In addition, later children have older siblings who are potential role models and can often supply them with ways to cope with the problems of childhood, especially those relating to adult expectations.

Family size per se affects the socialization process to the extent that it influences the kind and amount of interaction children have with other family members. Large families, in the main, decrease children's opportunity for interaction with adults and increase their opportunity for interaction with others of similar status. However, in extended families or families in which there are large age differences among siblings, the occasions in which children interact with adults are more numerous.

CULTURAL DIFFERENCES AMONG FAMILIES

Every family socializes its children to fit in with its own ongoing social system so that the behavior of each individual will contribute to the total family unit and cause it minimal disruption. In addition, most families give their children some preparation for the social roles they will hold in the larger society. Parents deliberately try to transmit what in their view are the most important elements of the dominant culture, whether or not they are similar to elements in the family's culture. The extent to which this anticipatory socialization is useful to children depends largely upon the accuracy of their parents' perception: children whose parents have had opportunity to learn the dominant culture firsthand usually have socialization advantages for their nonfamily roles.

Nonetheless, even in ideal circumstances, parents do not totally prepare children for later roles. However, they can aid them considerably by imparting some of the norms and values these roles will entail. That proportionately more middle-class than lower-class children experience success in educational institutions and in the occupational world is owed in large part to the familiarization with the dominant social values and norms that they receive in their early years at home.

Socioeconomic status

The most relevant cultural differences for participation in school and in the larger society are often related to family socioeconomic status. Even in the most democratic societies families are differentiated into a rank order. This is sometimes based on the prestige that is awarded to the occupational level of the family's chief breadwinner and other times, on the power that family members have to force their will on others in the society. In the United States status tends to be related to the size of income or wealth, years and quality of formal education, and the esteem one is granted by other people. These three indicators—wealth, education, and prestige—are so highly intercorrelated that it seldom matters which measure is used in describing subcultural differences among social strata.

An exception to this generalization is the occasional discrepancy between wealth and education found in the newly rich. However that may be, wealthy families are usually able to supply education to their children so that the balance among indicators of status can be restored in one or two generations. Another exception, not as easily remedied, is found among readily identifiable racial-ethnic groups that have been subjected to economic discrimination. Here educational level often outranks income and occupational prestige, and a balance can be attained only by a change in the norms of the general society.

The uniqueness of each social stratum arises out of the common interests, income, prestige, and kinds of tasks related to the work of the people who fall inside its boundaries. Within every group, a somewhat distinctive subculture—an adaptation of the general culture to the group's special circumstances and experiences—emerges and this subculture is transmitted to its children. The distinctive values and norms of each subculture serve to further isolate children of each social stratum from one another, thereby perpetuating their differences. Even in situations which provide socioeconomic heterogeneity, as for example some church, school, and youth groups, children tend to select their closest associates from their own socioeconomic background.

The number of strata into which a society is divided varies depending upon the theoretical reasons for division, and the refinements required by the analysis that is being made. Warner and his associates set the pattern for the analysis of social stratification in 1941, with the publication of the first of their community studies. They identified six social strata ranging from lower-lower to upper-upper classes, each with an associated life-style.[28] In the discussion that follows, six social strata are also described, but terminology and descriptions differ somewhat from Warner's. "Culture of poverty" and "working class" are substituted for "lower-lower" and "upper-lower" classes since these terms more nearly describe contemporary stratification. It should again be noted that descriptions of social strata provide only a general orientation and few families evince *all* of the patterns that are characteristic of the social stratum into which they are classified. Further, since each person's cumulative experiences are unique, social-class membership is not always useful in predicting and explaining the behavior of any one individual.

The upper classes. In the United States, the *upper classes* are in so favored a social position that little is known about the details of their personal lives. While members of the upper class receive some notice in news media, they usually have sufficient influence to "manage" the image that is projected and to protect their privacy from invasions by social scientists. The upper classes are often divided into two substrata: the *upper-upper class*, composed of those who inherit prestige and riches from ancestors who can be traced back through many generations of Americans of Northern European stock, and the *lower-upper class*, consisting of those who have accumulated great wealth in the comparatively recent past. The Joseph Kennedy family of Massachusetts is an example of this class.

The upper-upper class, made up exclusively of white Protestants, is more like a *caste* than a class in that one must be born into it or, occasionally, selected into it through marriage. The high social status of these families is based on lineage rather than family fortune or present-day achievement: family status usually remains even after the bulk of the family fortune is gone. Upper-upper-class members emphasize the extended more than the nuclear family. Members are admitted to elite social clubs, private schools, and are listed in the exclusive Social Register on the basis of their relatives. Individuals have been known to be dropped from the Social Register list following marriage to persons of lower social status, including Catholics, Jews, and nonwhites. Upper-upper-class women occupy themselves with a certain amount of charity work and upper-upper-class men are often members of the boards of directors of large public and private corporations which form the backbone of the power elite described by C. Wright Mills.[29]

Lower-upper-class families are also part of the "establishment," though they do not have the status of, say, Boston Brahmins or members of the Philadelphia Main Line. Unlike the upper-upper class, they include ethnic and religious minorities among their members; but they, too, join exclusive clubs and send their children to elite private schools. The patterns of consumption of the lower-upper class are usually more conspicuous than those of the older families, and they are often much richer in fact.

Members of the upper classes have an earmark of security and success. Individuality is highly stressed and both husbands and wives are often financially self-sufficient. Because they are heirs to the "good life" they tend to support the status quo and are usually, but not always, politically conservative. Since the social status of the children of the upper classes is assured, socialization is directed toward upholding family position and carrying on its life-style. Unlike the youth of the middle classes who are oriented to the future, upper-class children have been found to be remarkably oriented toward the past.[30] They receive no more education than midde-class children, and often less, but their education is carried out largely by nannies, governesses, tutors, and in the elite private schools and colleges that function mainly to transmit upper-class traditions.

Upper-middle-class families. Professionals and owners and managers of large business establishments comprise the *upper-middle class*. They are not as wealthy as the members of the upper classes, nor do they have as much social influence, although they are equally and sometimes better educated. Upper-middle-class families are concerned with individual success and self-fulfillment for both adults and children. Wives frequently have careers outside the home which can be either voluntary or of comparable status to those of their husbands. Children are expected to achieve in school and, later on, in some occupation. Upper-middle-class homes are marked by the strivings of individual parents and by their combined pressures on children to maintain the family's social position.

Formal socialization is carried out in the "best" schools—either public or private—and parents often purchase additional education for their children in music, athletics, the arts, and foreign languages. Upper-middle-class families are adult-directed since parents oversee their children's socialization, but do not necessarily participate in "togetherness," as is common in the lower-middle class.

Adults are highly educated, skilled in communication techniques, and are able to deal effectively with the secondary structures of society. They tend to be active in voluntary associations such as civic clubs and country clubs; they read books and journals in addition to the daily newspapers, travel frequently, and enjoy the arts and classical music. Upper-middle-class adults usually have strong feelings of personal efficacy and an aura of authority and responsibility which comes from their personal success. Women are commonly viewed as equal rather than subordinate to men, and boys and girls are treated similarly and given the same access to the abundant life-chances parents can provide.

Lower-middle-class families. Lower-middle-class families receive their incomes largely from skilled or clerical (white collar) jobs or from small businesses that they either own or manage. These families, compared to upper-middle-class families, are more likely to emphasize togetherness within the nuclear unit. However, although mother and father both take on household and socialization responsibilities, the mother is usually the major socializing agent. Family life is more important than friendship, which is more often between adult couples than between individuals. And to the extent that the extended family pattern has disappeared, it is most absent within the lower-middle class.

Parents in lower-middle-class families usually want upward mobility for their children and view education, self-discipline, and industry as a way of getting ahead. They often project their own ambitions onto their children and push them to succeed. Many lower-middle-class families move to suburban residential areas so that their children will have fuller opportunities to develop. They make use of voluntary associations to furnish additional sources for socialization: children join youth groups and church-related clubs, while adults are often active in churches and political organizations.

Working-class families. Working class families have much in common with members of the lower-middle class and often have an equivalent income as well. Mass communication, especially television, has made many middle-class norms known to working-class people and the mass production of consumer goods has enabled large numbers to acquire some of the accoutrements of middle-class life.

The culture of the working class reportedly differs from that of the lower-middle class in that it stresses stable interpersonal relations above long-range individual-achievement goals; its social interaction tends to be confined to long-time friends, neighbors, and the extended family; and individuals do not join large numbers of voluntary associations. Compared to middle-class people, working-class people are believed to have a lower sense of personal efficacy and less general faith in human nature.

Child-rearing practices within the working class are largely concerned with the physical care of young children and with socialization to their current roles more than to their future statuses; there is also a noted absence of detailed explanations to children about why some behaviors are preferred over others. Children are often raised in a male-dominated two-parent household in which the division of labor by sex is clearly manifest and the behavior appropriate to the child's own sex is stressed. The mother is the chief socializing agent; the father is the authority figure who backs her up, using physical force when necessary.

The working-class subculture has been described as a peer-group society since interaction with peers of the same age and sex occurs with great frequency.[31] Strong peer groups develop during adolescence and carry over into adult years: mothers and fathers each have their own social circles composed of relatives and neighbors of the same sex. Much adolescent as well as adult socialization occurs within these groups. The strong pressures of group life discourage individualism. As a consequence, social mobility out of the working class is most frequent among those who, for some reason, do not adopt their peers as reference groups.

Culture of poverty. The culture of poverty falls at the base of the American stratification system.[32] While it is found only among the poor, all poor people do not share this subculture. Culture of poverty sometimes develops among rural and urban families if their incomes are both extremely limited and fluctuate to such a degree that they are unable to predict economic conditions from one day to the next. This subculture provides norms and values that help them to contend with economic uncertainty and extreme privation. Families in the culture of poverty are sometimes known to welfare workers as multiproblem families because their total immersion in poverty has made it difficult for them to untangle themselves from its negative consequences. They are plagued disproportionately with family instability, crime, and physical and mental handicaps; many children from the culture of poverty have difficulty in adjusting to public schools.

According to Lewis, people in the culture of poverty have developed feelings of dependency, powerlessness, and inferiority which they hand on from generation to generation. Children who absorb the attitudes of this subculture cannot easily take advantage of changing conditions or extended opportunities which might occur during their lifetime. But other aspects permit people to cope with the strains of unrelieved crises:

. . . The "culture of poverty" is not only a matter of economic depriviation, of disorganization, or of the absence of something. It is also something positive and provides some rewards without which the poor could hardly carry on.[33]

This subculture arose as an adaptation to objective conditions and was an effort to cope with feelings of hopelessness that develop when success is improbable in terms of the values and goals of the larger society. Thus, uncertainty about the future has encouraged an emphasis on present rather than future gratification. This makes spontaneity and enjoyment possible. Low aspiration levels reduce frustration, and in some ways people in the culture of poverty suffer less from alienation than do those in the middle class.[34]

The culture of poverty is present in many societies where large discrepancies exist in the distribution of wealth, and in which the poor are comparatively isolated. In the United States it is probably more widespread than has been generally recognized.[35] Such a subculture located in the rural areas of the Appalachian Mountains came to the national attention in the early 1960s. The declining lumbering industry and changes in mining methods greatly curtailed the sources of income traditional to many mountaineer families. By 1968, Appalachia had grown its third welfare generation and "some were so far from their last job that it can be said that they had no trade at all."[36]

The subculture of the typical Appalachian family has been described in terms similar to those used by Lewis in detailing the lives of poor Mexicans in Mexico City and poor Puerto Ricans in New York: people tend to be oriented toward the present rather than the future and toward personal rather than impersonal relationships; social interaction tends to be more with people of the same age and sex than with other members of the nuclear family; child-rearing practices are more oriented toward custodial care than toward deliberate socialization; and the period of childhood compared to childhood in the larger society is considerably shortened.[37]

Many of the same characteristics have been attributed to poor black families living in the vast ghettos of northern cities. These families, like the rural poor of Appalachia, are isolated from the social mainstream and often have values and norms that stress present-time orientation and a sense of powerlessness. In addition, disproportionately often they are headed by a single parent, usually the mother.

In a moving anthropological account of 24 poor black men living in Washington, D.C., Liebow documents their feelings of economic insecurity and relates their seemingly negative attitudes toward their families to their inability to provide for them. According to Liebow, these men want to be "publicly, legally married, to support a family and be the head of it, because this is what it is to be a man in our society." They have had no evidence, however, that they will fare any better than their own fathers who had failed before them and who had to "cut out," or than the other men they know who have also failed. "Armed with models who have failed, convinced of his own worthlessness, illiterate and unskilled, he enters marriage and the job market with the smell of failure all around him."[38]

The lack of a successful role model perpetuates some of the disadvantages suffered by boys who are immersed in the culture of poverty. The socialization input of the black-power movement has been extremely wholesome in this regard, defining negro maleness as something strong, beautiful, and worthy. However, while this image helps to foster positive values about the role of the black man in society, it does not provide norms for the role. Boys who have grown up without fathers or father surrogates continue to be disadvantaged, since the content of a role must be observed in order to be learned. In addition, both boys and girls in single-parent homes do not have an opportunity to learn the roles of husband and wife and are further handicapped if, as adults, they want to establish traditional nuclear families of their own.

In sum, the culture of poverty offers reduced life-chances to the young; those who desire to escape from poverty get little from family socialization to assist them. Family values tend to deemphasize work —the legitimate route to upward mobility in the United States. And family norms do not usually contain prescriptions for dealing successfully with society's secondary structures such as schools, business institutions, the police, and the courts. Moreover, these children receive considerably less education, training, and information about employment opportunities than do those with whom they will have to compete. To make matters worse, poor people, both black and white, are often subjected to discrimination. Even when they are qualified, they are apt to be the last hired and the first fired. The American society has not yet learned how to intervene in this cycle that afflicts too many of its families.

Racial-ethnic groups

Racial and ethnic background usually creates cultural variations above and beyond those evolving from socioeconomic status. Aside from the initial differences in values and norms that stem from national and religious heritage, further differences arise from the economic and educational discrimination that is often thrust upon persons with readily observable racial-ethnic characteristics. In the United States, for example, blacks and American Indians, above all other physically identifiable groups, have suffered reduced life-chances. Because of a prejudiced society, many generations have had less geographic mobility and fewer educational and occupational opportunities than did other Americans. As a result, a disproportionate number of these and other similarly treated, readily distinguishable racial-ethnic groups are concentrated among the lower strata where sources for socialization to widely accepted American cultural patterns are restricted.

Racial-ethnic minorities from the middle classes are more likely than those from the lower classes to be exposed to influences of others who are unlike themselves. This is due to the fact that people who have had the most experience with *gesellschaft* social norms are the ones who most easily accept and establish relationships with people who are racially and ethnically different.[39] These norms tend to be more common to the middle than the lower classes. Accordingly, middle-class people do not find is as necessary to be similar to those with whom they establish viable relationships, and background differences do not limit social interaction to the same degree.

For some time it had been assumed that members of distinctive racial-ethnic groups attempt to shed their unique heritage as they attain middle-class status and become part of what affectionately used to be called the melting pot of American society. It now appears that one's fellow racial-ethnic group members have always formed a salient reference group.[40]

Thus, even among the middle classes, where much acculturation to dominant American patterns has assuredly taken place, there continues to be a parallel system of racial-ethnic social structures. Within many racial-ethnic groups there are networks of informal social systems and formal organizations that permit and encourage members to remain within the confines of their own group for all of their primary and some of their secondary relationships.[41] Many minority-group members live in neighborhoods with predominantly similar minority-group residents, and the people with whom they attend schools, churches, and clubs, and those whom they marry are from the same racial-ethnic background as their own.

Greatest cultural differences among racial-ethnic groups are found within the lower classes. Continuous struggle for economic security, *gemeinschaft* personal orientations, and isolation from *gesellschaft* secondary groups all work against contact with members of other racial-ethnic groups and with the middle class. Because of this, many channels of mutual influence are cut off. Nevertheless, some acculturation to the larger society does take place, and differences among racial-ethnic subcultures diminish with each American-born generation. In a study of an Italian working-class neighborhood in New England, Gans documented the acculturation of successive generations of Italians in the United States. He found that their traditional diet was more resistant to change than were other cultural characteristics, perhaps because eating is related to family ceremonial occasions. He also found that knowledge of the native language lasts only through the second generation. By the third generation there is even much anglicization of names.[42] Similar findings with respect to home language comes from a study by Anderson and Johnson of Mexican-American families in a small southwestern community. They observed that although families that have been in the United States for one or two genertaions communicate among themselves largely in Spanish, by the third generation many families have totally adopted the English language.[43]

To understand why some cultural patterns persist longer than others, it is useful to distinguish between *intrinsic* and *extrinsic* cultural traits.[44] Intrinsic traits derive from common heritage, and include religious practices, musical tastes, ethical values, and recreational patterns—all of which are greatly resistant to change. Extrinsic traits, on the other hand, develop as an adjustment to the local environment and to the kinds of secondary social structures in which the group finds itself. These include elements like dress, manners, and language, and are all readily modified. Differences among ethnic groups at the same socioeconomic level are largely intrinsic cultural differences, whereas those between different socioeconomic levels of the same ethnic group tend to be extrinsic differences. In other words, intrinsic cultural elements are more deeply imbedded in racial-ethnic background while extrinsic elements are imbedded in general social-class position.

An examination of the intrinsic cultural values of a racial-ethnic group can shed light on why disproportionately more members of some groups than others experience upward mobility. Respect for formal learning, importance of rational discussion, hard work, delayed-gratification patterns, and the like are cultural elements that have often fostered mobility for many Jewish and Oriental children in the United States. In the now classic study that attempted to explain why larger proportions of Jewish than Italian children were upwardly mobile, Strodtbeck documented differences between the intrinsic culture of the two groups which could be related to overall group mobility.[45] He found that more Jewish than Italian parents believed "the world is orderly and amenable to rational mastery" and more of them held that through education and individual striving people could control their destinies regardless of socioeconomic status. The orientation of Jewish parents was largely one of achievement motivation and deferred gratification, two characteristically middle-class values. The same cultural orientations have been reported in greater frequency for other racial-ethnic groups that have also experienced high rates of social mobility.

The emigration since the close of World War II of Spanish-speaking peoples from Mexico, Puerto Rico, Cuba, and other North American countries has considerably added to the ethnic variety of the United States. While there is much variation between as well as within the cultures of each of these national groups, many of the newer immigrants have come from the poorer social strata of their own countries and have some of the intrinsic cultural patterns associated with generations of poverty. For example, comparisons between the characteristics of Mexican-American and Anglo school children of similar socioeconomic status show that more Mexican-American children accept family authority of wide scope, view their fellow man with caution, and view their own destiny with resignation. These cultural orientations appear to be negatively associated with public school achievement and, consequently, with upward mobility. On the other hand, those Mexican-American children, regardless of social class, who more closely resemble middle-class Anglo children in their intrinsic cultural patterns are more likely to experience school success.[46]

CHANGING MODELS FOR THE SOCIALIZATION OF RACIAL-ETHNIC MINORITIES

Total assimilation

During the twentieth century the ideal model for the socialization of cultural minorities has undergone considerable modification. *Total assimiliation* of the immigrant was the predominant model until after 1920. Before that time it had largely been assumed that, wherever possible, immigrants would relinquish their ancestral heritage and adopt the dominant Anglo-Saxon patterns of the United States. This notion reached its zenith with the "Americanization" movement of World War I and was given legitimacy in official pronouncements. For example, the then president, Woodrow Wilson, has been quoted as saying "A man who thinks of himself as belonging to a particular national group in America has not yet become an American."[47]

The ideal was to acculturate and assimilate the immigrant population totally into existing social structures so that it would eventually be impossible to identify a person's ethnic background. This goal was never attained. While some ethnics were included in the secondary structures of the larger society, they were excluded from particularistic groups, such as social and recreational clubs, in which they could establish significant primary relationships. Physically identifiable minorities were excluded from secondary structures in greater proportions than other ethnics. Thus black, Indian, and Oriental Americans at the very least did not often interact in situations of equal status with people from other subcultures.

The melting pot

The movement for the Americanization of all immigrants assumed that acculturation was a one-way process. Individuals would give up their own cultural heritage, but would make no impact on the dominant culture of the society. This model was supplanted in popularity by the *melting-pot* theory of acculturation which held that there would be an interpenetration of all cultures brought into the United States and an eventual fusion into one homogeneous American culture. As in the total-assimilation model, the melting-pot model held that cultural differences would disappear, but not without transmitting some of their unique elements to an emerging common culture.

The melting pot model was in ascendancy between the two world wars. It had been fostered largely by social reformers and welfare workers who were moved by the personal hardships created by the expectations foisted upon new eastern- and southern-European immigrants. These reformers held that it was difficult, if not impossible, for many immigrants to shed the cultural characteristics in which their own identity lay and to adopt an alien Anglo–Saxon culture. They reported observations of the psychological damage inflicted on the immigrants by the dominant society—especially the development of social distance between foreign-born and native-born generations within the same family—and the growth of ethnic self-hatred as children struggled to reject the ways of their parents in favor of what they believed to be correct.

The theory of the melting pot held promise of equality of all cultures within the dominant American culture, but in essence what happened was that some elements of ethnic cultures disappeared without making any impact on the general American culture while others persisted little changed within ethnic subpopulations. Recently some observers noted that the point about the melting-pot model is that "it did not happen."[48] It did not happen because ethnic- and racial-minority people have been for the most part socially and physically isolated from the dominant culture, and also because those who did exhibit some of the widely held American behavior patterns were often cruelly penalized for it by more powerful members of society. This was especially true for racial minorities who lived in small towns dominated by bigoted whites. Other observers who maintain that there has, in fact, been a great deal of assimilation within the American society, admit that divisions remain along religious lines. People with the same religion may have merged their ethnic characteristics, but Americans continue to be divided into Protestant, Catholic, and Jewish subcultures, albeit with considerable overlap.[49]

Cultural pluralism

Since the end of World War II the concept of *cultural pluralism* has received wide notice and many social commentators suggest that this model is a more appropriate goal than either the Americanization model of total assimilation or the melting-pot model of reciprocal cultural influence. They point out that cultural pluralism has existed in the United States at least since the Germans, Norwegians, and Swedes settled on the plains of America to recreate a society in which they could communicate in their native tongue, maintain familiar institutions, and band together for mutual protection against the uncertainties of the strange environment.[50]

The conception of cultural pluralism asserts the legitimacy of the individual's right to be different with respect to certain cultural elements so long as cultural differences do not lead to dangerous national disunity. In accordance with this concept, racial-ethnic minority-group members are expected to adjust to generally agreed upon social values and norms which enable them to obtain and keep jobs that are commensurate with their potential and training, perform their political role as citizens, and raise their children in a way which will not subvert the process congenial to established patterns of child-rearing.[51]

While each of these expectations may require some modification in the extrinsic culture of racial-ethnic groups, the concept of cultural pluralism permits many of the intrinsic elements to go relatively untouched. It holds that people should be able to remain comfortably within traditional primary groups composed of people with a like heritage and should feel free to participate in parallel rather than integrated secondary structures. Although this model holds that individuals have the right to retain their intrinsic cultural patterns, it also holds that they have the right to reject them if they desire. It does not purport to foster cultural segregation.

The extent to which schools ought to encourage cultural pluralism has not yet been determined. At the time of the establishment of American public schools, socialization to a common culture was an articulated goal and formal education was directed at either total or partial acculturation of the culturally different. Since the late 1960s there has been considerable pressure by competing racial-ethnic groups to change the direction of school socialization and to modify the curriculum to reflect unique cultural differences of their pupils. If the model of cultural pluralism becomes widely accepted and its philosophy is implemented in schools, several significant questions relating to both pupils and the larger society arise. First, to what extent will emphasis on cultural variations exaggerate differences among racial-ethnic groups and foster diversity and conflict? Second, to what extent will the school's official recognition of these differences deny individual pupils freedom to choose between their family's heritage and common American cultural patterns? And third, will the study of racial-ethnic subcultures be undertaken at the expense of other skills such as language arts and *gesellschaft* interpersonal relations which will help pupils to participate effectively in the larger society at a later time?

The answers to these questions are basic to the socialization mission of schools and to their role as intermediary between the *gemeinschaft* culture of the child's family and the *gesellschaft* culture of the larger society. Schools are in an ideal position to redress many of the injustices that have historically been thrust upon the racially and ethnically different. Through an emphasis on cultural pluralism, they can foster a child's favorable identification with his or her own family and culture; they can reduce racial-ethnic self-hatred and increase self-esteem; and they can create greater tolerance for cultural diversity. At the same time, one must ask if it is possible for schools to do these things without denying children the right to be free of unwanted categorizations arising from family background and without depriving them of the opportunity to learn those things which will help them cope with the dominant society.[52]

NOTES

[1] George P. Murdock, *Social Structure*, New York, Macmillan, 1949, chap. 1.

[2] There can be no question about its existence in the United States if separate residence is a measure of independence. In 1966, for example, over 98 percent of all married couples reported that they maintain their own households. Theodore Caplow, *Elementary Sociology*, Englewood Cliffs, N.J., Prentice-Hall, 1971, pp. 484–485.

[3] Murdock, *op. cit.*, pp. 23 ff.

[4] Urie Bronfenbrenner, "Socialization and Social Class through Time and Space," in Eleanor E. Maccoby, *et al.*, eds. *Readings in Social Psychology*, 3rd ed., New York, Holt, Rinehart & Winston, 1958, p. 424, *passim*.

[5] Ralph Turner, *Family Interaction*, New York, Wiley, 1970, p. 420. Some sociologists now estimate that the traditional nuclear form in which the husband is the provider and the wife, the home maker, represents less than 35 percent of all households in the United States. See Marvin B. Sussman, ed., *Non-Traditional Family Forms in the 1970's*, Minneapolis, National Council on Family Relations, 1972, p. 3.

[6] Elaine Cummings and David M. Schneider, "Sibling Solidarity: A Property of American Kinship," *American Anthropologist*, 63, no. 3 (June 1961), 498–507.

[7] Wilbert E. Moore, *Social Change*, Englewood Cliffs, N.J., Prentice-Hall, 1963, p. 107.

[8] Charles Horton Cooley, *Social Organization: A Study of the Larger*

Mind, New York, Schocken, 1962, p. 23. First published 1909. Groups that have the characteristic *espirit de corps* of primary groups but not face-to-face interaction are also thought of as primary groups since their influence on members is profound. Thus, extended family members in fully modernized societies may be a primary group even though they live at great distances from one another. Nonetheless, young children must have face-to-face interaction in order to develop their initial social characteristics.

⁹ See Chap. 1.

¹⁰ For example, B. F. Skinner, *Science and Human Behavior,* New York, Macmillan, 1953.

¹¹ See Albert Bandura and Richard H. Walters, *Social Learning and Personality Development,* New York, Holt, Rinehart & Winston, 1963.

¹² C. L. Hull, *A Behavior System,* New Haven, Yale University Press, 1952.

¹³ Aase Gruda Skard, "Maternal Deprivation: The Research and Its Implications," *Journal of Marriage and the Family,* 27 (1965), 333–343.

¹⁴ René A. Spitz, "Hospitalism," in Rose L. Coser, ed., *The Family: Its Structure and Functions,* New York, St. Martin's Press, 1964, pp. 399–425.

¹⁵ *Ibid.,* pp. 424–425.

¹⁶ The influence of the middle-class mother on the child's behavior has been held up to ridicule by many American novelists; among them, Philip Roth. Yet this influence has been well-documented in fact. See Arnold W. Green, "The Middle Class Male Child and Neurosis," *American Sociological Review,* 11 (February 1946), 31–41.

¹⁷ Employment rates for American women living with their husbands have increased from 4 percent in 1890, to 15 percent in 1940, to 35 percent in 1966. Caplow, *op. cit.,* p. 492. Employment rates for all American women have moved from 29 percent in 1950 to 39.6 percent in 1970. Census Bureau statistics, in the *Los Angeles Times,* 15 October 1972, sect. A, p. 11.

¹⁸ Turner, *op. cit.,* p. 311.

¹⁹ Herbert Barry III, Margaret K. Bacon, and Irvin L. Child, "A Cross-Cultural Survey of Some Sex Differences in Socialization," *Journal of Abnormal and Social Psychology,* 55 (1957), 327–332.

²⁰ *Ibid.,* pp. 330–331.

²¹ Marion Shaycroft, *et al., The Identification, Development and Utilization of Human Talents: Studies of a Complete Age Group—Age 15,* Pittsburgh, Pa., University of Pittsburgh Press, 1965, p. 132; Alan Wilson, "Social Stratum Differences and Sex Differences," Berkeley, Calif., University of California, 1966, mimeograph.

²² Torsten Húsen, ed., *International Study of Achievement in Mathematics,* New York, Wiley, 1967, vol. 2, p. 258.

²³ Wilson, *op. cit.*

²⁴ See for example Gabriel A. Almond and Sidney Verba, *The Civic*

Culture: Political Attitudes and Democracy in Five Nations, Boston, Little, Brown, 1965, pp. 274–283. First published 1963.

25 For the relationship between compliance techniques, alienation, and learning, see Amitai Etzioni, *A Comparative Analysis of Complex Organizations: On Power, Involvement, and Their Correlates*, New York, Free Press, 1961, *passim*. For the importance of the nurturient authority figure see Philip Slater, "Parental Role Differentiation," *The American Journal of Sociology*, 67, no. 3 (November 1961), 296–308.

26 Glen H. Elder, "Parental Power Legitimation and Its Effects on the Adolescent," *Sociometry*, 26, no. 1 (March 1963), 50–65; Robin M. Williams, Jr., *American Society: A Sociological Interpretation*, 3rd ed., New York, Knopf, 1970, p. 80.

27 Bernard Berelson and Gary A. Steiner, *Human Behavior: An Inventory of Scientific Findings*, New York, Harcourt Brace Jovanovich, 1964, p. 254.

28 W. Lloyd Warner and Paul S. Lunt, *The Social Life of a Modern Community*, New Haven, Yale University Press, 1941.

29 C. Wright Mills, *The Power Elite*, New York, Oxford University Press, 1956. See also G. William Domhoff, *Who Rules America?*, Englewood Cliffs, N.J., Prentice-Hall, 1967.

30 Charles McArthur, "Personality Differences Between Middle and Upper Classes," *Journal of Abnormal and Social Psychology*, 50, no. 2, (March 1955), 247–254.

31 Herbert J. Gans, *The Urban Villagers: Group and Class in the Life of Italian-Americans*, New York, Free Press, 1962.

32 Oscar Lewis, *A Study of Slum Culture: Backgrounds for 'La Vida'*, New York, Random House, 1968. This concept has come under sharp attack because it implies to some that poverty is perpetuated by the poor themselves through the culture they transmit to their children. Critics of the culture of poverty notion claim that to place the onus of poverty on poor people discourages changes in the opportunity structure of the larger society. See Eleanor Burke Leacock, ed., *The Culture of Poverty: A Critique*, New York, Simon & Schuster, 1971; also Charles A. Valentine, *Culture and Poverty: Critique and Counterproposals*, Chicago, University of Chicago Press, 1968.

33 Lewis, *op. cit.*, p. 4.

34 Lewis, *op. cit.*, p. 18.

35 For example, Harrington claims that almost one-fourth of the American population is poor but has been relatively invisible to the general society because of the isolated conditions in which it lives. He adds that although poor, not all of these families fit into Lewis' description of culture of poverty. Michael Harrington, *The Other America: Poverty in the United States*, New York, Macmillan, 1963.

36 Peter Schrag, "Appalachia: Again the Forgotten Land," *Saturday Review* (27 January 1968), 14–18.

37 Jack E. Weller, *Yesterday's People: Life in Contemporary Appala-*

chia, Lexington, Ky., University of Kentucky, 1965. See also Richard A. Ball, "A Poverty Case: The Analgesic Subculture of the Southern Appalachians," *American Sociological Review*, 33, no. 6 (December 1968), 885–895.

[38] Elliot Liebow, *Tally's Corner: A Study of Negro Street-Corner Men*, Boston, Little, Brown, 1967, pp. 210–211.

[39] Robin M. Williams, Jr., *Strangers Next Door: Ethnic Relations in American Communities*, Englewood Cliffs, N.J., Prentice-Hall, 1964, pp. 358–359.

[40] Andrew M. Greeley, *Why Can't They Be Like Us?*, New York, Dutton, 1971, p. 18.

[41] Milton M. Gordon, *Assimilation in American Life: The Role of Race, Religion, and National Origins*, New York, Oxford University Press, 1964, p. 34.

[42] Gans, *op. cit.*, pp. 33–34.

[43] James G. Anderson and William H. Johnson, "Stability and Change among Three Generations of Mexican-Americans: Factors Affecting Achievement," *American Educational Research Journal*, 8, no. 2 (March 1971), 300.

[44] Gordon, *op. cit.*, p. 79.

[45] Fred L. Strodtbeck, "Family Interaction Values and Achievement," in David C McClelland, *et al.*, eds., *Talent and Society*, New York, Van Nostrand Reinhold, 1948, pp. 135–194.
On Japanese-Americans see Audrey James Schwartz, "The Culturally Advantaged: A Study of Japanese-American Pupils," *Sociology and Social Research*, 55, no. 3 (April 1971), 341–353.

[46] Audrey James Schwartz, "A Comparative Study of Values and Achievement: Mexican-American and Anglo Youth," *Sociology of Education*, 44, no. 4 (Fall 1971), 438–462. See also Francis B. Evans and James G. Anderson, "The Psychocultural Origins of Achievement and Achievement Motivation: The Mexican-American Family," *Sociology of Education*, 46, no. 4 (Fall 1973), 396–416.

[47] Quoted in Gordon, *op. cit.*, p. 101. Original source given as *President Wilson's Addresses*, G. M. Harper, ed., New York, 1918.

[48] Nathan Glazer and Daniel P. Moynihan, *Beyond the Melting Pot: The Negroes, Puerto Ricans, Jews, Italians, and Irish of New York City*, Cambridge, MIT Press, 1963, p.v. See also Williams, 1964, *op. cit.*; Gordon, *op. cit.*

[49] See Will Herberg, *Protestant-Catholic-Jew: An Essay in American Religious Sociology*, Garden City, N.Y., Doubleday, 1955.

[50] Gordon, *op. cit.*, p. 134.

[51] *Ibid.*, p. 243.

[52] The federal government is supplying impetus in this direction through the Ethnic Heritage Program which provides grants and contracts to educational agencies to "assist them in planning, developing, establishing and operating ethnic heritage studies programs. . . ." This provision

was added to the Elementary and Secondary Education Act in 1972 "in recognition of the heterogeneous composition of the Nation and of the fact that in a multiethnic society a greater understanding of the contributions of one's own heritage and those of one's fellow citizens can contribute to a more harmonious, patriotic, and committed populace. . . ." Elementary and Secondary Education Act of 1965, Sec. 504 (a), Title IX.

4
The formal school

SCHOOL FUNCTIONS FROM DIFFERENT PERSPECTIVES

Society

From the point of view of a society, formal educational institutions
are developed to prepare younger members to effectively carry
out the legitimate roles of adult social life: to meet the expectations mature members of society have of them and to perpetuate the existing social order after older generations die out.
Schools do, in fact, usually transmit much of the dominant
culture of the society and, at the same time, imbue some level
of commitment to that society and to its culture. The content of
the transmitted culture includes, in large measure, the values,
norms, knowledge, beliefs, and symbols upon which there is
general social agreement. In the case of disagreement, it includes
those characteristics that the most powerful groups in the society
want to perpetuate.

When school socialization is effective, many social expectations
are widely shared. This simplifies communication, fosters consensus, and encourages individuals to conform voluntarily to the
established requirements of group life. A major consequence of
public education, then, is that it minimizes the extent to which
power and extrinsic rewards are needed to maintain the dominant
social order.

Transmission of the civic culture. Another important function of public education, at least in democratic societies, is the transmission of the civic culture. In the United States, public schools attempt to prepare young people to participate in political processes both by cultivating their commitment to the ideology of democracy and by giving them the knowledge and skills they need for the satisfactory performance of civic roles.

Political socialization within schools is largely anticipatory, however, since few pupils have the opportunity to exercise these roles until after they leave school. Nevertheless, many observers view this function as a necessary condition for participatory democracy. The relationship between education on the one hand, and subsequent political attitudes and political participation on the other, has been shown to be a fact in many countries. For example, Almond and Verba found in their studies of the civic cultures of five nations including the United States that, within each nation, those with more education were most likely as adults:

1. to be aware of the impact of government on the individual.
2. to follow politics and to pay attention to election campaigns.
3. to have a fund of political information.
4. to have opinions on a wide range of political subjects.
5. to engage in political discussions.
6. to consider themselves capable of influencing the government.[1]

The development of human resources. The development of these resources, which are needed for economic growth and the maintenance of an industrial society, is another important function of formal education. From this perspective, socialization includes both the acquisition of knowledge and skills required for occupational and other public roles and the acquisition of a world view which is consistent with the social organization of formal adult life. A *gesellschaft* orientation composed of the patterns of affective-neutrality, universalism, specificity, and achievement,[2] and the capacity to move easily from one role to another are usually associated with social organizations in technological societies such as the United States.

Since formal education sets the overall quality of a labor force by bringing most workers to some minimum stage of competence, many scholars believe that the kind and amount of education available to the members of a society are directly related to its level of economic productivity. Studies relating educational attainment to economic development usually show that those nations with extensive educational systems have relatively large gross national products per capita, high rates of economic growth, or both. Harbison and Myers, for instance, correlated the relationship between a composite index of human-resource development, based on the percentages of students currently enrolled in secondary and higher education with measures of national economic development for each of 75 different countries. They found a high positive correlation between the index of human-resource development and gross national product per capita (0.888) and a high negative correlation between the index of human development and the percentage of the active population engaged in agriculture (−0.814).[3]

Strong correlations between amount of education and national economic well-being have led many economists to the conclusion that an educated population is a necessary condition for national prosperity. Some, such as Harbison and Myers, have concluded that it is its principal cause. Even if this is not the case (for correlation is not the same as causation), most economists hold that schooling does contribute to the material level of a society; it provides technical training which produces workers with highly developed skills, and it provides general education which creates flexible workers who can adapt to changed circumstances within the society.[4]

The contributions of education to the economy also come through the part it plays in generating a cadre of elites. Schools identify and develop the talent of many of those who hold higher positions in key social structures such as the economy, government, the military, politics, religion, and education.[5] This function is not unlike that proposed by early national leaders who sought universal education for the discovery and proper education of a national intellectual elite.[6]

Underlying the goals of public education pertaining to the identification and development of talent are the following assumptions:

1. Some children are innately more able than others.
2. Public schools give all children equal opportunity to demonstrate their innate abilities.
3. Schools select the most able of their pupils and prepare them for the leadership positions they will eventually hold.
4. The entire society benefits from the fact that different pupils receive different kinds of socialization.

Although there is much room for debate about each of these assumptions, many of the influential positions in modern societies do demand high levels of technical knowledge which are acquired only after years of formal education or its equivalent.

Influential social positions often demand, in addition, less easily definable social-psychological traits that, coming together, tend to characterize the "innovative" personality. These include need for personal achievement, tolerance of ambiguity, openness to new experience, high energy levels, initiative, risk-taking, flexibility, creativity, and insight.[7] The contribution of schools to the development of these characteristics can never be as great as their contribution to the development of technological adequacy, for, although knowledge and skills are often obtained through formal study, innovative traits are derived more from initial home than from school socialization.

The extent to which schools are actually involved in fostering innovative personalities is open to question. While there is no doubt that highly intelligent pupils, as defined by traditional I.Q. measures, are selected for formal socialization that leads to elite roles, I.Q. scores and innovative thinking are not the same thing. In a well-known study that compares the attitudes of secondary-school teachers toward high-I.Q. pupils with their attitudes toward highly creative pupils, Getzels and Jackson discovered that teachers show special preference for high-I.Q. pupils even though both groups have equivalent school grades. The reasons that high-I.Q. pupils are preferred were not investigated, but Getzels and Jackson note that creative pupils are more likely to view objects and events differently from other pupils and that their wit is often perceived as hostile and threatening to teachers. They suggest that "if we wish to foster intellectual inventiveness, we may have to risk granting the creative student greater autonomy, and perhaps even reward behavior that fails to comply with what we were prepared to reward."[8]

Influences over educational programs. In the United States influences over educational programs come from national, state, and local sources. As a result, there are variations in the formal socialization experiences provided to children throughout the nation. Individual states have traditionally assumed the major responsibility for public education. They delegate their authority in different degrees to local school districts, which in turn delegate some authority to individual schools. States typically set guidelines containing standards for many aspects of public education; for example, requirements for teacher certification and pupil graduation, years of compulsory school attendance, curricular offerings, physical qualities of the school plant, and minimum dollar expenditure per pupil. Some states' guidelines are extremely detailed, whereas those of other states give wide discretion to local districts.

The federal government has only slowly entered into the affairs of elementary and secondary schools. It was briefly involved when following the Civil War, the Freedman's Bureau was established in the South; and, through the passage and implementation of the Smith-Hughes Act of 1917, it played a part in agriculture and industrial education. However, until recently the influence of the federal government on schools has been largely to ensure that they remain secular.

During the past several decades there have been contradictory tendencies in the locus of control of educational policy. At the same time that there have been pressures for standardization of educational programs, countervailing pressures have developed for local diversity. Pressures for standardization have come from state and national levels. At the state level there has been a continuous trend toward the merging of small, local school districts into larger units. In 1969-70 for example, the total number of school districts in the United States was less than one-half the number of districts in 1959-60, and less than one-fourth the number of districts in 1949-50.[9]

At the federal level, both Congress and the courts have made decisions that are applicable to all of the nation's schools. The Elementary and Secondary Education Act of 1965 was the first large-scale federal legislative involvement in local public schools. Its influence has been felt through grants that can only be received by school districts which comply with the provisions of the legislation. The Supreme Court has had far-reaching effects on schools through its 1954 decision in the case of *Brown* v. *The Board of Education of Topeka, Kansas,* in which it declared that "schools which segregate pupils on the basis of race, even though other facilities are equal, deprive children of minority groups of equal educational opportunity."[10] As a result of that judicial opinion, most *de jure,* or legally mandated, segregated schools in every section of the country are being eliminated. The Brown decision also paved the way for litigation directed at eliminating *de facto* school segregation, that is, segregation created by residential patterns.

National associations of professional educators and tax-exempt foundations are two other potent forces for standardization of educational practice. Their influence is felt through well-publicized conferences and through their publications. And commercial producers of textbooks and other educational materials, as well as other subject-matter experts, make significant impact on curricula by the content they include and the kinds of presentations they make.

At the same time, increased pressures for local diversity in educational programs are emerging. With the growing acceptance of cultural pluralism, racial-ethnic-group identification, and the right to be different, many members of the black, Mexican-American, and other minority groups make considerable input into the educational programs of their children. The notion of "maximum feasible participation" in community affairs, fostered by the "war against poverty" of the 1960s, has led to greater involvement in schools by people who are from the same racial-ethnic and socioeconomic background as the student body. An increasing number of school districts, in addition, sponsor "alternative" schools in which teachers, parents, and pupils cooperate in an atmosphere more or less free of traditional constraints to build their own preferred educational program.

The ecological characteristics of local districts stimulate variation in the socialization experiences provided by schools. Communities differ from one another in many ways: in their average levels of income, education, and occupational prestige; in their life styles, racial composition, religious and moral orientations; and in the general aspirations and expectations they hold for their children. These factors converge to create a somewhat distinctive social climate which, in combination with the district's physical location, economic and political structures, and especially the way it views the purposes of a school, are reflected in the kind of education it supplies. The influence of local communities on schools is felt directly through the amount of resources they make available, the way in which they allocate these resources, and their selection of school-board members. It is felt indirectly through the educational environment they create and through the pupils and other personnel they provide.

Even within a single district, variations in local characteristics can modify the functions of the school. Some schools stress the culture of the dominant society, others stress subcultural variations. The curricula of some schools are predominantly academic, others are vocational. And some schools concentrate on the development of elites, whereas others are geared to the production of workers for local industry and agriculture. However, despite these differences, public schools are usually expected to transmit broad societal values, provide some minimum level of knowledge and skills, and train future leaders.

The individual

The many functions education performs for the larger society should not obscure its influence on the lives of individuals. By providing socialization, schools can help people cope with the demands that society makes upon them and can add to the quality of personal life. The traditional *humanistic* orientation toward education sees schooling as "liberating" and holds that it is a basic human right, desirable in and of itself, which should be available to all. The *human-resource-development* orientation toward education also sees schooling as desirable, but primarily because it leads to higher individual productivity and increases one's range of choices for employment.[11] The implications of these two views lead to somewhat different educational programs. Humanists advocate a generalized, liberal-arts curriculum believing that it enhances the dignity and the intrinsic worth of the individual. Developmental economists stress specialized occupational preparation because it leads to higher levels of productivity and consumption by each member of society.

These two views of education have long competed for representation in the policies of American public schools. Each in turn has dominated as schools have alternated between one orientation and the other. Thus, at the beginning of the twentieth century, secondary schools moved from elite institutions providing liberal education for the few who planned to continue their schooling, to mass institutions which stressed vocational requirements for the many who would not. As college attendance became more common in the years following the Second World War, schools retained their mass institutional characteristics, but again provided liberal education for the majority of their pupils who were once more preparing for higher education. The current educational mood is toward a compromise between the two orientations, with pupils encouraged to study both liberal and vocational, or career, education.

It is interesting to note that a similar compromise was reflected two centuries ago in the curriculum of Benjamin Franklin's academy. Franklin was so pleased with this concept he proposed that it be extended to all the youth of Pennsylvania:

As to their Studies, *it would be well if they could be taught* every Thing *that is useful, and* every Thing *that is ornamental: But Art is long, and their time is Short. It is therefore propos'd that they learn those Things that are likely to be* most useful *and* most ornamental. *Regard being had to the several Professions for which they are intended.*[12]

However noble the sentiments of the humanistic tradition, they do not supply the common rationale for the many hours students spend in formal classrooms. Education is pursued by most Americans for its instrumental more than for its intrinsic value. Except for the economically secure for whom high social status is assured, individual decisions about school attendance and educational programs are largely informed by the opportunities they provide for subsequent occupational placement.

That there is a relationship in fact between the amount of education one has had and earned income is repeatedly demonstrated. One example, from U.S. Bureau of the Census data, is that in 1969 the annual median income for white families in which the prime wage earner had less than 8 years of school was $5,799, but the income for families in which the wage earner completed 4 or more years of college was $14,685. Positive associations between education and income, as well as between education and occupational prestige, have fostered wide faith in the efficacy of public schools for occupational opportunity and upward mobility.

According to the American dream, universal free schools provide all citizens with an equal opportunity to develop their initial talents and prepare those who are most able and most industrious to assume leadership positions. It holds that there is always "room at the top"; all persons, regardless of circumstances of birth, can rise to whatever societal level their intelligence, training, and motivation entitle them. Public education is an essential element of the articulated American value of equality: ideally, the achievement orientation of schools supplies criteria that emphasize *what* individuals are able to do rather than *who* they are, and their universalistic orientation reduces the effect of family background on future social status.

Nevertheless, family environment and, perhaps, genetic inheritance figure strongly in a child's scholastic attainment. In spite of opportunities for formal education, most children end up in about the same relative social position as their parents. Although it is true that education provides social and occupational mobility for some people, schooling by and large is a transmission belt, in that initial advantages stemming from the family are maintained for the fortunate and initial disadvantages are perpetuated for the unfortunate.[13]

The family

Schools are often viewed by parents as an extension of the family. They support formal education because they know that, if their children are to be successful in the larger society, they must have socialization experiences beyond those they themselves are able to provide. However, although parents believe that schools should give children tools that will enable them to earn their livelihood and perhaps move upward socially, many are reluctant to delegate other socialization responsibilities for fear that children will be exposed to values and norms that are antithetical to their own.

Two frequently controversial curricular issues relate to sex education and the absence or presence of religious instruction or observance. The origin of human life is an especially sensitive issue and a source of perennial controversy. Thus, in Tennessee in 1929, J. T. Scopes was convicted of the crime of teaching the Darwinian theory of evolution in a public school, and in California in 1972, religious fundamentalists fought unsuccessfully to introduce the biblical explanation of creation into state-approved textbooks as an alternative to the theory of evolution.

The obligation that parents send children to schools that are potentially disruptive to family culture has recently been questioned in several camps. One argument against compulsory schooling is grounded in the protection given to religious liberty by the First Amendment of the Constitution. In this regard, the United States Supreme Court ruled in 1972 that, despite a Wisconsin state law compelling school attendance by all children until age 16, Amish parents were not obligated to have their children attend school beyond the eighth grade because this "would gravely endanger if not destroy the free exercise of their religious belief."[14]　　　•

Another argument against compulsory public-school attendance is based on the notion of ethnic pluralism and on the responsibility of public schools to provide equal educational opportunities for all children. This position was elaborated in 1969 by the founders of the National Association of Afro-American Educators, who concluded that public schools are not "legitimate" institutions in the American society. Because many black children receive inadequate education and because schools are not responsive to the wishes of the black community, they have "criminally" failed the black youth of this country.[15] Similar grievances have been presented by other black and ethnic minority groups and many are attempting to gain sufficient political and economic power to control the education of their own children.

A third argument against compulsory schooling holds that education which provides no more than minimum-level skills does not directly affect a child's ultimate social position. The vast differences in income among adults who have had the same amount of education is used to support this argument. Those who take this position often ignore the functions formal education performs for the larger society or view these functions as undesirable in that they perpetuate existing inequalities. Some critics of compulsory schooling suggest that the money that is allocated for education be given to business and industry to establish apprenticeships or to individuals so that they can have a "stake" of their own when they start out in the world which they could use for education or not, as they see fit.[16]

However valid the arguments against universal free education may be, in the United States, schools have been established and are supported for what is believed to be the *collective* good. The formal socialization that schools provide is directed toward the development of competent adult citizens who can meet the needs of the dominant society.[17] Faith in public education is so widespread that schools are generally viewed as the road to social progress and the panacea for most social problems. Reciprocally, education is seen by pupils and their families as a way of equalizing individual opportunity and maximizing personal options.

Interests of society, individuals, and families

Theoretically these interests coincide and ideally schools serve all three as they go about the business of transmitting the dominant culture. For some children and their families, there is no conflict between the school's function as a seeker-out and developer of talent and their own personal aspirations. These include both children who start school with initial advantages and are selected to be prepared for high social positions, and those who are content to be prepared for occupational opportunities which yield some minimum acceptable social status and standard of living. However, other children who appear less talented yet have high aspirations are often excluded from occupational opportunities because of school practices.

Children from the middle classes have traditionally been well-served by public education. The achievement values they acquire from their families and those stressed by school are mutually supportive and most are able to meet the school's academic demands in a satisfactory manner. Teachers have been shown generally to prefer to teach children from this group: they are perceived as better behaved and as having greater "moral acceptability" than children from poorer families. Even though upper-middle-class children do not always meet teacher expectations, their misbehavior tends to be interpreted as a natural concomitant of brightness or as evidence that they are spoiled. Compared with other children they do not threaten the authority or the basic values of their teachers.[18] Disproportionately more of them are identified among the talented and more receive special socialization leading to high social positions. The generally high levels of school achievement of middle-class pupils, combined with the additional opportunities provided by their families, assures that the majority of them will be able to meet or surpass the social status of their parents.

Many children of late-nineteenth and early-twentieth century European immigrants were also well-served by public schools. Although their educational experiences were not as trouble-free as those of the native-born middle classes, newly arrived parents often encouraged their children to acquire American ways so that the rags-to-riches theme that permeated the political oratory and public-school curricula of the day would be played out in their own lives.[19]

The socialization provided by schools often differed from that provided by families and, no doubt, many parents and children suffered the attendant pain of culture conflict. This is not to say that immigrant adults were not subjected to socialization influences as well. Political parties courted immigrants for their votes, and political participation was a source of socialization for many. The influence of mass communication was another source of socialization. It has been said, with more than a grain of truth, that it was Hollywood that Americanized the immigrant family.

First-generation pupils often had a difficult time in school. Although there was much variation among national groups, immigrant children compared with native-born were grossly overrepresented in retarded classes, were more likely to receive low scores on intelligence tests, and were less likely to complete high school.[20] For those who succeeded, however, formal education was a legitimate avenue to upward mobility. Analyses of the educational and occupational achievement of Americans by nationality show that, as of now, most white children with comparable education have an equal chance to enter higher levels of the occupational structure regardless of the birthplace of their forebears. The notion of "equal opportunity irrespective of national origins is a near reality."[21]

Schooling has not, however, been as salutary to the occupational success of those who come from physically identifiable racial-ethnic groups; it does not lead to the same opportunities for employment that it does for comparable whites. The economic disadvantage of nonwhites is reflected in national income differentials: U.S. Census reports of 1970 show that the median annual income of nonwhite families headed by high school graduates is $7,875 contrasted with an income of $10,563 for comparable white families. Difference in income between races is less among college graduates, but it does not disappear: the median incomes are $13,682 and $14,685 for non-white and white families respectively. These differences may be even larger because statistics by family income hide the fact that since more members of minority families work, their reported family incomes are produced by a greater number of people. Such findings are due in large part to discriminatory practices against nonwhite and Spanish-surnamed populations in the competition for jobs. No matter how much one strives for mobility or how well one conforms to the behavior that usually attains it, there is no American dream when irrelevant criteria such as physical characteristics are utilized in selecting people to fill occupational positions.

Some of the differences in occupational achievement between white and other subpopulations is also due to the differences in the *kind* of education they receive. Local variations among school programs provide some pupils more than others with the skills needed to attain higher-level positions. Because of the commonly found patterns of racial and ethnic separation in housing, minority children often attend schools that are less effective in transmitting dominant social values and in training them for leadership roles. Further, schools have been generally less effective in developing the abilities of many racial-ethnic–minority pupils as a group in the critical areas of language and computational skills.[22] Moreover, the use of schools of objective and universalistic criteria on the one hand prepares children to compete on merit, but on the other denies some the opportunity to be selected for socialization experiences which will give them a chance to get ahead. This topic is pursued in greater detail in Chapter 7.

THE FORMAL ORGANIZATION OF THE SCHOOLS

Schools are deliberately planned social systems created primarily to attain the collectively held goal of socializing the young. The formal features of American public schools are usually organized around a set of roles such as administrators, teachers, and pupils. That was thought by many nineteenth-century school reformers to be the most efficient division of labor to achieve this goal.[23] The most significant of the formal features of schools are their rules prescribing the rights, duties, and obligations of each role. Rules introduce rationality and provide the basis for many repetitive patterns of behavior. To some extent, they reduce extraneous behavior which might impede formal education.

Bureaucracy

Schools, like other deliberately planned social systems, typically take a *bureaucratic* form. That is to say, they have among other formal features: a division of labor, a hierarchical structure of authority, a set of explicit rules, and a system of evaluation based on achievement criteria.[24] The term, bureaucracy, technically refers to these elements.

In popular discourse, however, bureaucracy sometimes means a formal social system in which bureaucratic elements have produced negative consequences. Two common examples of the popular meaning of bureaucracy are schools where compliance to rules is emphasized to the detriment of educational goals and where rigid adherence to rules makes response to changing conditions impossible. Bureaucracies are also associated in the public view with social systems that are characterized by extreme impersonality and a lack of sensitivity to the personal needs of the people who come into contact with them.

None of these undesirable consequences must necessarily accompany bureaucracies, but they occur sufficiently often to suggest that no matter how rational the structure appears to be on paper, when implemented it has a tendency to foster behavior which undermines the initial purpose of the organization. Despite these dysfunctions, however, the bureaucracy of public schools, like those of other large social systems, assists in the management of large numbers of people and in the organization of activities that help bring about educational goals.

The extent to which school bureaucracies directly affect pupils differs from classroom to classroom. Most teachers have considerable discretion in their relationships with pupils, if only because ordinarily they are solo practitioners. This gives them leeway to adhere to bureaucratic rules, to adapt these rules to their own situations, or to ignore them in part as they see fit. In addition, the ideal of professionalization which is increasingly pursued by contemporary educators goes counter to bureaucratization in many respects. As will be seen in the discussion of the roles of educators in Chapter 5, the concept of professionalism requires that professionals have autonomy from organizational restraints that interfere with the exercise of their best judgment.

Informal social systems

The need for rationality, efficiency, and predictability in public schools is met by their formal structures, which create the bureaucratic milieu —a social climate that is distinct from that of the home and of informal peer groups. Formal structure creates only a part of the educational environment, however, since it is people with their many different idiosyncracies who occupy formal roles and implement formal rules. How individuals play out organizational roles depends upon their personalities, their previous and concurrent socialization, and their other social roles, as well as on the prescriptions imposed on them by organizational rules. It also depends upon the influence which other people in the school have upon them and upon one another, on their patterns of interaction, and on the values and norms they develop.

Each school has its own social system created out of the unique blend of people who happened to be assigned or recruited into it. Although most schools start out with similar plans of organization, dissimilar social systems emerge as informal patterns of behavior develop among school personnel and pupils. Schools that appear identical in structure may have different internal environments which, in return, support, neutralize, or even subvert the school organization and its socialization goals.

Although the informal relationships among the people in a school sometimes interfere with socialization, schools, like all formal organizations, cannot get along without them. The informal system, which is characterized by spontaneous, *gemeinschaft* behavior, in contrast to the rational, *gesellschaft* behavior of the formal system, assists both the formal system and the people who participate in it in several ways. One of its functions is to interpret, modify, and communicate general rules so that individuals can meet their expectations. Another is to develop norms and values which assist those who occupy similar roles in dealing with their common concerns and which socialize newer members to this subculture. Still another function is to provide emotional support which helps people participate in the otherwise impersonal milieu.

From the standpoint of the individual, the last of these functions is the most significant since, in addition to being treated as occupants of formal roles, people like to be related to as unique personalities. Regardless of age, experience, and social status, people usually seek primary relationships among those with whom they work and often come to value the organization solely because of them. School personnel and pupils sometimes participate in school activities and comply with formal demands because of these relationships, even when they are otherwise dissatisfied. Principals often go out of their way to foster informal ties among teachers, and teachers attempt to cultivate pupil peer groups in the belief that higher morale and fuller participation results.

On the other hand, emotional attachments within informal groups can become so valued that they are subversive to the organization. Pupils' satisfaction from peers, for instance, may so outweigh those from formal education that they ignore the tasks and goals of the school. The ideal school attains a delicate balance between the rewards of the formal and informal systems. It is one in which participants know how to separate the expectations of their formal roles from those of their informal ones and how to shift easily from one role to another.

School goals

Presumably the behavior fostered by a school's bureaucratic organization is the most rational means of attaining stated educational goals. However, the specifications of these goals, compared to those of other organizations, are very loose. In reality, they give little direction to educational activity, and, what is more, it is extremely difficult to determine when and if school goals have been attained. A major difficulty in knowing whether school goals are reached lodges in the problem of arriving at common interpretations of their meanings. Another difficulty is the result of the future orientation of the socialization process itself. Since most school goals are concerned more with preparation for adult than for contemporaneous childhood roles, one must often have a historian's view to evaluate school effectiveness. Evaluation of school activities is further complicated by the fact that schools are but one of many sources of socialization; it is often impossible to identify their unique contributions to the development of their pupils.

Most goal statements have been modeled after the prototype developed in 1918, by the National Educational Association's Commission on the Reorganization of Secondary Education. This document, entitled *Cardinal Principles of Secondary Education*, recommends that secondary education should "develop in each individual the knowledge, interests, ideals, habits and powers whereby he will find his place and use that place to shape both himself and society toward ever nobler ends."[25] It offers as a guide the now well-known seven "cardinal principles" of health, command of the fundamental processes, worthy home membership, vocation, citizenship, worthy use of leisure, and ethical character.[26] One should note the extent to which these goals are couched in broad generalities and their lack of direction for implementation. The functions of statements like these are mostly to set the organizational "tone" of schools and to give them legitimacy in the eyes of their communities. They do not suggest the means by which these goals can be accomplished.

Policymakers are reluctant to state precisely what ends a school serves because it must appear to be responsive to the many and varied demands of the public which supports it. The American people's traditional faith in public education has given schools a heavy burden. One of its many publics inevitably pressures the school to deal with almost every social problem. Consequently, schools are held responsible for more functions than time and resources allow, and for some which are mutually contradictory.

Examples of the former arise out of separate demands for liberal and vocational curricula or for the transmission of national and local cultures. Examples of the latter come from pressures leading to education for social change at the same time that there are pressures for the transmission of traditional values and education for the status quo. Increasingly common examples of contradictory aims originate in the goal fed by the American dream of minimizing differences in life-chances among all children. This goal competes with other often-stated goals such as provision of the opportunity for all pupils to develop their ability to the maximum and the fostering of cultural pluralism and ethnic identity.

Diffuse goals such as the cardinal principles are likely to be accepted by most members of the community. They contain few specifics over which individuals can differ and offer many generalities on which they can pin their hopes. School goals are concerned with an ideal society; they are grounded in values and tend to be impervious to empirical verification. For these reasons, schools shy away from controversial issues in their public statements and reflect only those values upon which there is community consensus. Because most American school districts emphasize generally agreed-upon values of the dominant American society, many school goal statements are remarkably similar.[27]

This is not to suggest that schools are without operating goals, but to emphasize that they are not necessarily the same as articulated goals. Operational goals arise out of the specific commitments or obligations to which schools pledge themselves. Examples of these include the provision of education for all children until age 16, driver education, and education for the gifted. They do not include general statements concerning topics like "life-adjustment" education. Corwin hypothesizes that a real goal comes about as a result of a "bargaining process among the power blocks within the school and between those power blocks and certain outsiders who are able to exercise constraint."[28] The implication of his view is that school operating goals are identical to the settlements made between conflicting groups. To discern what local operating goals are, one must look at priorities in the allocation of resources within the school district since these represent the culmination of decisions that have been made at all levels of the school organization.

NOTES

[1] Gabriel A. Almond and Sidney Verba, *The Civic Culture: Political Attitudes in Five Nations*, Boston, Little, Brown, 1965, pp. 317–318.

[2] For a discussion of these and other pattern variables, see Chap. 1.

[3] Frederick Harbison and Charles A. Meyers, *Education, Manpower, and Economic Growth: Strategies of Human Resource Development*, New York, McGraw-Hill, 1964, p. 40. Noted exceptions to this relationship exist in Kuwait and other oil-rich nations that rely on external entrepreneurs and labor for the initial exploitation of their mineral wealth.

[4] John Vaizey and Michael Debeauvais, "Economic Aspects of Educational Development," in A. H. Halsey, J. Floud, and C. A. Anderson, eds., *Education, Economy and Society*, New York, Free Press, 1961, pp. 37–49.

[5] "Elite" is employed here in the manner developed by S. M. Lipset and A. Solari, eds., *Elites in Latin American*, New York, Oxford University Press, 1967, preface.

[6] See James Mulhern, *A History of Education*, New York, Ronald Press, 1946, pp. 472–473, who commented that although the educational writings of most of the early national leaders contain some of the "noblest and most inspiring liberal thoughts to be found in democratic educational literature . . . there is a touch of the aristocratic tradition in their view."

[7] Everett E. Hagen, *On the Theory of Social Change: How Economic Growth Begins*, Homewood, Ill., Dorsey Press, 1962, pp. 88–95.

[8] Jacob W. Getzels and Philip W. Jackson, *Creativity and Intelligence: Explorations with Gifted Students*, New York, Wiley, 1962, p. 125.

[9] Kenneth A. Simon and W. Vance Grant, *Digest of Educational Statistics: 1971 Edition*, Washington, D.C., U.S. Department of Health, Education, and Welfare, 1972, p. 44.

[10] Brown v. Board of Education of Topeka, *U.S. Official Reports*, 347 (1954), p. 483.

[11] For this view see Theodore W. Schultz, "Investment in Human Capital," *The American Economic Review*, 51, no. 1 (March 1961), 1–17. Demands for manual training and vocational education in public secondary schools began as early as 1880. These culminated in the 1917 Smith-Hughes Act providing federal funds to train a national work force. See Norton W. Grubb and Marvin Lazerson, "Vocational Education in American Schooling: Historical Perspectives," *Inequality in Education*, 16, March 1974, pp. 5–18. Contemporary emphasis on human resource development is expressed in calls for career education to begin in primary schools. See U.S. Commissioner of Education Sidney P. Marland, "Career Education Now," address to National Association of Secondary School Principals, 23 January, 1971.

[12] Benjamin Franklin, *Proposals Relating to the Education of Youth in Pennsylvania*, Philadelphia, 1749, p. 11, as cited by Mulhern, *op. cit.*, p. 273. A review of historical efforts for technological education is found in Arthur G. Wirth, *Education in the Technological Society*, Scranton, Pa., Intext Educational Publishers, 1972.

[13] *Toward a Social Report*, Washington, D.C., U.S. Department of Health, Education, and Welfare, 1969, p. 19.

[14] State of Wisconsin v. Jonas Yoder, *et al.*, *Supreme Court Reporter*, 92, no. 15 (June 1972), 1526–1550.

[15] Charles V. Hamilton, "Race and Education: A Search for Legitimacy," *Harvard Educational Review*, 38, no. 4 (Fall 1968), 675–676.

[16] For example, see Christopher Jencks, *et al.*, *Inequality: A Reassessment of the Effect of Family and Schooling in America*, New York, Basic Books, 1972; Ivan Illich, *Deschooling Society*, New York, Harper & Row, 1970; Paul Goodman, *New Reformation: Notes of a Neolithic Conservative*, New York, Random House, 1972; Everett Reimer, *School is Dead: Alternatives in Education*, Garden City, N.Y., Doubleday, 1972. The Panel on Youth of the President's Science Advisory Committee recently proposed that educational vouchers equivalent to the cost of schooling through 4 years of college be given directly to youth at age 16 "to be used at their discretion for schooling and other skill acquisition at any subsequent time of their life." Any unused portion would be reflected in payments received upon retirement. *Youth: Transition to Adulthood*, Washington, D.C., Office of Science and Technology, Executive Office of the President, 1973, pp. 77–78.

[17] The functional needs of a society are discussed in Chap. 1.

[18] Howard S. Becker, "Social Class Variation in the Teacher-Pupil Relationship," *Journal of Educational Sociology*, 25 (April 1952), 451–465.

[19] Materials presented in schools of the early twentieth century often stressed the theme that relentless striving, scrupulous honesty, and the development of inborn talent are rewarded by an appreciative American society. The McGuffy Readers and Horatio Alger stories are noted ex-

amples of this delayed-gratification theme that was presented to pupils. In contrast is the immediate-gratification theme of more recent works by Edward Stratemeyer, which detail the adventures of ordinary young people. Written under a variety of pseudonyms, these books include among others: *Rover Boys*, *Motor Boys*, *Racer Boys*, *Radio Boys*, the Barton books for girls, *Moving Picture Girls*, *Honey Bunch*, *Bobsey Twins*, *Tom Swift*, and *Nancy Drew*. The extent to which the shift away from delayed gratification in popular children's literature has affected the work orientation of those who are now in their middle– and early–adult years makes interesting speculation. On Stratemeyer see Arthur Prager, *Rascals at Large*, Garden City, N.Y., Doubleday, 1971.

[20] David K. Cohen, "Immigrants and the Schools," *Review of Educational Research*, 40, no. 1 (February 1970), 24. For a different interpretation of the effectiveness of American schools in providing opportunities to immigrant children see Colin Greer, *The Great School Legend: A Revisionist Interpretation of American Public School*, New York, Basic Books, 1972; Michael B. Katz, *Class, Bureaucracy and Schools: The Illusion of Educational Change in America*, New York, Praeger, 1971.

[21] Beverly Duncan and Otis Dudley Duncan, "Minorities and the Process of Stratification," *American Sociological Review*, 33, no. 3 (June 1968), 356–364. Exceptions to this generalization are the over-achievement typical of Russian-Americans and the under-achievement typical of Latin Americans.

[22] James S. Coleman, *et al.*, *Equality of Educational Opportunity*, Washington, D.C., U.S. Office of Education, 1966, p. 20. An exception is the academic achievement of Oriental-Americans. This national survey found the mean achievement of Orientals to be about the same as that of whites (see Table 6.1, Chap. 6) and a Los Angeles survey found the mean of Japanese-Americans to be much higher. See Audrey James Schwartz, *Traditional Values and Contemporary Achievement of Japanese-American Pupils*, Los Angeles, Calif., Center for the Study of Evaluation, University of California, 1970.

[23] On the influence of the organizational form taken by industry on the development of public school bureaucracy, see Raymond E. Callahan, *Education and the Cult of Efficiency*, Chicago, University of Chicago Press, 1962; also see Katz, *op. cit.*

[24] According to German sociologist Max Weber, the essentials of bureaucratic organization include: a structure of hierarchical and stratified offices containing explicit definitions of official activities; an authority system in which authority resides in the office rather than in the person who occupies it; a division of labor and specialization of functions, tasks, and duties; and formal and impersonal rules of procedure. This ideal type has become known as the "classical" model of bureaucracy and it exists to some extent in all formal organizations. Hans H. Gerth and C. Wright Mills, *From Max Weber: Essays in Sociology*, New York, Oxford University Press, 1946, chap. 8.

[25] Commission on the Reorganization of Secondary Education, *Cardinal Principles of Secondary Education*, Washington, D.C. National Education Association, 1918.

[26] *Ibid.*, pp. 9–16.

[27] For a summary of American values, see Chap. 1.

[28] Ronald G. Corwin, *A Sociology of Education*, New York, Appleton, 1965, pp. 434–435.

5
Role expectations in local school districts

THE FORMAL ROLES

Typically the organizational roles of a school district are stratified into a pyramid of hierarchical positions in which those at the top are expected to direct and evaluate much of the work of their subordinates. *Boards of education* stand above the pyramid and function as boards of directors. Members of the board are theoretically responsible to the people who elect them or, in some districts, to the mayor or political body that appoints them, and are presumed to represent the interests of most of their constituents when they formulate school district policy. (See Figure 5.1.)

Superintendents are the highest ranking professional educators employed by school districts. They are the schools' chief executive officers and are in charge of all operations. Among the most significant responsibilities built into the superintendency are: the district's relationships with its external community, acquisition and allocation of resources including personnel, translation of policy statements into operational goals, and the development of educational practices to attain them. Superintendents often delegate many of these responsibilities to members of their administrative staffs.

Principals and similar administrators compromise the organiza-

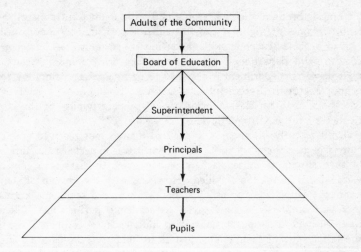

FIGURE 5.1 Traditional Channels of Authority in Local School Districts

tional levels between the superintendent who is at the apex of the school district's formal structure and classroom teachers who form its base. Large districts sometimes require a number of lesser superintendents, supervisors, and "line" personnel to assist with the direction of district-wide affairs; and most districts, regardless of size, assign a principal to manage each school unit.

The responsibilities of principals with respect to individual schools are very much like those of superintendents with respect to the entire district. The principal is the highest ranking professional in the school building and is accountable for its total management. Duties of principals typically include the acquisition and allocation of personnel and tangible resources for the school, maintenance of the school's relationship with parents and other groups within its attendance boundaries, and management of the school staff and pupils. Because of their proximity to the classrooms where formal socialization takes place, principals are usually more concerned than are other administrators with immediate educational objectives and the means to attain them.

Teachers are the foremost socializing agents in every school district and they carry the greatest responsibility for the educational progress of individual pupils. The organizational task of teachers is to manage the classroom environment in such a way that maximum learning is brought about. Learning is usually defined in terms of the twin outcomes of cognitive growth which is measured by the acquisition of specific academic skills, and "moral" socialization, shown by correct pupil deportment.[1] These two goals are commonly seen as related in that deportment is assumed to be a necessary condition for cognitive growth. Successful teachers have traditionally been those who both maintain classroom order and prepare pupils for the curriculum of the next grade level.

Until recently, the goal of order had many times received greater emphasis than the academic achievement it was expected to facilitate; in such situations those teachers who excelled in classroom control were viewed as the most skilled.[2] However, with the growth of standardized testing and the establishment of national scholastic norms, increased emphasis is now given to academic performance. There have even been serious proposals to link teachers' compensation to the test results of their pupils, just as in industry salaries are sometimes contingent on workers' productivity. But because socialization of children does not lend itself as easily to quantifiability as do products off an assembly line, there are significant flaws in many of the plans that demand this kind of teacher accountability.

The most serious flaw is that easily measured achievement tends to be narrowly circumscribed and overly concerned with short-term cognitive gains, whereas teachers, in theory at least, are interested in long-term development of the whole child. If teachers are encouraged to stress certain kinds of learning such as language and computational skills, some of the less easily measured components of socialization may be disregarded. Since public schools have been created to serve the larger society which requires that they develop people who will contribute to it, schools presumably foster the growth of many of the other attributes of well-functioning adults. These include, in addition to established knowledge and skills, the ability to learn on a continuing basis, the capacity to solve problems, intellectual curiosity, and interpersonal skills—not to mention other attributes such as an understanding of social justice and the political process, and a sense of aesthetics.

PROFESSIONAL VERSUS LAY CONTROL OF EDUCATION

There are two sources of conflict that affect the work of educators, both deriving from the concept of professionalism. One pertains to the relationship between professional and lay control over educational policy and practice; the other pertains to the relationship between the requirements of professionals for independence in their work and those of school districts for standardization. Regardless of the occupation that is making the claim of professionalism, the concept has similar assumptions:

1. The work of professionals requires a body of specialized knowledge that has been gained only after a long preparatory period.
2. Professionals have a monopoly over the kind of work they have been trained to do and have authority over the policies that control it.
3. Only like professionals are competent to evaluate the behavior of professionals.
4. Professionals are obligated to improve the services their occupations offer.
5. Professionals guard the welfare of their clients.

The lay school board

Professionally oriented educators look to their colleagues, to work-related associations, and to schools of education more than they do to lay members of their school district for advice and approval. Manifestly, there is an inescapable conflict between the concept of professional educator and that of lay boards of directors, a conflict that may become more acute if efforts for community participation in school policy and practice continue to grow.

Lay control over education is built into the concept of American public schools. Not only are boards of education composed of lay people, their meetings are usually open to the public. Reporters, individuals, and diverse lay groups attend board meetings to learn what is going on and to pressure for their own educational programs. Local boards are constrained to some extent by superordinate state policies, but they generally have authority to issue broad policy statements pertaining to educational goals, to monitor school expenditures, and to appoint the superintendent of schools.

In recent years, school districts have so grown in size and complexity that boards have increasingly delegated responsibility for critical policy to professional educators and have retained for themselves the functions of monitor for the public and mediator between the public and the schools in time of conflict and crises.[3] How authority is divided between school boards and superintendents differs among school districts and often differs temporally within the same district. Under normal conditions, most superintendents have a great deal of autonomy in the selection and implementation of educational practices. McCarty and Ramsey conclude from their study of the political structures of 51 school districts that school boards rubber stamp the policies of superintendents when tranquility reigns, but take an active part in school affairs when conflict erupts.[4] Similarly, Kerr concludes from his study of two northern suburban districts that the chief function of school boards is to legitimate the policies of professional school administrators to the lay community, rather than to represent various segments of the community to the school administration.[5]

In spite of the fact that most boards have the formal authority to hire and fire superintendents, the superintendent has certain advantages over the board that make it difficult for board members to retain strong control of the district. Because superintendents are professionals, they have specialized knowledge of school systems in general and their own systems in particular; they have access to a supporting staff for research, planning, and information; and, most importantly, the superintendency is a full-time occupation.

In contrast, members of school boards are laymen; they have other occupations with which they are equally or more concerned, and they seldom have an independent staff on which to rely for information and guidance about school matters. They look to superintendents even though superintendents are in a position to "manage" and interpret the data given to them. It has been said that when board members are not overawed by the superintendent's personality, they are overwhelmed by the complexity of the issues they must face.[6] Except when there is a credibility crisis in local districts, superintendents are usually in charge.

Local community control

One of the most important functions retained by school boards is that of buffer between lay citizens and schools. Through this function they supply schools with autonomy to pursue long-range socialization objectives. This buffer has become so effective against political, economic, and other pressures that the claim is commonly heard that contemporary public education takes place within "fortress" schools which are unresponsive to the socialization needs of the day. Because of schools' relative insulation from many contemporary social concerns and because board members often represent the well-established and conservative sectors of the school district,[7] a number of telling arguments have been made for giving residents of local communities a direct voice in the development of local school policy. The arguments that follow are particularly germane to the concerns of low-income and some minority-group members:

1. The "people" are the trustees of the school and schools should be accountable directly to them.
2. Minority and low-socioeconomic groups have traditionally been excluded from decisions involving their members and their participation should be encouraged.
3. Cultural differences between the expectations of the home and the school lead to a disjointed socialization process whereas greater continuity in socialization occurs when parents and schools join together.
4. Community participation fosters cultural diversity and shows children that their own culture does not have to be replaced by that of the dominant society.[8]

Changes in the locus of school decision making are in fact being brought about as a result of demands from both minority and white community groups with the support of diverse and influential forces. For example, many civil-rights advocates view administrative decentralization and local control of schools as a way of increasing the quality of schooling for minority pupils until that time when school integration comes about. Other social reformers view these changes as a way of providing "maximum feasible participation" by the poor in institutions that have been designed to serve them. Not only will education be more relevant to the special needs of low-income children, the participation of low-income adults provides opportunities for the development of both leadership skills and a base for political and economic power. Many social scientists see increased school district efficiency and the provision of greater access to school administrators as decided advantages stemming from decentralization. In addition, local control of schools stimulates parental involvement in school affairs, which in itself has been shown to enhance children's academic achievement.[9]

The long-range effects of direct community participation cannot now be ascertained, but it seems clear that the interest of lay people in public schools has shaken the traditional fortress posture. Even more, it has underscored the reality that, in the final analysis, schools are accountable to the society that creates and supports them. One might speculate that an increase or even a continuation of general lay participation in the internal affairs of schools over a long period will be extremely threatening to school personnel.

For one thing, most lay persons are not as tutored in educational affairs as their confidence sometimes suggests. They are not usually knowledgeable, for example, in educational technologies and in how, when, and for which pupils each technique is most appropriate. In addition, evaluations of educational programs by lay people tend to stress short-term over long-term outcomes, with the result that easily measured cognitive skills and the deportment of pupils are often disproportionately emphasized.

Also, direct involvement of lay persons in educational practice may have negative effects on the development and maintenance of a cadre of professional educators, since professional personnel require some independence from lay control in order to carry out their occupational roles. If educators are unable to use their special knowledge and experience because they lack autonomy, it is likely that the most skilled among them will change to more productive and rewarding work, to say nothing of the problem of recruiting comparable replacements.

In this connection, Becker concluded long ago from his well-known study of school teachers in Chicago that entrance of the parents on the scene is always potentially "dangerous" in that parents and educators do not usually share the same understandings about the legitimate role of the teacher. He found that teachers build defenses against parents who complain about school practices and that they expect their principals to help them to maintain their automony. Teachers wish to avoid disputes about their authority and feel that this can be accomplished best when parents do not get "involved in the school's operation" any more than absolutely necessary.[10]

Perhaps most important from the standpoint of traditional public schools, the direct involvement of lay persons in school affairs makes the irresolvable inconsistencies in popularly held goals of public education painfully apparent. Responses to the recognition that schools must necessarily fall short of some expectations can undermine support of public education.

Indeed, dissatisfaction with public schools has already led to serious proposals for alternative forms. One plan is to issue educational "vouchers" for the amount of money customarily spent on a child's education which parents can take to a public or private school of their choice.[11] Another plan is to give tax exemptions or tax credits to parents in some proportion to the amount they spend on their children's education in private schools. Proposals such as these have already done a great deal to stimulate responses by professional educators to pressures from lay communities.

PROFESSIONALISM WITHIN THE SCHOOL

At the same time that there has been increasing involvement of lay persons in the development of educational policy and practice, there has been a growing trend toward the inclusion in decision making of educational personnel from all organizational levels. It is consistent with the rights and responsibilities of professional educators for teachers and principals to share in the formation of policy: to control their own work and to improve the quality of schooling for their clients. It has in fact been largely in response to demands by professional teacher associations that such changes in the formal structure of authority are coming about.[12]

There are, however, two different kinds of expectations that govern the roles of educators and they sometimes have conflicting implications. One set derives from professionalism; it stresses teacher participation in the formation of school policy, their occupational autonomy, and the socialization of children. The other derives from the school-district bureaucracy and emphasizes the implementation of policy that has been created by boards of education and superintendents. These two sets of demands often cause confusion in how educational roles should be carried out.

Professional expectations of school principals

These include, for example, staff development and the exercise of informal leadership among teachers. At the same time, principals are expected to be administrative agents of the district bureaucracy and to evaluate the performance of teachers according to district criteria. Unlike the headmaster in traditional English schools who is given full freedom regarding internal educational policy, American principals are both professional educational leaders and administrative representatives.[13] Since the career advancement of American principals usually resides in moving up the administrative ladder, principals often assign higher priority to bureaucratic than to professional role expectations.

Nonetheless, a national study of elementary school principals by

Gross and Herriott makes clear that professional leadership by principals has an important effect on teacher morale and classroom performance; and, more significantly, it influences pupil achievement. These leadership qualities include the ability to impart to teachers an attitude of professionalism, a feeling of importance about their work, and a belief in their own competence to improve the educational performance of pupils. Effective principals work to develop an *esprit de corps* among members of the faculty and make maximum use of the skills of individual teachers by offering them constructive criticism, by encouraging classroom innovation, and by rewarding those who do an outstanding job. The extent to which principals exhibit professional leadership characteristics was found to be positively related to the professional leadership style of their immediate superiors and to the quality of their own undergraduate education. Principals who had attended small, private liberal-arts colleges, for instance, seem to stress professional leadership.[14]

These findings take on special significance when they are considered in the light of charges that attempts by principals to influence the performance of teachers are an invasion of the teachers' own professional autonomy. According to Gross and Herriott, principals should develop their professional leadership, for, if they were to do no more than engage in routine bureaucratic management, "a strong force conducive to improved teaching and learning would be eliminated."[15] Perhaps the extent to which it is useful for principals to become directly involved with the socialization function depends upon the excellence of their teachers. It is likely, for example, that, whereas the creativity of the imaginative teacher would suffer from outside interference, the performance of the average teacher would benefit from the interest of an administrator.

In similar vein, Janowitz agrees that principals cannot be solely administrative agents and suggests that they "represent and personify the teaching function." He proposes a role of "principal-teacher," somewhat like the chief-of-service doctor in the hospital, in which principals act as training officers for the staff, engage in classroom teaching, and are available to pupils, parents, and other community members.[16] These changes in the role expectations of the principal are part of his larger plan to give inner-city schools greater flexibility in carrying out their socialization goals.

Janowitz proposes that schools develop close working relationships with all community agencies: that they house complete records about each child, and that they take on the responsibility of referring children to other community services as needed. In short, Janowitz would like to see inner-city schools become the central "coordinating mechanism" for formal and informal programs of "intervention" in the personal and social development of their pupils.[17]

Classroom teachers

Classroom teachers are more affected than other school-district personnel by the inherent conflict between the district's requirements for bureaucratic conformity and professional requirements for autonomy. From a bureaucratic perspective, teachers are the lowest-ranking educators: all rules, directions, and evaluations come from administrative layers above. The formal position of the teacher within the school district is of great concern to many professionally oriented teachers, since low organizational status can reduce classroom autonomy below the level needed for optimum performance.

Role expectations of teachers like those of other school personnel vary from district to district. Compared with smaller districts, larger districts usually accord teachers more prestige, pay higher salaries, require that they be better educated, and allow them more ideological deviance in their personal lives. But larger districts are also inclined to be more bureaucratic and to have clearer status divisions between teaching staff and administrators. Teacher expectations held by school districts range along a continuum with bureaucratic-employee at one end and autonomous-professional at the other. In employee-oriented districts, the teacher role is explicitly defined and only slight variations are tolerated; in professionally oriented districts, expectations are very general and teachers are given great flexibility.

Teachers themselves can also be categorized as employee- and professionally-oriented. According to Corwin, the "employee" teacher believes that what is best for the school organization is best for education, that curriculum should be planned so that every child taking the same course throughout a state covers the same subject matter, and that teachers take into account the opinion of their community to guide what they say and do in the classroom. In contrast, the "professional" teacher believes that it is permissible for a teacher to violate rules if it is in the best interest of the pupils, that teachers should live up to the standards of their profession even if the school administration or the community do not seem to respect them, and that they should be evaluated on their knowledge of the subject matter they teach and their ability to communicate it.[18]

Each of these orientations presents different kinds of problems since school districts need both professional expertise in pursuing socialization goals and loyalty among their employees.

To the extent that there is general agreement or disagreement in the interpretation of a particular role, there is role *consensus* or *dissensus*. Teachers who have been socialized to a professional orientation but work in bureaucratic-employee districts, or who have acquired bureaucratic-employee orientations and work in professionally oriented districts, are faced with role dissensus. Role dissensus for professionally oriented teachers usually leads to conflict with administrators since they typically attempt to expand their own authority. Dissensus for bureaucratic-oriented teachers leads to *anomie*, or normlessness, since they never receive the guidance they want and expect. Professionally oriented teachers may be disliked or distrusted by other personnel, but they are seldom viewed as incompetent. On the other hand, the ability of bureaucratic-employees is often questioned in professionally oriented districts.

In order to minimize role dissensus, school districts try to employ teachers with role expectations that are similar to those of district administrators. Districts often prefer personnel who share similar background, including preparation in professional schools that are known to put forth a particular interpretation of the teacher role. In-service training sessions provide additional socialization to preferred role definitions and reinforce expectations that are already shared. Although careful hiring and training practices substantially reduce role dissensus, they seldom eliminate it entirely. A moderate amount of conflict works to the ultimate advantage of pupils, however, because it forces educators to look for new solutions to educational problems. But a great deal of conflict has a negative impact since it consumes energy needed for the attainment of socialization goals.

Educators are not unique in the tensions they experience between bureaucratic and professional requirements. These tensions are also felt by professionals in hospitals, large law firms, research and development corporations, social–service agencies, and indeed, by all professionals who work in large organizations. Gouldner distinguishes between the *cosmopolitan* and *local* orientations found among people in many different occupational groups. Cosmopolitans are oriented primarily toward their professional specialization and toward affiliations beyond their employing organization, whereas locals are committed to their own organizations and to the people with whom they work.[19]

The loyalty of teachers and administrators to particular schools and school districts differs depending upon their view of the educator's role. A cosmopolitan is usually willing to change institutional affiliation in order to exercise professional judgment, but a local is constrained by loyalty to the school and to current associates. To the extent that educators have a cosmopolitan outlook, they potentially undermine bureaucratic structure. On the other hand, cosmopolitans tend to be more creative in their responses to educational challenge and to stimulate change in educational practice.[20]

Studies of teacher attitudes suggest that, regardless of a teacher's role definition, those employed by highly bureaucratic school districts compared with those in less bureaucratic districts feel greater sense of power to influence organizational forces. Moeller examined the formal organization of 20 school districts in the St. Louis metropolitan area and ranked them according to their bureaucratic characteristics, including school policies, clearly delimitated areas of responsibility, and specified lines of authority. He then determined the extent to which teachers of each district had a feeling of efficacy in relation to textbook selection, participation in school committees, and general ability to influence district-wide teaching policies. Finding that teachers in highly bureaucratic systems experience a significantly higher sense of power than those in less bureaucratic districts, Moeller concludes that bureaucracy provides teachers with "an understandable and predictable ethos" in which to pursue their profession.[21]

Bureaucratic structures give educators protection from some of the nonrational elements within school districts, allowing them to use organizational rules to circumvent unreasonable pressures from pupils, parents, colleagues, and superiors. Rules also discourage administrators from employing particularistic criteria such as racial-ethnic, social, and religious origins, as well as sex, age, and educational institution attended in the allocation of tasks and rewards. Further, bureaucratic structures enhance professional performance by prescribing the amount and circumstances under which superiors are permitted to intervene with role performance and by granting tenure and other forms of job security so that professionals have the autonomy to carry out their roles.

Negative consequences of bureaucracy

Bureaucratic protections are not unmixed blessings, however, for universalism and affective-neutrality have negative as well as positive consequences on individual personality and on the performance of formal roles. With respect to the consequences on personality, sociologist Robert Merton has noted that individuals who work within bureaucratic settings often demonstrate certain characteristic behavior patterns including "overconformity" to rules and formal role expectations.

According to Merton, "bureaucratic personalities" develop because formal organizations typically reward conformity through salary increments, promotions, and the like, and provide no reinforcements for innovative behavior. He points out that conformity is frequently dysfunctional for attaining organizational goals since traditional expectations tend to be carried out even when the original circumstances that made them effective have materially changed.[22] The phenomenon of bureaucratic personality goes a long way in explaining why schools have typically been slow in responding to changed social conditions: the expectations that are rigidified in school roles are comfortable for most role occupants and receive highest organizational rewards.

With respect to the negative consequences of bureaucracy on role performance, Gross and Herriott have shown that teachers as well as principals seem to benefit from some affective support from those above them.[23] While it is true that teachers are partly sustained in their work by their colleagues, that support usually helps them to cope more with common problems *vis-à-vis* the school bureaucracy than with their relations with their pupils. Moreover, teachers are often isolated from other teachers for most of their work day unless they are members of a teaching team or are housed in the architecturally newer "open-space" buildings. If they are to receive affective sustenance within the classroom it must usually come from principals and other administrators. Yet bureaucratic structures militate against personal styles of administration in spite of the fact that teachers have higher morale and are more productive when they are present.

Teachers are also expected to behave in accordance with organizational rules that call for affective–neutrality and universalism when dealing with pupils even though the development of cognitive achievement and deportment require varying amounts of affective support. Wide variations in the out-of-school socialization of their pupils create differences in the kind and amount of reinforcements each pupil requires; and the more difficult the learning tasks are for pupils, the more affect they seem to need.[24] Successful teachers are sensitive to such differences and respond with at least some particularistic behavior and some manifestations of affect.

A partial solution to the conflict between the district's formal demand for universalism and the pupils' need for particularism is to sort pupils on the basis of those characteristics that are most relevant to their formal socialization. In this way each teacher is responsible for a somewhat homogeneous group with relatively similar educational requirements. Empirical support for this practice comes from several sources. First, extremely able or gifted children seem to achieve at higher levels when they are grouped with other pupils who are also very able even though average pupils in homogeneous classes are not similarly advantaged.[25] This seems to come about because many teachers set expectations for all pupils at the level of the class average, with the result that the most able are not always challenged sufficiently.

Second, and more importantly, different kinds of teachers have been shown to affect different kinds of pupils in varying ways. In one study, St. John divided the behavior of 36 white teachers of interracial sixth-grade classes into groups she termed child-oriented and task-oriented and discovered that similar teacher behavior influences the academic growth and conduct of pupils in dissimilar ways. She defined the child-oriented teacher as one who is "kindly, optimistic, responsive, understanding, democratic and adaptable," and the task-oriented teacher as "fluent, broad, stimulating and confident." Black pupils who were taught by child-oriented teachers exhibited considerably more growth in reading than those who were taught by task-oriented teachers, whereas white pupils learned most with task-oriented teachers. She also found that the conduct of both black and white pupils was more favorable in classrooms of child-oriented teachers.[26] This and other research into the same question strongly suggests that the right teacher or method for some children may be wrong for others.

Tracking pupils, nevertheless, is not a totally satisfactory way to reduce particularism in the teacher role. By separating pupils according to educational needs, schools tend to assign those who share a common background to the same classroom. In reality, pupils become segregated by socioeconomic status and racial-ethnic–group membership, a practice which severely limits their educational opportunities.[27]

Some schools are experimenting with other ways to organize education which take into account individual differences among pupils as well as among teachers. One technique is to divide pupils into different groups for different purposes so that pupils receive the kind and level of instruction in each subject within the educational context that best fills their unique needs at the time. Another technique is to maintain heterogeneous classes but to highly individualize instruction by personalizing educational tasks so that they will contribute as much as possible to the total development of each specific child. Many innovative schools also employ "differential" staffing, in which a team of teachers and assistants take responsibility for a large cohort of pupils. Teachers with diversified talents and teaching styles are then assigned to a single team, thereby providing some teacher specialization by type of child.

Personalized teaching style

The need for particularism on the part of teachers also arises because many beginning pupils have not yet learned the implications of universalism.[28] Since children's treatment at home is largely particularistic and their outside-the-home experiences with universalism are relatively limited, they often have no conception of impersonal rules and do not respond to formal school sanctions. Indeed, an important component of school socialization is to teach pupils to comply with impersonal regulations.

In order to transmit universalistic norms to young pupils, teachers initially employ particularistic methods and administer positive and negative affect as reinforcements. Teachers soon learn that a smile here and an encouraging word there, an appropriate scowl or gentle word of derision, are affective sanctions in a formal setting. These noninstitutional rewards and punishments are highly personal; they arise out of the personality of teachers and are applied to pupils as teachers see fit. Proficiency in the application of affective sanctions seems to be an important component of the art of teaching.

Personalized teaching styles are also used to great advantage with older pupils. By emphasizing personality at the expense of institutional sanctions, some teachers can gain greater pupil compliance and increase the chances that they will become significant others. Teachers so viewed are powerful socializing agents in that pupils actively seek their approval and consciously or unconsciously internalize many of their behaviors.

However all teachers are not equally able to develop personalized styles. The need to constantly discriminate in the application of

affect is potentially exhausting, especially for those whose personalities tend toward affective-neutrality. Young enthusiastic teachers
are most likely to employ personalized leadership, but, as they settle
into their occupational roles, they begin to routinize their behavior
and turn to bureaucratic procedures.

Formal teaching styles sometimes enhance teacher effectiveness,
especially for those with personal characteristics that irritate pupils
and/or those who do not have sufficient energy to consistently maintain a highly personalized style. Formality provides pupils with protection against teachers they dislike and reduces the negative consequences of unpleasant teacher-pupil interaction. So-called "teacher
proof" materials which offer skillfully organized learning experiences
such as programmed instruction and film or audio tapes, have similar
advantages in that they reduce teacher-pupil contact that might
interfere with learning. The research by St. John also suggests that
some pupils learn most when teachers rely on a formal style that
emphasizes universalism and achievement, although other pupils—
most notably those for whom the cultures of school and home are
different—learn most when personalized styles dominate.[29]

In general, teachers tend to emphasize particularism and affective
reinforcements when they first socialize their pupils to the formal
requirements of the school and classroom and rely more heavily on
institutional rules and sanctions as pupils come to understand their
interpretation of universalism. Neither teaching style is found in
pure form, however, for each teacher combines them in varying
amounts into a role which is most comfortable to maintain.[30]

Formal rewards and punishments

Even the formal grading process is not immune from the conflicts
between universalism and particularism and between neutrality and
affectivity. The most common of all institutional sanctions is, in
fact, school grades, which are used as much as rewards and punishments as they are as indicators of educational progress. In their early
years at school most children learn to value grades or the equivalent
symbols of achievement that are awarded to them. They learn from
the combined responses of school personnel, family, and peers that
high evaluations bring prestige and approval and low evaluations
are viewed as signs of inadequacy. Although testing was initially
conceived as a way to gain information about pupils that could be
used in diagnosing educational treatment, the practice of translating

test results into grades has provided teachers with powerful sanctions. Like a carrot to a donkey, grades often have the power to motivate pupils to comply with their teachers' demands.

Teachers will sometimes exploit the reinforcement properties of evaluation by awarding grades on the basis not only of scholastic achievement but of effort, improvement, and deportment as well. And pupils often study more for the purpose of receiving high grades than they do because of interest in the subject. (Witness how quickly some subject matter is forgotten after examinations.) It should also be added that many pupils learn to successfully manipulate their teachers in order to receive high grades. Regardless of whether or not favorable deportment is really the precondition for achievement that it is popularly assumed to be, school grades, at least as they are awarded in elementary school, show that good and bright pupils seem to be one and the same.[31]

It has been seriously suggested that tangible rewards such as candy, script, and money be included among positive institutional sanctions and that they be dispensed to all pupils who perform at satisfactory levels. The purpose would be to provide incentives for achievement to pupils who have not internalized the value of school grades and are consequently not motivated by them. The proponents of one plan expect that monetary rewards would be extremely effective with low-income pupils, since money has an especially high value for them. They also believe that, because money is generally valued more than grades, peer groups would be likely to grant high status to those who achieve in school.[32]

In addition to grades and other rewards, teachers in some school districts quite literally have a "stick" to obtain pupil compliance. There are a variety of institutional punishments available, including the infliction of physical pain, withdrawal of privileges and participation in special events, and public humiliation. Also, as foolish as these may appear, punishments include extra hours of schooling and extra homework assignments on the one hand, and expulsion from school on the other. Suspension has been criticized widely by parents on the logical grounds that, if children are excluded from the classroom, they cannot learn what is expected of them. This kind of treatment not only punishes errant pupils, it is assumed by those who initiate it to act as a deterent to other pupils who tend toward nonconformity.

Even if the threat of punishment compels pupils to comply with school regulations, it is not an optimum way to modify behavior. One reason is that coercive sanctions tend to alienate punished pupils from their teachers and from school and thereby reduce the extent of their participation. Positive rather than negative sanctions are more effective in social systems such as schools and families that have socialization as their primary goal.[33]

Another reason that punishment is often ineffective is that what is conceived as punishment by educators is sometimes a reward for pupils. Ability to withstand bureaucratic sanctions and to come through the punishment ordeal with dignity is often a source of peer approval. Unless teachers have carefully noted the values in pupil subcultures, they may find that to inflict some kinds of punishment is to further undermine their own authority.

Institutional punishments are usually employed as a last resort after more subtle sanctions have failed. Despite their noted dysfunctions however, they do have some important attributes. Negative sanctions delineate aberrant behaviors, thereby informing all pupils about what is essentially taboo; they make it possible for teachers to legitimately remove offending pupils from the classroom; and they give teachers an opportunity to vent pent-up anger before it erupts into uncontrollable hostility.

This chapter has been primarily concerned with the organizational roles of the members of the board of education, of administrators, and of teachers, and with many of the conflicting expectations in each. The next chapter examines the role of pupils within the school, the development of pupil peer groups, and, finally, the reevaluation of family culture by adolescent children.

NOTES

[1] It is assumed that moral socialization is demonstrated by "responsible citizenship in the school community." This includes respect for teachers, cooperativeness in relation to fellow students, good work habits, and the like. Talcott Parsons, "The School Class as a Social System: Some of Its Functions in American Society," *Harvard Educational Review*, 29, no. 4 (Fall, 1959), 303.

[2] Willard Waller, *The Sociology of Teaching*, 1st science ed., New York, Wiley, 1965. Originally published 1932. C. Wayne Gordon, "The Role of the Teacher in the Social Structure of the High School," *Journal of Educational Sociology*, 29 (September 1955), 21–29.

[3] Raymond C. Hummel and John M. Nagle, *Urban Education in America: Problems and Prospects*, New York, Oxford University Press, 1973, p. 138.

[4] Donald J. McCarty and Charles E. Ramsey, *The School Managers:*

Power and Conflict in American Public Education, Westport, Conn., Greenwood, 1971.

[5] Norman D. Kerr, "The School Board as an Agency of Legitimation," *Sociology of Education*, 38 (Fall 1964), p. 36.

[6] Morris Janowitz, *Institution Building in Urban Education*, Chicago, University of Chicago Press (Phoenix), 1969, p. 69.

[7] Hummel and Nagle, *op. cit.*, 138.

[8] For a full discussion of these points see Mario D. Fantini, *The Reform of Urban Schools*, Washington, D.C., National Educational Association, Center for the Study of Instruction, 1970, pp. 54–58.

[9] Edward L. McDill and Leo C. Rigsby, *Structure and Process in Secondary Schools: The Academic Impact of Educational Climates*, Baltimore, The Johns Hopkins University Press, 1973.

[10] Howard S. Becker, "The Teacher in the Authority System of the Public School," *Journal of Educational Sociology*, 27 (November 1953), 128–141. The United Federation of Teachers strongly opposed decentralization and lay control of New York City schools in the 1960s. However, once these changes became inevitable the union lobbied effectively for legislation providing that local school districts have over 20,000 pupils in average daily attendance, thereby diluting the impact of any single community group. In addition, 46 union members were elected to the first community school boards in New York, and most of them opposed lay judgment of teacher competence. See Marilyn Gittell, *et al.*, *School Boards and School Policy: An Evaluation of Decentralization in New York City*, New York, Praeger, 1973.

[11] *Educational Vouchers: A Report on Financing Elementary Education by Grants to Parents*, Cambridge, Mass., Center for the Study of Public Policy, 1970.

[12] Ronald G. Corwin, *Militant Professionalism: A Study of Organizational Conflict in High Schools*, New York, Appleton, 1970, p. 358.

[13] George Baron and Asher Tropp, "Teachers in England and America," in A. H. Halsey, Jean Floud, and C. Arnold Anderson, eds., *Education, Economy, and Society*, New York, Free Press, 1961, p. 551.

[14] Neal Gross and Robert E. Herriott, *Staff Leadership in Public Schools*, New York, Wiley, 1965.

[15] *Ibid.*, p. 151.

[16] Janowitz, *op. cit.*, p. 74.

[17] *Ibid.*, p. 56–57.

[18] Corwin, *op. cit.*, pp. 76–77.

[19] Alvin W. Gouldner, "Organizational Analysis," in Robert K. Merton *et al.*, eds., *Sociology Today: Problems and Prospects*, New York, Basic Books, 1959, pp. 415–417.

[20] Etzioni characterizes teaching as a "semi-profession" which takes into account both professional and bureaucratic requirements. The professional is more involved in the creation of new knowledge than the semiprofessional who is primarily concerned with the communication of

knowledge. Amitai Etzioni, ed., *The Semi-Professions and Their Organization: Teachers, Nurses, Social Workers,* New York, Free Press, 1969, preface.

[21] Gerald H. Moeller, "Bureaucracy and Teachers' Sense of Power," *School Review,* 72, no. 3 (Summer 1964), 157. But see Joanna Jenny Samuels, *Bureaucracy of School Districts and Teacher Autonomy,* Los Angeles, Calif., University of California Doctoral Dissertation, 1966, who found that regardless of the degree of bureaucratization, only 4 percent of the teachers in her sample were dissatisfied with teaching in their school districts.

[22] Robert K. Merton, "Bureaucratic Structure and Personality," *Social Theory and Social Structure,* rev. ed., New York, Free Press, 1957. See also Chris Argyris, "The Individual and Organization: Some Problems of Mutual Adjustment," *Administrative Science Quarterly,* 2, no. 1 (June 1957), 1–24.

[23] Gross and Herriott, *loc. cit.*

[24] Evidence for this statement is not strong, mainly because it is not a common area of inquiry. But one study that related affective teacher behavior to pupil performance found it to be a better predictor of achievement in arithmetic than in easier subjects. See C. Wayne Gordon and Leta McKinney Adler, *Dimensions of Teacher Leadership in Classroom Social Systems,* Los Angeles, Calif., University of California, Department of Education, 1963, p. 179.

[25] Miriam Goldberg, A. H. Passow, and J. Justman, *The Effects of Ability Groups,* New York, Teachers College Press, Columbia University, 1966; Dominick Esposito, *Consequences of Ability Grouping: Ethnic and Socioeconomic Separation of Children,* New York, Teachers College, Columbia University, 1971.

[26] Nancy H. St. John, "Thirty-Six Teachers: Their Characteristics and Outcomes for Black and White Pupils," *American Educational Research Journal,* 8, no. 4 (November 1971), 635–648. For similar conclusions see Stephan Michaelson, "The Association of Teacher Resourceness with Children's Characteristics," *Do Teachers Make A Difference?,* Washington, D.C., U.S. Office of Education, 1970, pp. 151–152.

[27] District Court of Appeals Judge Skelly Wright ruled that to place children in academic tracks within a school is a violation of the Fourteenth Amendment to the U.S. Constitution because it perpetuates segregation and fosters a hereditary intellectual elite. See Julius W. Hobton, *et al.* v. Carl F. Hansen, *Federal Supplement* 269, no. 4 (4 September 1967), 401–519.

[28] For a discussion of this topic, see Robert Dreeben, *On What Is Learned in School,* Reading, Mass., Addison-Wesley, 1968.

[29] St. John, *loc. cit.*

[30] Gordon and Adler, *op. cit.* identified 12 different teaching styles among their sample of 74 seventh-grade teachers.

[31] Parsons, *op. cit.,* p. 304.

[32] Andrew Effrat, Roy E. Feldman, and Harvey M. Sapolsky, "Inducing Poor Children to Learn," *The Public Interest* 15 (Spring 1969), 109.

[33] This problem is extreme in prisons which attempt both to punish and rehabilitate prisoners. Their very existence implies punishment to the inmates, yet inmates must identify with the organization to become re-socialized by it. For a general discussion of the relationship between compliance measures and organizational goals see Amitai Etzioni, *A Comparative Analysis of Complex Organizations: Power, Involvement, and Their Correlates*, New York, Free Press, 1961.

6
Pupils and their peers

THE PUPIL ROLE

Between the ages of about 5 and 18 years most American children are ascribed the role of pupil. Unless they fall outside the range of normality, children are not only expected to attend school, for most of these years they are compelled by law to do so.[1] Schools have been established to provide children with some special treatment which is generally thought to benefit them and society as a whole. Pupils (and sometimes their parents) are *clients* of the school in spite of the fact that school attendance is compulsory and sometimes involuntary. In this sense, schools are similar to other "people-processing" organizations such as hospitals, prisons, and mental institutions, all of which are expected to change their often unwilling clients in designated ways.[2]

Curiously, success in reaching the objectives of people-processing organizations depends greatly upon the extent to which clients assist in their own socialization. Those who internalize their formal roles and voluntarily submit to the influences of the organization are obviously most preferred, for they give the organization an aura of success. This is shown by the fact that organizations that have control over the selection of their clients tend to choose people with whom they seem best to succeed. With respect to schools, the most academically selective institutions give the appearance of being the most effective although their high levels of achievement are often due more to the initial motivation and other personal characteristics of their pupils than to the quality of education they provide.

The compulsory and often nonselective character of public schools is related to problems concerning classroom order and academic achievement. Although these properties ensure that there are sufficient numbers to keep most schools going, they do not guarantee that children will perform their pupil roles adequately. Reluctant pupils are seldom motivated to conform to all of the activities designed to lead toward school objectives. Much rebellious behavior within secondary schools has been traced to youth who reject notions of academic achievement and proper school deportment because they can see no relationship between these requirements and the roles they believe will be available to them as adults.[3]

Anticipatory socialization to school

By the time they enter school, most children have some notion of what it is about. They usually receive such information from their families, playmates, and the communications media, and most children have had experiences with kindergarten and perhaps nursery school. Parental attitudes strongly influence children's attitudes toward school. Those parents who view it as a place they have helped to create and support, and one that is directed toward the same socialization objectives they hold for their own children usually furnish children with confidence in their ability to perform the pupil role. On the other hand, parents who view school as an agency of alien culture, and one which they have little power to affect may inadvertantly teach children to be fearful of it, no matter how much they agree with what it tries to do. Contemporary efforts to develop community advisory boards and to use community residents as auxiliary personnel are partly addressed to reducing estrangement between some families and schools. Although channels for communication with parents have long been available through voluntary associations such as the Parent-Teachers Association, participation in these organizations has been largely limited to middle-class parents. It is hoped that increased involvement by pupils' families will make schools less threatening to both parents and children.

The culture of some families more than others provides useful anticipatory socialization for the pupil role. For example, middle-class families compared to low-income families usually have more experience with the norms of specificity, universalism, and affective-neutrality and consequently, their children have greater opportunity to observe these norms in practice. Middle-class parents also commonly have more years of formal education, which gives their children socialization advantages such as a larger fund of information and greater familiarity with the vocabulary and language patterns of their teachers. In addition, the expectations middle-class compared with low-income families hold for their children tend to be more consistent with expectations held by school personnel. All in all, middle-class children have less to learn than other children upon school entry.

Although all parents are more sophisticated than their children about schooling, the advice they offer concerning the pupil role is frequently obsolete or has become idealized with time. Those children who have older siblings or friends currently in school have a more valuable source of information. The attitudes as well as the information transmitted by older children is an important part of anticipatory socialization.

Anticipatory socialization to school is also provided by television. From about age three on, the average child watches television at least two hours every day.[4] Viewing is even higher among poor families: it has been estimated that about three-fourths of six-year-old urban inner-city children spend between two and five hours watching programs in their homes.[5] Some of these programs have socialization to school as their primary objective. One example, "Sesame Street," has been widely acclaimed in many countries and is translated into other languages and produced throughout the world. An evaluation of the knowledge acquired by the viewers of "Sesame Street" concluded that, for younger children at least, the more they watched, the more they learned.[6] The extent to which children acquire information and attitudes from a variety of television programs—including commercials—should not be underestimated. Most observers believe that television viewing increases vocabulary and extends the horizons of young children, and that both these factors influence the capacity to carry out the pupil role.[7]

In addition most children have had some experience with schooling before they enter first grade. In 1970 an estimated 70 percent of all five-year-olds were enrolled in kindergarten and 30 percent of all four-year-olds attended preschool.[8] Early-childhood education varies in the extent to which it prepares children for primary school. Some preschools seem to provide only custodial care, whereas others emphasize emotional, social, or intellectual development. Evaluations of Head Start programs (preschools supported by the federal government to compensate young children for educational disadvantages that derive from poverty) suggest that early childhood programs that emphasize cognitive over affective and social objectives are considerably more effective in helping the subsequent academic performance of low-income children.[9]

The conception of the pupil role which children first bring to school affects their initial school behavior and thereby, their total educational career. This view colors their expectations of school as a formal institution, their interprepations of the behavior of their teachers, and their perception of their own adequacy in the school environment. Nevertheless, the transition from the primary *gemeinschaft* milieu of family to the increasingly *gesellschaft* milieu of school is not an easy one, even for children who have received a great deal of anticipatory socialization. Although schools attempt to reduce the contrast between home and school in the lower grades, there are, nonetheless, important differences to which pupils must adjust.

First, the child is but one of many children of similar status, all of whom relate and seem to receive similar attention from the same adult who is their teacher. The child, therefore, is immediately exposed to the norm of universalism.

Second, schools rely on affective-neutrality to a much greater extent than do families; many of their tasks such as reading and computation can only be performed when emotions are held in check. Although young pupils are given frequent opportunity for expression, when and how they do so are specified by teachers and school regulations. Even periods of play are often organized into games which are constrained by formal rules. In this same vein, pupils are expected to learn to be motivated by delayed more than immediate gratification. Except to the extent that they are intrinsically motivated, that is, to the extent that they enjoy doing the assigned tasks, or are given ongoing rewards such as teacher approval, gratification comes after school work is completed—perhaps from the knowledge that it is over and done with, or more hopefully, from the knowledge that it has been performed with some competence.

Third, adults other than parents have the right to exercise authority over the child. Most children have been exposed in their homes to the hierarchical authority of adults (although this may appear at times to be egalitarian) and transition presents little difficulty at first. As children approach adolescence, however, the legitimacy of hierarchical authority is sometimes questioned. The extent to which pupils are able to internalize the authority of their teachers in early grades possibly affects the degree to which they accept this authority during their adolescence.

Individual differences in scholastic achievement

Although the American dream holds that personal success is due largely to one's innate intellectual ability in combination with the effort one puts forth, most sociologists believe that socialization, in and out of school, is the crucial component of academic achievement. They believe that both ability and effort are, in fact, products of socialization experiences. Further, many sociologists view the socialization provided to children during their early formative years as the most critical factor in their achievement, although they also recognize that quality of schooling is important.

Early family socialization determines children's personalities, their orientations toward the physical world and the people in it, and their self-concepts. It also determines the language they speak and at what level of competence. And evidence is gathering to suggest that it determines cognitive ability as well.[10] Added to all of these, family socialization provides information, knowledge, and skills which assist or undermine children's adaptation to their schools.

The wide range of variations among families with respect to family organization, division of labor by sex, authority structure, and subculture have been discussed in detail in Chapter 3. Many of these differences are commonly associated with family socioeconomic status or with racial-ethnic background. It should be reiterated, however, that there are variations within every subpopulation and although some characteristics relating to school success are more common among one subgroup than another, there are sufficient counterexamples to suggest that subpopulation membership alone is not a good predictor of scholastic achievement.

A classic example of differences within working-class families that relate to academic attainment is provided by Kahl's study of the college expectations of 4000 secondary-school boys in the Boston metropolitan area.[11] Noting that almost 90 percent of high-ability, high-status pupils, compared with about 50 percent of high-ability, lower-status pupils, expected to attend college, Kahl attempted to find out why only some of the academically successful working-class boys planned to continue their education. From interviews with a sample of their parents he discovered that working-class parents were oriented either toward "getting by" or "getting ahead," and, further, that only sons from "getting ahead" families had college expectations. "Getting by" parents had little personal knowledge of college graduates or professional people. They viewed high school completion as important for their children's future work opportunities, but did not consider college education as a viable option. Moreover, they remembered their own high school days as "the time of their lives" and encouraged their sons to "enjoy life" while they could before they had to take up the responsibilities of regular employment.

The "getting ahead" parents, although also part of the working class, looked to the middle classes as their reference groups. Some of them felt handicapped by their own poor education and some even felt guilty for not doing better in their occupational careers. Most of the "getting ahead" parents, especially the mothers, pressured their sons to achieve in school so that they would have a greater opportunity later on. Kahl concluded that although schools provide a means for social mobility, they do not initiate it. Social mobility begins in the home.

Another classic example of differences within subpopulations is provided by Miller and Swanson in their study of the child-rearing practices of middle-class parents. They related the structure within which the father works to the value orientations of his children and found that children of entrepreneurs differ from children of fathers who work in bureaucratic settings. Entrepreneurial children have a more optimistic orientation toward the future and a more manipulative approach to life, whereas children from bureaucratic families are more accommodative and are less likely to engage in activities which will bring their goals about. These characteristics of entrepreneurial children are those that are most often associated with high scholastic achievement.[12]

Other examples of differences within socioeconomic status as well as within racial-ethnic groups could be cited to illustrate variations within each of these classifications. Such classifications are nonetheless useful, since people are most likely to have the characteristics of those with whom they associate frequently. Socioeconomic status and racial-ethnic background can each independently influence a child's achievement. In looking at subpopulation membership in relation to school performance it is often instructive to take both into account.

The independent influence of racial-ethnic background on the one hand, and socioeconomic status on the other, is dramatically illustrated in the work of Lesser and his colleagues who studied patterns of mental abilities among 320 first-grade New York City school children. The researchers administered a battery of tests, measuring

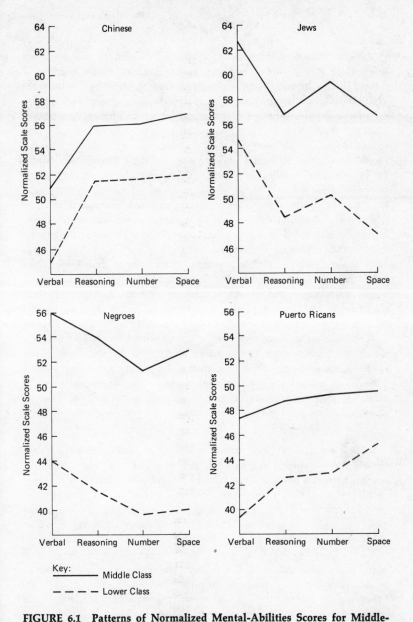

FIGURE 6.1 Patterns of Normalized Mental-Abilities Scores for Middle-Class Children by Ethnic Group
SOURCE: Gerald S. Lesser, Gordon Fifer, and Donald H. Clark, *Mental Abilities of Children from Different Social-Class and Cultural Groups*, University of Chicago Press, 1965, pp. 65–68.

reasoning, verbal, numerical, and spatial abilities to a sample of lower-class and middle-class pupils from Chinese, Jewish, black, and Puerto Rican homes. They discovered that the average pattern of abilities differed for pupils in each racial-ethnic group (see Figure 6.1). For example, although Chinese and Jewish children scored higher than either of the other two groups on each of the tests, the highest mean score for Chinese children was in spatial relations and the lowest score was in verbal ability, whereas the opposite was found for Jewish children. Black children, like Jewish children, scored highest in verbal ability, but differed in that they were weakest in numerical ability. The pattern for Puerto Rican children resembled that of Chinese children, but the level of their performance was much lower. Lesser, et al., found that regardless of the social status of the child's family, the pattern of abilities for each group was the same, but that middle-class children on the average scored higher than lower-class children on every test. They concluded that "at least several mental abilities are organized in ways that are determined culturally and that higher social class produces differences in the *level* of mental ability.[13]

These differences are reflected in school achievement. The national Equality of Educational Opportunity study, for example, found that with the notable exceptions of Oriental-Americans and some Indian-Americans, minority pupils on the average score significantly below majority pupils on all tests of achievement in their first year of school and this discrepancy grows larger with each subsequent grade (see Table 6.1).[14]

Language ability and value orientations. These characteristics should receive special emphasis in any discussion of school achievement since each plays a large part in the school behavior of children and in their ability to perform academic tasks. It was brought out in the discussion of language in Chapter 2 that theorists differ in the extent to which they believe that language determines thought and in the extent they believe that one precedes the other in human development. They do agree, however, that language is an important tool for dealing with others and for understanding oneself, and that it is also the common medium through which role expectations and other aspects of culture are communicated and stored. Language is given an even more salient place in the explanation of achievement by those who hold that thought cannot occur before language is acquired.

Hess and Shipman are among those who argue that language shapes thought, including the *cognitive style* one uses for solving

TABLE 6.1 Nationwide Median Test Scores for First and Twelfth Grade Pupils, Fall, 1965

| Test | Racial or ethnic group | | | | | |
	Puerto Ricans	Indian Americans	Mexican Americans	Oriental Americans	Negro	Majority
1st grade:						
Nonverbal	45.8	53.0	50.1	56.6	43.4	54.1
Verbal	44.9	47.8	46.5	51.6	45.4	53.2
12th grade:						
Nonverbal	43.3	47.1	45.0	51.6	40.9	52.0
Verbal	43.1	43.7	43.8	49.6	40.9	52.1
Reading	42.6	44.3	44.2	48.8	42.2	51.9
Mathematics	43.7	45.9	45.5	51.3	41.8	51.8
General information	41.7	44.7	43.3	49.0	40.6	52.2
Average of the 5 tests	43.1	45.1	44.4	50.1	41.1	52.0

SOURCE: James S. Coleman, *et al.*, *Equality of Educational Opportunity*, Washington, D.C., U.S. Department of Health, Education, and Welfare, 1966, p. 20.

problems.[15] According to them, language and cognitive abilities result from the kind of control system parents employ in raising their children. Parents who present a range of "alternatives of action and thought" foster reflective and rational thinking; those who restrict available alternatives encourage impulsive thinking and present orientation.

From their observations of 163 black mothers from four different socioeconomic levels who were teaching their own four-year-old children identical tasks, Hess and Shipman concluded that parents of different social status employ different socialization techniques. Mothers from lower-socioeconomic levels tend to stress their own authority, whereas mothers from higher levels stress the rationale behind desired behavior and, thereby, contribute to their children's ability to conceptualize verbally and perform complex tasks. These researchers also suggest that the social, educational, and economic poverty common to lower-status families is owed largely to the cognitive styles they acquire from their early socialization.[16]

Studies by Bernstein show that children from lower-status families tend to rely exclusively on "restricted" speech patterns which inhibit the verbal expression of abstract ideas and subjective feelings.

This is supposedly due to the fact that more people in lower-status than in higher-status families depend on gestures and other non-verbal communication, and that, as a consequence, their verbal language is relatively terse and grammatically simple. Because spoken language is a more important means of communication within the middle class, children from higher-status families acquire both these "restricted" patterns and also "elaborated," or more complex, patterns which allow for the expression of abstractions.[17]

Restricted patterns are informal and rich in idioms and are used at all socioeconomic levels in communication among equals. Elaborated patterns are formal and are appropriate for use within schools and other secondary groups. If Bernstein is correct in his observations that elaborated speech patterns are more common in middle and upper classes, then lower-status children are again disadvantaged at school entry because they have limited knowledge of the speech that forms the foundation of much educational instruction.

Extreme isolation of some racial-ethnic groups has created even greater communication difficulties for children in their schools. One example comes from the language spoken by Mexican-American agricultural workers in the Southwest; another, from the language spoken by blacks in rural areas of the South. "Black English," or "Negro nonstandard English," which has become increasingly evident in Northern cities with the migration of blacks out of the South, is a form of English with a distinctive grammatical structure and many variations in vocabulary. Although black English is a fully viable language containing the same linguistic concepts found in standard English, it is sufficiently different to create an obstacle to the formal education of many black youngsters in public schools. A few special educational programs have overcome this educational disadvantage by teaching the grammar of standard English as if it were a "quasi-foreign" language instead of the more common practice of assuming that black English is merely an incorrect version of the language of the general society.[18]

The most extreme form of language disadvantage for achievement in public schools is found among the 10 percent of American children who are totally non-English speaking upon school entry. These include not only sizable numbers of Spanish-speaking children from Cuba, Mexico, and Puerto Rico, but many American Indian and Oriental children as well. Official school policy had often viewed the teaching of English and cultural assimilation as more important than educating children in whatever language they understand. Many children were therefore encouraged at school to renounce their original language, which to some is the same as renouncing their families' culture and part of their own identity.

Hopefully this is a policy of the past for schools are increasingly seeking ways to teach children of non-English-speaking families both the language skills they need to participate effectively in the main-stream of American life and to increase their knowledge of their native tongue. One promising program is *bilingual education* which attempts to develop high-level skills in both. This program provides continuity between the family and the school by reducing tensions between the two languages and the cultures they imply, and by providing instruction based upon skills that children already have. Although bilingual educational programs are in the developmental stage, results thus far are encouraging. Where bilingual education has been introduced in the earliest grades, pupils acquire literacy in both English and their native language and seem to avoid feelings of inferiority and alienation which have been a common experience among non-English-speaking children in American schools.[19]

Studies that attempt to differentiate successful from less successful pupils who, at least from outward appearances, have equal oppor-tunity for school achievement, have shown that personal values are extremely salient factors.[20] This conclusion should be expected since values orient people toward what in their personal views is most worthwhile. If pupils are to be committed to the performance of school tasks, the objectives they seek from school must be consistent with those that schools attempt to bring about, and the formal activi-ties put forth by the schools must be seen as appropriate means for attaining these objectives. Extent and quality of academic per-formance are most often contingent on the pupil's evaluation of its usefulness.

The interpretation pupils give to their own situation within the school is also related to academic performance. Pupils' motivations toward school-prescribed behaviors is affected by their confidence both in their abilities to perform the activities required for school achievement and in the willingness of others to assist them. In addi-tion, some pupils must so value school achievement that they are willing to sacrifice friendship if their peer groups supply norms which undermine it. The importance of role models and reference groups which value scholastic achievement is extreme in the case of pupils for whom school success implies upward mobility and possible sep-aration from their present primary groups

Perhaps the most important value for school success for many pupils is the belief that one can control factors external to oneself and can thereby influence the environment. This value has been variously described as "fate control," "future orientation," "destiny control," "personal efficacy," and the like. Pupils with an optimistic orientation toward the future and with a manipulative rather than a fatalistic approach toward life are most likely to engage in activities which bring about their personal goals. Exceptions to this generalization, however, are found among American school children of Oriental ancestry. For example, one study of Japanese-American children in Southern California concludes that future orientation is unrelated to the achievement of Japanese-American pupils, although it is positively related to the achievement of their Anglo peers.[21] Nevertheless, pupils who see their own goals as realistic are usually motivated to perform the required activities at an adequate level of competence.

These crucial values—agreement with school goals and the formally prescribed means to attain them, confidence in one's own ability, faith in human nature, independence from restrictive interpersonal ties, and a feeling of personal efficacy—combined with an ability to defer gratification and a rational, intellectual approach toward the formal school create an *achievement orientation* which typically leads pupils to academic success.

The functions of competition

Once children enter school, their teachers are their primary formal socializing agents who, by means of advice, assistance, support, praise, and punishment, attempt to transmit the formal expectations of the school. Most pupils learn these expectations, but some do not learn to value them and others do not learn how to meet them. Peers also help children to acquire knowledge of their role by providing them with an opportunity to observe the behavior of others, and by exerting social pressure for conformity to accepted behavior. Pupils whom teachers believe are desirable role models are given official school approval in the form of public praise, high grades, and other symbolic awards. When these awards are seen as attractive, other pupils emulate their behavior and often compete among themselves for similar recognition.

At first blush, the fostering of competition by teachers appears to be an effective method for obtaining compliance, at least for those who value the rewards the school can offer. However, research findings suggest that competition does not always lead to long-range changes in pupil behavior and that in many ways it is contrary to what schools are set up to do.[22] Some of the common criticisms of competition follow:

1. Schools encourage pupils to spur one another on to such an extent that the most motivated have little opportunity to develop their other skills.
2. Competition pits child against child and sometimes creates conflict situations in which the denial of rewards to the competitor becomes as important as the attainment of rewards for oneself.
3. Success in competition is related to the ability of the cohort with whom one competes; grades are determined more by how one compares with others than by how much one has learned.
4. Competition has a negative effect on one's sense of self if pupils have made their best efforts and have not succeeded. Self-evaluations of ability gained by comparing oneself with one's peers are not necessarily accurate when classmates are unusually gifted or limited in academic ability. Overestimations of competency can lead to unrealistically high aspirations just as an underestimation can lead to low aspirations.
5. Competition leads pupils to spend more effort in attaining the symbols of achievement than in acquiring its content. It has long been suspected that pupils who consistently come out on top may have learned the art of competition more than they have internalized the knowledge, skills, and behavior symbolized by its rewards.

Supporters of the use of competition point to the parallels between classroom competition in the achievement-oriented society for which pupils are being prepared. They claim that by making each school or classroom an arena for achievement, children learn to compete before they move into the wider, highly competitive society: if children are to function in the adult world in which highest status is available to only a few, they must have internalized the norms of universalism and achievement, and must have learned to both win and lose.

A proposal to avoid the destructive aspects of competition but retain its motivating qualities is to substitute rivalry among groups for rivalry among individuals. Coleman has noted that interscholastic athletic competitions seem to foster group cohesion even among spectators who do not directly participate. He suggests that schools develop similar systems of scholastic competition along the line of public debates, group-discussion tournaments, and academic "gaming."[23] The advantages of group rivalry are first, they shift the locus of competition so that pupils come to support and cooperate with each other, and second, they change the goals of competition from trying to satisfy the teacher (who is the custodian of school rewards) to winning in an encounter with another team.[24]

Another proposal is to eliminate competition among individuals and groups altogether. To the extent that competition is employed, pupils compete with themselves and attempt to top their previous performances. The use of *criterion-referenced* tests as measures of accomplishment is becoming common for this purpose; pupils succeed by meeting the criteria or standards that have been set out for them in advance. Critics of the criterion-reference technique usually charge that it discourages excellence since a ceiling is placed on expectations. This problem could be remedied by basing expectations on a person's previous performance, rather than on some preconceived standard of competency.

Finally, those critics of competition who are concerned with its negative effects on the educational aspirations of academically proficient pupils who rank near the bottom of their classes suggest that individual ability be measured against the norms of a national cohort of peers rather than against their own classmates. In this way a pupil's aspirations will not be influenced as much by who his or her classmates happen to be.

While there is much that can be said about the abuses of competition, for many pupils peer groups provide some protection against its potentially harmful effects. If academic achievement is excessively emphasized by the school staff, pupil subcultures tend to downgrade it in importance or undermine it completely. Their values and norms are transmitted to individuals through peer pressures, thereby socializing them to a peer-approved version of the pupil role. These values and norms are usually made known to the staff as well, and sometimes academic expectations are realigned as a result.

PEER GROUPS

The collective influence of other pupils in the classroom is felt by individual children as early as the first grade. This influence expands as children mature and become increasingly independent of adults. Peers attain more and more significance and by the time children reach secondary school, fellow classmates constitute potent reference groups that often rival families in authority.

Although large numbers of children are thrust together into an educational cohort, they do not stay undifferentiated. Smaller, informal peer groups, or cliques, emerge which frequently have characteristics of primary groups, such as great intimacy, communication, and loyalty among their members. In terms of the pattern variables, the norms of these, like other primary groups, encourage diffuseness, particularism, affectivity, and ascription.[25] Peer groups differ from deliberately planned student organizations such as clubs and athletic teams because of their primary group characteristics and because they emerge spontaneously. They also differ from families in that membership is voluntary; each person typically accepts and is accepted by the others.

There is no monolithic student peer group, but rather many groups, each with a somewhat distinctive subculture created out of the background, interests, and abilities of its members. Since choice of friends is most often from among those whom previous socialization has made most alike, peer groups tend to include people from similar socioeconomic, religious, and racial-ethnic backgrounds, albeit with some exceptions. Group membership also leans toward those whose own responses to formal school expectations are similar. Some groups emphasize academic requirements and have reputations such as "curve-raisers" or "apple-polishers." Other groups are more interested in school extracurricular activities and are perhaps known as "jocks" or "politicos." Still others totally reject all school expectations and are frequently thought of as delinquent.

Ambiguities of adolescence

Peer groups are of special importance to secondary school pupils because of the ambiguities that inhere in adolescent status. Adolescence begins approximately with the onset of puberty, but it is more a social than a physical classification. The idea of adolescence was probably introduced by Rousseau when he characterized it in *Émile* as a second birth beyond the earlier period of childhood weakness.[26] But in the United States the conversion of that idea into a commonly accepted reality did not occur until the end of the nineteenth century with the advent of urban industrial life.[27]

Adolescence usually starts when children, regardless of age, grade level, or physical development, enroll in a secondary school which is distinct from elementary school; it concludes when they acquire some adult occupational role or when they marry, also regardless of age. Hollingshead put it this way:

Sociologically, the important thing about adolescent years is the way people regard the maturing individual . . . adolescence is the period in the life of a person when the society in which he functions ceases to regard him as a child and does not accord him full adult status, roles, and functions.[28]

It follows, then, that the adolescent period is longest in societies that offer most years of formal schooling; within each society, it is longest for children from higher-status families which can supply them with more years of education. In the United States, where high-school graduation is the norm and higher education is increasingly accessible, adolescence is notably prolonged. The relatively recent extension of the adolescent period, plus the large proportion of the American population in the student age group,[29] have focused popular and scholarly attention on adolescents.

However, despite the sizeable notice paid to adolescence and its general acceptance, for many it is a perplexing interval typified by "storm and stress."[30] It begins inauspiciously with promotion from elementary to secondary school and is only occasionally marked by "rites of passage" such as Catholic confirmations and Jewish *bar mitzvahs*. There is no clear and consistent view of the rights, duties, and obligations of adolescents, and they are intermittently treated as children, adults, or as people in some unique stage. Little wonder many adolescents are uncertain about the expectations others have of them and about their own ability to meet these expectations in the event they are discerned. Added to these problems are the private uncertainties of adolescents about their abilities to cope physically and socially with radical body and mental changes and with their rapidly developing sexuality.

Changing adult expectations

Responses of individual pupils to the expectations of their teachers and parents influence the quality of their adolescent experiences. Once recognized as adolescent, it is incumbent on pupils to put aside childish musing and realistically decide about some future occupational role and the educational preparation it entails. Adolescence is a time when one is supposed to reconcile personal and parental aspirations with past records of performance and prospects for future success. It is perhaps the first time in the life of young people that they are asked to make choices that lead them toward or away from specific adult roles. Although some of these decisions can be reversed later on, planning for adult life is a formidable process for many.

Adolescents are also expected to develop some autonomy from their families and to become physically, psychologically, and sometimes economically self-sufficient. They are granted more freedom from adult control than they had previously and are expected to assume greater responsibility for their own behavior. The amount of independence adults are willing to grant and how much their children are willing to accept varies. Adolescents must somehow define what independence means in the context of their own lives; to assume too little or too much is an added source of stress.

In addition, adolescents are expected to develop criteria for a choice of mate, since in the United States they, rather than their parents, most often make this selection. Given the ethos of romantic love and the American ethic of social equality, almost any marriage can be justified to the larger society. Parents, nevertheless, typically expect their children to select marital partners from roughly the same background as their own—which is what usually occurs—and they anxiously monitor their children's dating behavior up to the time some special friend emerges who is just like mom or dad. On the other hand, adolescents are often steeped in notions of romance and sincerely believe that the choice rests with them. Many are therefore stunned by parental opposition to their seemingly legitimate behavior, until they realize that this choice, like so many others, is theirs only within certain parameters.

Functions of peer groups

Peer groups support individual pupils through their adolescence by supplying them with social norms and offering them affective support. Since these groups are most often composed of persons of like status with similar interests and concerns, they tend to develop solutions to their members' most pressing problems. Further, peer groups provide a social arena away from adults where members can work out new social identities. Adolescents "try on" various accommodations to adult expectations and experiment with new social roles within the circle of their friends.

The norms of peer groups provide guidelines for interaction among peers as well as between adolescents and adults. One of their most important functions is to limit conflict within the peer group. Norms control competition among members by imposing ceilings on the extent to which they should comply with adult expectations and by defining areas in which conflict is acceptable. For example, a peer group may view it as perfectly legitimate for a boy to outplay a friend in tennis or chess, but not to outwit him in romance. Each group develops its own code of conduct prescribing limits to competition and cooperation. Many of these codes also contain norms which provide upper and lower limits to school work. Therefore they have the additional function of permitting members an acceptable level of school performance while leaving them with time and energy to devote to other aspects of their development.

Although peer groups usually support members during their adolescence, they do not always contribute to their adjustment as adults. Some groups develop subcultures which are antithetical to those of the school and the larger society. Membership in these groups encourages behaviors which deviate from society at large. This is especially apparent among adolescents who have not been able to come to terms with adult demands and for whom a peer group is the chief source of emotional support.

The socialization provided by peer groups differs depending upon their special subcultures; and their impact on individuals also differs depending upon the social background and probable social destiny of each. For example, a fun-oriented subculture will introduce adolescents from high-achievement-oriented families to supplementary values that may enrich the quality of their lives, whereas an academic-oriented subculture will introduce below-average pupils to some of the achievement norms that can influence their own academic performance. Predominantly middle-class peer groups usually provide some anticipatory socialization to their lower-class members who are upwardly mobile.

The powerful effect of peer groups on academic performance has been shown by the comparatively higher achievement of lower-class pupils who attend predominantly middle-class rather than lower-class schools.[31] Because children carry the values and norms of their families into school situations, those whose backgrounds are conducive to academic achievement make a favorable adaptation to school demands. To the extent that less scholastically advantaged pupils learn these adaptations, their school achievement increases.

The national "adolescent society"

Much has been made in communications media of what appears to be a national youth culture that superimposes its values and norms on adolescents throughout the country. This "adolescent society" has become visibly stronger in recent years because of the growth in the absolute number of people who fall into the adolescent category and the increased buying power of the group as a whole. Since its chief concerns relate to the development of desirable sex roles, emphasis is placed on clothing, erotic love, music, and the like. However, many scholars doubt that this society was created entirely, if at all, by adolescents. They allege that commercial interests for whom adolescent consumers are the principal target participated in its development. But whatever its source, the national adolescent society influences the behaviors and tastes of many Americans.[32]

The general adolescent society differs from a particular peer group both in its origin and its impact on individuals. As previously noted, a peer group's values and norms emerge out of the specific needs of its members. However those of the national adolescent society are ongoing and are external in origin. As children move into adolescence they are met with preexisting norms, as well as older adolescents who intolerantly enforce them.[33] To the extent that the adolescent society provides general norms, they are at a sufficiently low level for most adolescents to meet comfortably. Peer groups, on the other hand, are concerned with norms relating to local situations. Indeed, one function of peer groups is to translate general national norms to meet the special circumstances of their members.

Role conflict

Once peer-group norms have become established, peer groups tend to be intolerant of members who deviate from them. Nonetheless, people hold many social roles and some inevitably have norms that are at odds with those of their peers. Adolescents must somehow learn to reconcile conflicting expectations among their pupil, peer, and family roles.

Pupils, more than other people in the school, experience conflict between formal school expectations and the informal expectations of their peers. Role conflict arises for many pupils when group norms for academic performance are lower than those set by adults and they are forced to choose between the demands of teachers and those of fellow pupils. They must decide, for example, whether to conform with peers or to be independent from them, whether to cooperate with peers (i.e., cheat) or to compete with them, and whether to emphasize play and immediate gratification or to attend to educational chores.

This is not to say that all peer groups are unconcerned with academic performance, nor to imply that all groups devalue it. The achievement of members is irrelevant to some groups, whereas other groups are organized around mutual scholastic interests. But peers often set a ceiling on the amount of work one is expected to do. Their restrictive norms present a common source of conflict in adolescence, since strongest personal gratification typically come from peers, and schools are limited in the valued rewards they can provide.

A constant concern of schools is how to use peer groups to the socialization advantage of their pupils. Many schools have successfully set up semiformal student clubs in which faculty have an opportunity to participate. Faculty members also try to influence peer-group leaders directly through cooptation so that they can indirectly mold the values and norms of other pupils. Where schools fail to bring about some reconciliation between formal and informal pupil roles there is often hostility and mutual distrust between pupils and the school staff. Low levels of academic achievement and high levels of pupil delinquency are often attributed to role conflict.

As difficult as the conflict between pupil and peer roles may be, an even greater conflict arises for adolescents outside of school if the collective behavior of their peers is contrary to the behavior approved by their families. Because of the deep emotional ties children have with family members, the resolution of this kind of conflict is often very painful.

During adolescence individuals develop lifelong patterns for coping with role conflicts. Since no one technique is totally adequate, they experiment with different ways to balance competing demands. One common technique is to place social roles in a hierarchy and then be guided by the expectations in the most valued role. For example, a girl who aspires to become a great scientist might choose to work in the school chemistry laboratory on weekends rather than to attend sporting events and parties with her friends or outings with her family.

Another technique for dealing with role conflict is to evaluate the cost of nonconformity and comply with those norms that have the most negative sanctions. Adolescents who consistently favor peer over adult-approved behavior may have rationally concluded that, with regard to sanctions concerning deviance, peers are more severe than are families. Since it is not uncommon for peer groups to renounce transgressors and families to offer only verbal admonishments, children sometimes act against family wishes more out of expedience than conviction. If peer-group membership is sufficiently rewarding, pupils often conform merely to belong, in spite of any private reservations they may have.

Still another technique is to attend to one role at a time rather than to reconcile conflicting demands. This solution is most effective when roles are isolated from one another and played out in different social settings. There is reason to believe that many adolescents have dual orientations in which peer and family roles are totally separated. Middle-class youth, for example, may value the middle-class adult life of their parents, even though they do not employ these same norms in their peer-group relationships.

From a reanalysis of empirical studies that treat this issue, Schwartz and Merten conclude that adolescents' conceptions of adult roles and values are "largely independent of the standards they use to estimate the relative excellence of their peers."[34] The criteria set forth by adults are not rejected, they are just not important to the adolescent group. While the separation of roles can often be an effective solution to family-peer conflict, it is not usually satisfactory for reconciling conflict between individual pupils and peers since one's school behavior is simultaneously observed by school officials and friends.

A final technique is to compromise between competing demands. The success of this method depends upon the extent to which the roles are basically compatible. One's ability to handle role conflict develops through experimentation. Mistakes in balancing social roles are frequent among adolescents, but the consequences of these errors are not usually as serious for them as they would be for adults. In general, adolescents are allowed to explore the arena of interpersonal relationships through trial and error and are held responsible only for extreme deviations.

INTERGENERATIONAL CONFLICT

During the adolescent period, all family members work out new relationships with one another. Not only must children develop autonomy from their families, but their parents, most of whom have entered middle age, must learn to deal with the problems presented by their own change of status.[35] Ironically, the quest by children for independence often occurs about the time that parents have more leisure and increased desire to associate with their adolescent children. Mothers who are freed from providing custodial care to young children and fathers, from the initial concerns of building an occupational career typically turn to their children for companionship just as children begin to move out from the family to form other emotional attachments. Therefore, some conflict between parents and children is endemic to the adolescent period.

One major source of conflict lies with parents' difficulties in adjusting to their new status *vis-à-vis* their children; namely, in changing from the role of socializing agent to adviser and in recognizing that they and their children are of relatively equal status. These problems are acute in periods of rapid social and technological change which make much of the parents' own socialization obsolete so that their function as socializing agents is problematic in any event.

Another source of conflict lies with the adolescent's independent and sometimes negative assessment of general social values. Parents are often thought to be representatives of adult society and are forced to bear the brunt of their children's reactions as they become aware of discontinuities between the simplistic view of what they learned to be right and the complexities of social reality. Moreover, the capacity of adolescents for criticism is enhanced by the anticipatory nature of much of their socialization which provides them with knowledge of adult roles but with few opportunities to experiment with them.

General impatience, frustration, and disappointment of adolescents are often directed toward their parents who are then put into the position of defending an adult society they may not even have helped to make. To make matters worse, this often happens just as there is conclusive evidence in many parents' lives that some values such as impersonal justice, work, and equality, that they have transmitted to their children, may not have paid off. But if parents respond to adolescent criticism defensively and vigorously defend the status quo, parent-child relationships are usually thrust headlong into conflict. At the other extreme, if they respond by agreeing to those criticisms they can conceivably force children to take even more critical positions merely to assert their own independence.[36]

The potential for parent-child conflict is enhanced to the extent to which adolescents are exposed to values and norms that differ from those of their parents. Children such as those from immigrant and migrant families who are headed for upward mobility, are often keenly aware of discrepancies between many of the values they acquire inside and outside the home. Some children may feel, rightly or wrongly, that in order to resolve these conflicts they must shed the cultural characteristics they believe will hold them back. Children who are headed for downward mobility, likewise acquire values and norms that differ from those of their parents. Both of these situations intensify the endemic sources of intergenerational strain.

However, some overt conflict within the family is usually functional. It identifies for both parents and children areas in which there is cultural lag and encourages both parties to come to grips with it. Conflict permits them to air disagreements over concrete issues instead of burying differences until they emerge in uncontrollable hostility. Further, it provides children with a channel through which to assert their independence.

All the same, conflict which occurs within systems of open and affective communication such as the family can easily get out of hand. When tempers are unrestrained thoughtless and cruel behavior can scar subsequent relationships for life. There are many examples in literature and life of bad blood between siblings or between parents and children which endure long after provoking incidents are forgotten.

Evidence to support strong and lasting conflict between parents and adolescent children is not as full as some of the preceding discussion might imply, however. The so-called counterculture that gained attention during the 1960s and early 1970s was composed of many middle-class youths and is a case in point. This subculture was initially interpreted as an example of intergenerational conflict, but it later came as a great surprise to some to discover that most of the youths of "new left" student movements were representing their parents' values more than rebelling against them. From a review of empirical literature that looked into the family backgrounds of these youths, Flacks concluded that their parents tend to be "more consistent and principled than most parents," and that they desire to impart to their children a commitment to intellectualism and a critical attitude to prevailing cultural goals. Although most of these parents hoped that their children would maintain the family's social status by filling useful occupational roles, they stressed the "necessity of living in accordance with one's values more consistently than they themselves had done."[37] In addition to studies of the new left a host of earlier studies pertaining to political socialization reviewed by Hyman presents considerable evidence to refute the notion that political attitudes, at least, are formed in terms of rebellion and opposition to parents.[38]

Families seem to survive the stresses of the adolescent period and even prodigal sons are often welcomed back. As Campbell points out, for many people, family structures do indeed endure as residential, affectional, and companionship units:

. . . Parents attend their child's high school graduation and give gifts gladly received, engage mutually and concernedly with the child in selecting a college, are invited to the child's wedding and do in fact attend, exchange visits and Christmas presents across the generations, are welcomed and eager guests in their child's home, fondle and indulge the grandchild, and eventually are mourned upon their death.[39]

Family bonds are relatively deep and lasting, and in spite of disputes over behavior, the family is more likely than any other group to accept adolescents when they violate important norms. Some overt family conflict may result because children are *more* rather than *less* certain of family support. In the case of competing demands between family and other social systems, children often bow to external pressures just because they know that they can always fall back on family members.

NOTES

[1] The number of years of compulsory schooling vary among the states. Seven to 16 is the modal range. Arizona requires the fewest number of years. There, children must attend schools between ages 8 and 16. Ohio and Utah require school for the greatest number of years. There, attendance is compulsory between ages 6 and 18. Kenneth A. Simon and W. Vance Grant, *Digest of Educational Statistics*, Washington, D.C., U.S. Department of Health, Education, and Welfare, 1972, table 30, p. 27.

[2] Morris Janowitz, *Institution Building in Urban Education*, Chicago, University of Chicago Press (Phoenix), 1969, pp. 3–4.

[3] Stinchcombe calls this kind of behavior "expressive alienation" and has shown that it is most common among pupils for whom the rewards offered by the school have the least meaning. Arthur L. Stinchcombe, *Rebellion in a High School*, Chicago, Quadrangle Books, 1964.

[4] Surgeon General's Scientific Advisory Committee on Television and Social Behavior, *Television and Growing Up: The Impact of Televised Violence*, Washington, D.C., U.S. Public Health Service, 1972, p. 83.

[5] Suzanne Keller, "The Social World of the Urban Slum Child: Some Early Findings," *American Journal of Orthopsychiatry*, 33, no. 5 (October 1963), 823–831.

[6] For a description of how educational goals are translated into television programming for "Sesame Street," see Gerald S. Lesser, "Learning, Teaching, and Television Production for Children: The Experience of Sesame Street," *Harvard Educational Review*, 42, no. 2 (May 1972), 232–272. For an evaluation of what is learned by "Sesame Street" viewers see

Samuel Ball and Gerry Ann Bogatz, *The First Year of Sesame Street: An Evaluation*, Princeton, Educational Testing Service, 1970, pp. 352–354.

[7] Surgeon General's Advisory Committee, *op. cit.*, p. 69.

[8] Simon and Grant, *op. cit.*, table 41, p. 34.

[9] For a description of a preschool model that meets these criteria, see Carl Bereiter and Siegfried Engelmann, *Teaching Disadvantaged Children in the Preschool*, Englewood Cliffs, N.J., Prentice-Hall, 1966. For evaluations of Head Start programs see Westinghouse Learning Corporation, *The Impact of Head Start and Evaluation of the Effect of Head Start on Children's Cognitive and Affective Development*, Washington, D.C., U.S. Office of Economic Opportunity, 1969; Marshall S. Smith and Joan S. Bissell, "Report Analysis: The Impact of Head Start," *Harvard Educational Review*, 40, no. 1 (February 1970), 98–99.

[10] For example, see Benjamin S. Bloom, *Stability and Change in Human Characteristics*, New York, Wiley, 1964; Robert D. Hess and Virginia D. Shipman, "Early Experience and the Socialization of Cognitive Modes in Children," *Child Development*, 36, no. 4 (December 1965), 869–886.

[11] Joseph A. Kahl, "Educational and Occupational Aspirations of 'Common Man' Boys," *Harvard Educational Review*, 23, no. 3 (Summer 1953), 186–203.

[12] Dan Miller and Guy E. Swanson, *Changing American Parent*, New York, 1958.

[13] Susan S. Stodolsky and Gerald Lesser, "Learning Patterns in the Disadvantaged," *Harvard Educational Review*, 37, no. 4 (Fall 1967), 578; Gerald S. Lesser, Gordon Fifer, and Donald Clark, *Mental Abilities of Children from Different Social Class and Cultural Groups*, University of Chicago Press, 1965.

[14] James S. Coleman, *et al.*, *Equality of Educational Opportunity*, Washington, D.C., U.S. Office of Education, 1966, p. 20. See also Marion F. Shaycroft, *The High School Years, Growth in Cognitive Skills*, Pittsburgh, Pa., University of Pittsburgh Press, 1967.

[15] Hess and Shipman, *op. cit.*

[16] *Ibid.*, p. 870.

[17] Basil Bernstein, "Social Class and Linguistic Development: A Theory of Social Learning," in A. H. Halsy, J. Floud, and C. A. Anderson, *op. cit.*, pp. 288–314. But see Dillard who points out that Bernstein overlooked the fact that lower-status groups have elaborated codes of their own. J. L. Dillard, *Black English: Its History and Usage in the United States*, New York, Random House, 1972, p. 38.

[18] For a discussion of some of these programs see Dillard, *ibid.*, pp. 265–294. On black English see William Labov, *Language of the Inner City*, Philadelphia, University of Pennsylvania Press, 1972.

[19] See Theodore Anderson and Mildred Boyer, *Bilingual Schooling in the United States*, Washington, D.C., U.S. Office of Education, 1970, vols. I and II. The U.S. Supreme Court recently ruled that school districts receiving federal funds are obligated to provide special English language

instruction to pupils who do not speak English. Failure to do so "denies them of meaningful opportunity to participate in public educational programs in violation of Civil Rights Act of 1964." See Lau v. Nichols, *et al.*, *Supreme Court Reporter*, 94, no. 8 (February 1974), 786–791.

[20] See, among others, Coleman, *et al.*, *op. cit.*, Kahl, *op. cit.*, Miller and Swanson, *op. cit.*, Bernard Rosen, "The Achievement Syndrome: A Psychocultural Dimension of Social Stratification," *American Sociological Review*, 21, no. 2 (April 1956), 203–211; Audrey James Schwartz, "A Comparative Study of Values and Achievement: Mexican-American and Anglo Youth," *Sociology of Education*, 44, no. 4 (Fall 1971), 438–462; Fred L. Strodbeck, "Family Integration, Values, and Achievement," in David McClelland, *et al.*, eds., *Talent and Society*, New York, Van Nostrand Reinhold, 1948, pp. 135–194; Alan B. Wilson, "Sociological Perspectives on the Development of Academic Competence in Urban Areas," in A. Harry Passow, ed., *Urban Education in the 1970's: Reflections and a Look Ahead*, New York, Teachers College Press, Columbia University, 1971, pp. 120–140.

[21] Audrey James Schwartz, "The Culturally Advantaged: A Study of Japanese-American Pupils," *Sociology and Social Research*, 55, no. 3 (April 1971), 341–355.

[22] Justin Aronfreed, "The Concept of Internalization," in David A. Goslin, ed., *Handbook of Socialization Theory and Research*, Skokie, Ill., Rand McNally, 1969, p. 272. Critics of competition as a means of fostering academic achievement include James Davis, "The Campus as a Frog Pond: An Application of the Theory of Relative Deprivation to Career Decisions of College Men," *American Journal of Sociology*, 72, no. 1 (July 1966), 17–31; John W. Meyer, "High School Effects on College Intensions," *American Journal of Sociology*, 76, no. 1 (July 1970), 59–70; Joel I. Nelson," High School Context and College Plans: The Impact of Social Structure on Aspirations," *American Sociological Review*, 37, no. 2 (April 1972), 143–148.

[23] James S. Coleman, "Academic Achievement and the Structure of Competition," *Harvard Educational Review*, 29, no. 4 (Fall 1959), 349.

[24] James S. Coleman, "New Incentives for Schools," in J. W. Guthrie and E. Wynne, eds., *New Models for American Education*, Englewood Cliffs, N.J., Prentice-Hall, 1971, p. 83. According to several observers, the Soviet Union is using intergroup competition and collective rewards in their schools to great effect. *Ibid.*, p. 84. However, none of these proposals address the question of how team members are selected in the first place.

[25] On pattern variables, see chap. 1.

[26] Jean Jacques Rousseau, *Émile*, trans. William H. Payne, New York, Appleton, 1918.

[27] David Bakan, "Adolescence in America: From Idea to Social Fact," in Jerome Kagan and Robert Coles, eds., *Twelve to Sixteen: Early Adolescence*, New York, Norton, p. 73.

[28] August B. Hollingshead, *Elmtown's Youth*, New York, Wiley, 1949, p. 6.

[29] For example, in the decade of 1960s there were 13.8 million more people in the 14 to 24 year-old age group than in the 1950s. This represents a 52 percent increase in the number of adolescents—a reflection of the post-World War II "baby boom." On the demography of youth see Report of the Panel on Youth of the President's Science Advisory Committee, *Youth: Transition to Adulthood*, Washington, D.C., Office of Science and Technology, Executive Office of the President, 1973, pp. 45–64.

[30] G. Stanley Hall, *Adolescence: Its Psychology and Its Relations to Physiology, Anthropology, Sociology, Sex, Crime, Religion, and Education*, New York, Appleton, 1904. In this influential two-volume work Hall depicts adolescence as a period of "storm and stress" in which the individual's biological stage of development brings him into "inescapable" conflict with society and in which his uncontrollable alternation between contradictory emotional tendencies brings him into conflict with himself. Hall's view of tempestuous adolescence as a biological inevitability has persisted in many quarters although empirical evidence to support his thesis has not been forthcoming.

[31] Coleman, *et al.*, *op. cit.*, "Equality"; Alan B. Wilson, "Educational Consequences of Segregation in a California Community," in U.S. Commission on Civil Rights, *Racial Isolation in the Public Schools*, appendix, Washington, D.C., 1967, pp. 165–206.

[32] The extent of national adolescent norms is shown in a study of 10 Illinois high schools of varying urbanization and socioeconomic status: most pupils in every school granted social prestige on the basis of participation in sporting and social events and on general physical attractiveness. James S. Coleman, *The Adolescent Society: The Social Life of the Teenager and Its Impact on Education*, New York, Free Press, 1961. For similar findings from two separate case studies see Hollingshead, *op. cit.*; C. Wayne Gordon, *The Social System of the High School*, New York, Free Press, 1957.

[33] Ralph H. Turner, *The Social Context of Ambition*, San Francisco, Chandler, 1964.

[34] Gary Schwartz and Don Merton, "The Language of Adolescents: An Anthropological Approach to the Youth Subculture," *American Sociological Review*, 72, no. 5 (March 1967), 453–468.

[35] Ralph H. Turner, *Family Interaction*, New York, Wiley, 1970, pp. 396–397.

[36] This point is made by Campbell in discussing parents who, by adopting adolescent slang and other fads, undermine their symbolic significance for peer-group identification. "More extreme instances of expressive behavior are encouraged by adults who, by imitating adolescent conduct and language, rob them of their meaning and value." Ernest Q. Campbell, "Adolescent Socialization," in David A. Goslin, ed., *Handbook*

of Socialization Theory and Research, New York, Rand McNally, 1969, p. 831.

[37] Richard Flacks, *Youth and Social Change*, Chicago, Markham, 1971, pp. 55–56.

[38] Herbert H. Hyman, *Political Socialization: A Study in the Psychology of Political Behavior*, New York, Free Press, 1959.

[39] Campbell, *op. cit.*, p. 829.

7
Toward the equalization of educational opportunity

THE ALLOCATION FUNCTION OF SCHOOLS

The American system of free public schools has traditionally provided one of the few ways to prepare children to move up the occupational ladder and for some to ultimately pass the socioeconomic status of their parents. Paradoxically, schools have also functioned to lock other children into the relative social positions of their birth. Thus school allocation processes take two different and conflicting directions: social mobility for a few on the one hand, and maintenance of the status quo for many on the other.

In his influential paper "The School Class as a Social System," Talcott Parsons points out that schools, in addition to transmitting the dominant culture of a society, perform the function of "manpower allocation."[1] Schools engage in a "sorting and selecting" of pupils for different socialization experiences and, at the conclusion of formal schooling, direct them to the adult social positions for which they have been prepared and are presumably best qualified. In so doing, schools provide societies with personnel to fill their roles, and at the same time, define the life chances of individuals.

Allocation to occupational roles through formal education occurs to some extent in all societies that have separate educational institutions, but this function of schools is most prevalent in complex, industrial nations which require high levels of technological skills in many of their occupations. Schools in these societies not only have the responsibility for giving most people a minimum level of competence, but for selecting people to receive advanced formal education and for certifying their capabilities.

In the United States, elementary and secondary schools sort and select pupils, screening them for entry into traditional institutions of higher education. The U.S. Office of Education estimates that of the cohort of pupils enrolled in fifth grade in 1961, three-fourths graduated from high school in 1969, and about 45 percent entered college the following fall.[2] Colleges and universities also perform sorting and selecting functions. It was estimated that about half these entering freshmen would not complete their degree requirements.[3] Of those who did, some would be channeled into further education in graduate schools.

By the time pupils reach secondary school, variations in aptitudes, talents, and interests have become manifest. Presumably it is on this basis that they are encouraged through guidance procedures, school grades, and other reinforcements to choose educational programs in which they seem to have the highest probabilities for success. Pupils who by the ninth grade demonstrate little academic ability are usually encouraged to choose practical courses to prepare them for the world of work, whereas others are prepared for further studies. However, low-achieving pupils who want and expect to go to college are often allowed to enter academic programs if they can master college preparatory courses such as advanced mathematics and foreign languages.

Unless they have demonstrated unusual academic talent, college attendance is not as readily expected of lower-class and some racial-ethnic-minority children as it is of those with middle-class backgrounds. Even then the proportion of high-ability, low-income children who attend college is smaller than the proportion of low-ability, high-income children who do.[4] Counselors are reluctant to start pupils on a college-bound track which might lead them to "frustration and despair," and many assert that it is kinder to provide career education to pupils from low-income families so that they will have salable skills upon school completion. Some inner-city schools carry this view to extreme: one black college student reported to the author that not only was there no college information available to her from her racially segregated secondary school, but that the counselor had arranged for a spokesman from a local employment agency for domestics to address the senior girls in her graduation class.

Malcolm X records a similar attitude on the part of a white

teacher in his racially integrated junior high school. Upon being told that young Malcolm, who was a top pupil in the class, wanted to be a lawyer, the teacher reportedly gave him the following advice: "But you've got to be realistic about being a nigger. You need to think about something you *can* be. . . . Why don't you plan on carpentry . . . you'd get all kinds of work."[5]

Pupils from higher-status homes, regardless of academic performance, usually go to college. This is due to a number of factors. Not the least among them is that college-going is ascribed to children from the upper-middle and upper classes. Everyone assumes they will acquire high levels of education and gain occupational positions equivalent to those of their parents. Parents, school counselors, and teachers cooperate to find one of the many suitable institutions from which the baccalaureate can be attained, if necessary, with minimal academic performance.[6]

While it is becoming increasingly common for decisions about college preparatory studies to be made by school counselors who take into account pupils' expectations, grades, standardized test scores, and deportment, Parsons suggests that the decision between going to college and not going to college is significantly influenced by the pupil's record of performance in elementary school.[7] Evaluations by elementary-school teachers and principals are, in effect, self-fulfilling prophecies because teachers acquire expectations of their pupils from information given them by previous teachers, and they then relate to their pupils and judge them accordingly.

The self-fulfilling prophecy

In education, the self-fulfilling prophecy is extremely poignant since children from different backgrounds differ in their initial abilities to meet school expectations. Many teachers begin to evaluate the educational potential of pupils upon school entry, little realizing that predictions are probably based more on deportment and developed talent than on innate capability. Self-fulfilling prophecies occasionally work to the advantage of pupils who exhibit unexpected ability and conforming behavior. Children from low-income families who perform at average levels, for example, may be perceived as extremely able by those who prejudge them in accordance with social-class stereotypes. A quite average performance in this instance can initiate positive prophecies about a child's future.

Teachers often communicate their expectations to individual pupils and to other pupils in their classes. Pupils then shape expectations about themselves to be more in line with those of their teachers and peers. In this manner they fashion their behavior. The effects of positive self-fulfilling prophecies in the primary grades of a predominantly Mexican-American school were investigated by Rosenthal and Jacobson. They gave teachers fictitious test results to indicate that selected pupils were entering into a period of rapid intellectual growth and should be expected to show considerable academic progress. Although there is some dispute about all of the authors' conclusions, it seems clear that many of the first- and second-grade pupils whom teachers expected to bloom did in fact gain significantly in intelligence-test scores over the year compared to pupils for whom similar predictions had not been made. This research is reported in a book appropriately titled *Pygmalion in the Classroom* after the play of George Bernard Shaw. It closes with Shaw's famous words: ". . . the difference between a lady and a flower girl is not how she behaves, but how she's treated."[8]

Many studies have documented the phenomenon that school allocation is not independent of children's home background and that sorting and selecting often stratify them in very much the same positions their families hold in the larger society. From the community studies of the Lynds' and Warner before World War II to the massive Equality of Educational Opportunity survey by the U.S. Office of Education in the 1960s, schools have been shown to be a transmission belt for many pupils in which they are generally allocated out into society in about the same rank order in which they entered into school.[9] There are exceptions to be sure, but, in the main, schools do not seem to fulfill the American dream for very many children from lower-socioeconomic–status families.

LOCAL INFLUENCES ON THE QUALITY OF SCHOOLING

Of the factors that contribute to unequal educational opportunities within American public schools, the geographic area in which the school is situated is perhaps the most significant. Where a school is located strongly influences tangible and intangible resources available for education, personal qualities and behaviors of the school staff, characteristics of the student body, and the formal curriculum. These factors interact and greatly affect one another. In combination they create the school social climate which is in a very real sense a latent curriculum that rivals the formal school curriculum in its socialization impact.

Local resources

Some neighborhoods provide a more hospitable educational environment than others, both because of the resources they allocate to formal socialization in and out of school and because of their normative milieu. Children who grow up in higher-status compared with lower-status areas have more libraries, museums, concerts, and theaters available to them, as well as a greater range of adult-supervised activities. They also attend more expensive schools which attract teachers with greater skills and have pupils who demonstrate high levels of academic achievement when they enter school and show large gains at every grade level.[10]

Segregated living patterns in American cities create residential neighborhoods which are homogeneous within themselves and often radically different from one another. Homogeneity is further reinforced by families that elect to live in a given area because of its social character. For example, educationally aware parents who are economically able to do so are attracted and move to areas with rich socialization resources for their children.

Since schools reflect the overall culture within their attendance boundaries, individual families with unique characteristics will either reap the benefits or the misfortunes of their place of residence, depending on their point of view. Thus, some lower-income families may enjoy the quality of education offered in white middle-class neighborhoods and other families may feel alien and oppressed by the social climate of middle-class schools.

The socialization objectives of schools differ somewhat in different locales. Schools in low-income areas tend to be concerned with custodial care and with meeting some of the physical needs of their pupils. They are also concerned to a large extent with socialization to the norms of the middle classes. This is one reason that minority parents who want their children to have strong racial or ethnic identification often advocate local neighborhood schools, with control of educational policy in their own hands. In this regard it is important to note that many black and Spanish-surnamed adults, among others, argue that to stress only the dominant American culture in school severely impedes the self-worth and identity of minority children and is largely responsible for their high rate of academic failure. They view local control of neighborhood schools as the only way to bring about needed educational reform.[11]

Schools in affluent areas typically place greater stress on high levels of cognitive achievement since the physical well-being and normative socialization of their pupils are assumed to be provided elsewhere. Mastery of basic studies is sometimes taken for granted in higher-status schools, which are more likely than lower-status schools to introduce esoteric academic studies and some of the "frills" that are assumed to enrich education and add to the quality of life. Stress on athletics may be one of the few activities that most public schools have in common.

The financial resources available for public education also vary from school to school. Expenditures in the United States have been shown to vary among geographic regions, states, school districts, and even among local neighborhoods. In 1970–71, estimated expenditures by state ranged from a high in New York of $1561 per pupil to a low in Alabama of $572.[12] Even when differences in cost of living are taken into account, it seems clear that the state of New York provides more educational opportunities. Gross differences in expenditures appear within states as well. For example, in the county of Los Angeles in 1971–72, the district of Baldwin Park spent an estimated $732 per pupil and Beverly Hills spent $1567.[13]

The fact that the amount of money spent on children's public-school education depends upon where they live has been interpreted by some state courts as a denial of equal opportunity, and therefore, unconstitutional.[14] Even so, socioeconomic bias in the allocation of school resources remains, and children who live in wealthier neighborhoods usually receive a more expensive education than do children who live in poorer ones.

The school staff

The personnel available to schools is largely determined by the area in which schools are located. Since teachers typically prefer assignments in urban or suburban middle-class neighborhoods over poor inner-city or rural areas, these schools usually have first choice. If it is assumed that verbal ability is a measure of teacher quality—and it has been shown to be positively related to pupil achievement—[15] then data from the Equality of Educational Opportunity survey support the view that able teachers are disproportionately distributed to affluent white schools. The average verbal scores of teachers in white schools were found to be consistently higher than those in black schools. These data also show that scores for teachers in the metropolitan compared with nonmetropolitan areas of the South are higher, although differences in teacher ability were not great within other regions of the country.[16]

The effectiveness of teachers as socializing agents is influenced by noncognitive factors as well. The most important of these are teachers' general orientations toward themselves and society and their specific orientations toward their pupils. Once assigned to a school, the attitudes of teachers are sometimes modified by its student body, including its socioeconomic and racial-ethnic composition and the pupil subculture it has developed. Many teachers relate differently to pupils from one peer group or subpopulation than they do to pupils from another. For instance, a study by the U.S. Commission on Civil Rights dealing with teachers' classroom interaction with Anglo and Mexican-American pupils found that the 429 teachers in their sample have more frequent verbal interaction with the Anglo than the Mexican-American pupils. The report also states that ". . . teachers respond positively to Anglos about 40 percent more than they do to Chicano students, [and they] direct questions to Anglo students 21 percent more often than they direct them to Mexican-Americans."[17]

Teachers, in general, prefer to work in schools that have many middle-class pupils, high salary schedules, large fringe benefits, quality resources, and are close to their own homes. They frequently move from school to school in an effort to meet these conditions. It should be noted, however, that the estimated annual teacher turnover rate of one out of three is not entirely the result of movement to better schools. Of the 30 percent of the classroom teachers who are men, many hope to be school administrators and either climb up the organizational ranks of the school or, if they find vertical occupational mobility closed to them, change to different careers. Of the women teachers, two-thirds are married and living with their husbands; they often move in and out of teaching as maternal obligations allow, or move from school to school to accommodate to their husbands' occupational needs.[18]

The location of schools, then, affects their teachers in important ways: it determines who is available and who is selected as part of the staff; it shapes how teachers perform their roles once employed; and it influences the interaction among teachers and between teachers and pupils. These factors, in turn, influence the school's social climate.

The pupils

The most important socialization resources that schools offer pupils is not their teaching staff, but the other pupils in the school. This is due partly to the influence of the student body on the recruitment and behavior of teachers, but, more importantly, it is due to the influence of pupils on one another. The academic expectations, the cognitive and social skills, the values and norms, and the behaviors of individual pupils combine to form a peer subculture which affects most of the student body. It was noted in Chapter 6, that academic behavior is determined not only by home environment, scholastic ability, and academic values, but by the social pressures of classmates as well. In schools where academic performance, intellectualism, and subject-matter competence are emphasized and rewarded, individuals tend to conform to the scholastic norms of the majority and achieve at high levels.[19]

Pupils are most likely to attend college, for example, when they are enrolled in secondary schools with a large proportion of middle-class pupils. In addition to peer pressure toward achievement, these schools usually have many college-oriented pupils, teachers, and counselors, as well as courses that provide practical information about college admission. By contrast, lower-status schools are oriented toward immediate employment upon leaving school. Their teachers often have low expectations of pupils, and pupils have low expectations of themselves and of one another. Information pertaining to college is commonly lacking and courses required by colleges may be absent. Further, the occasional pupil who applies to college is sometimes disadvantaged because of the stigma college-admission officers attach to lower-status schools. Once admitted, he or she may be handicapped by poor preparation for higher level work.

Accordingly, many educational reformers advocate that every school be socioeconomically integrated so that all children have the opportunity to share in whatever advantages are provided by middle-class schools. However, since some racial and ethnic minorities are disproportionately represented among low-income families, socioeconomic integration of schools cannot come about unless there is racial-ethnic integration as well. This is seen by some as the major stumbling block to socioeconomic integration. Others view racial-ethnic integration as a desirable social policy in and of itself which is in keeping with articulated American values.[20]

In any event, racial-ethnic and socioeconomic integration make the educational resources of higher-status schools equally available to all children. Studies of low-income minority children who have attended integrated schools—which are presumably of higher socioeconomic status and more supportive of formal education[21]—indicate that integration is conducive to academic achievement. For example, the Equality of Educational Opportunity survey shows that racial-ethnic-minority pupils in desegregated schools score significantly higher on objective tests of achievement than comparable pupils in segregated schools.[22] Preliminary evaluations of programs that transport low-income minority children out of local ghetto schools to schools in middle-class communities also indicate that, compared with siblings who stayed behind, more of them attend college and more of these colleges are of high quality.[23] In addition, studies show that adults, both black and white, who went to desegregated schools as children are more tolerant of people from other races than are those who did not.[24]

On the other hand, integrated education seems to have little if any adverse effects on the achievement of white middle-class children, although a few studies suggest that when percentages of low-income minority pupils in a school are very large—70 percent or more—the achievement of some white pupils is negatively affected.[25]

There are several practical problems that sometimes undermine the socialization opportunities of low-income children when they attend desegregated schools. One is the problem already discussed: the effects of the achievement of classmates on pupils' aspirations. It is not uncommon for low-income pupils in desegregated schools to have an appreciably lower conception of their academic abilities than do low-income pupils of comparable achievement who attend segregated schools. This is due to the fact that in integrated schools, low-income pupils often fall in disproportionate numbers to the bottom of the academic pecking order. Their comparative classroom standing then forms the basis for their expectations about themselves, expectations that are reinformed by the expectations they perceive their teachers and classmates have of them. It is sometimes suggested that the elimination of report cards can reduce invidious public comparisons that foster erroneous definitions of the situation and depress educational aspirations. Instead, parent-teacher conferences could substitute for letter grades, and test scores normed on a national student population could provide a more realistic evaluation for individual pupils.

Another problem that sometimes occurs in desegregated schools is that cleavages among adults within school-attendance boundaries are reflected in the school. For example, the disfavor with which some parents view racial-ethnic integration affects the adjustment of their children in desegregated settings. Added to this is the fact that children, like adults, tend to select companions whose background, interest, and educational development are similar to their own. The result of these forces is that desegregated schools often become resegregated, at least informally, and the influences that foster academic achievement never have a chance to permeate the school social climate fully. When this happens it would be well if the school staff could actively encourage social interaction. One argument for the elimination of ability grouping is, in fact, that it often precipitates socioeconomic and racial-ethnic isolation in the classroom.[26]

An integrated teaching staff might also assist in maintaining an integrated student body and perhaps raise the academic achievement and aspirations of low-income minority pupils as well. The presence of faculty members from many subpopulations demonstrates to pupils (and to adults) that people from different backgrounds can and do work together. Further, it makes it easier for pupils to identify viable role models from among the staff, a phenomenon that is usually to their educational advantage. Some of these same benefits could also come from the use of older pupils as tutors and classroom aides, especially since participation in the education of younger classmates increases the sense of efficacy of older pupils.

A NEW INTERPRETATION OF EQUAL EDUCATIONAL OPPORTUNITY

The American system of allocating people to social statuses through education has been characterized by Turner as a "contest" in which higher education and elite social positions are the prizes awarded after many years of competition. Unlike Parsons who suggests that allocation for higher education actually begins in elementary school, Turner believes that the decision to enter college is postponed as long as possible in the belief that pupils will be able to overcome their initial educational disadvantages. The relative lateness of the college decision for American students—European schools often sort pupils as early as age eleven—fosters the faith that anyone regardless of background can earn high social status if he or she is sufficiently motivated. Turner also sees late college-going decisions as contributing to social stability, since pupils are afforded time to acquire American values such as belief in equal opportunity, all the while hoping that they will be chosen to be part of the elite. By the time the selection is formally made, those who are losers in the contest, along with those who are winners, have become too committed to the selection system to rebel against it; they have accepted social mobility as an outcome of schooling and view the prescribed means of attaining it as legitimate.[27]

Experience has shown, however, that to delay sorting pupils until late in their public-school careers does not greatly modify their opportunity to be chosen for further education leading to high status. On the contrary, discrepancies in the average scholastic achievement of children from different subpopulations seem to grow larger as children move through school.[28] Even when children from low-income families are provided with educational resources equal in dollar value to those provided to children from higher-income families, many of the achievement differences between them remain.[29]

This disheartening phenomenon has led to a new interpretation of the concept of equal educational opportunity: one that associates equality with the *outcome* of schooling instead of the traditional view that associates equality with the resources allocated to it.[30] These two interpretations of equality have different underlying assumptions leading to different educational policies. The traditional interpretation is lodged in the notion of fixed intelligence: it holds that all children, regardless of background, should be provided with the same chance to demonstrate and develop their innate talents. On that basis, all have equal opportunity to be selected for further education and for elite social roles.

The newer interpretation puts greater store in the influence of environment on the manifestation of talent: it holds that schools are responsible for developing all of their pupils to the same high level regardless of initially demonstrated ability. It recognizes that pupils do not begin school with the same amount of developed talent, but holds that schools must create educational programs which compensate for the earlier absence of important environmental factors. According to the traditional view, if pupils do not achieve in schools it is because they lack the cognitive ability or the motivation. If they do not achieve in school according to the newer view, it is because schools are inadequate.

Also implicit in the newer interpretation of equality of educational opportunity is the assumption that resources should be diverted from the most to the least able pupils so that those who are educationally disadvantaged will have a fuller opportunity to catch up. This view has led to *Compensatory Education* programs in which schools supply additional resources to some pupils in order to help them to succeed in school. Beginning with the Head Start provision of the Economic Opportunity Act of 1964 and the Elementary and Secondary Education Act of 1965, the policy of the federal government has been to support compensatory education by providing money to be used directly in the education of children from low-income families. In recent years the bulk of expenditures by the U.S. Office of Education has gone for this purpose.[31]

Evaluations of Compensatory Education suggest that the goal of equal educational outcome (defined as the same mean achievement for every subpopulation group of pupils) is not easily, if at all, attainable. A summary compiled by the Rand Corporation of studies of a large number of elementary-school programs concluded that although some of the smaller surveys tend to show modest short-run gains, large surveys of national programs "have shown no beneficial results on average."[32] The Rand review of elementary-school programs, like reviews of Head Start, indicates that educationally disadvantaged pupils show greatest progress in highly structured educational environments with carefully designed programs of "intervention."

UNDERMINING FAMILY INFLUENCE

It is hardly likely that schooling, even if it begins in very early childhood, will ever totally eliminate the effects of home socialization on school achievement. From a review of social mobility studies throughout the world Lipset concludes:

In the Soviet bloc, in Western Europe, in Israel, in the United States, sociologists have found that increased educational resources and access to more and better schooling are not sufficient to make up for the cultural situation of the family and the norms and values the child receives.[33]

How much influence American schools have which is independent of their pupils' home life is difficult to asses since ability to function in school is closely intertwined with prior socialization. Estimates of the unique impact of formal education vary, but most empirical evidence indicates that the influence of schools on pupils' academic achievement is contingent on family background. The bulk of empirical evidence leads to the conclusion that equality of educational opportunity, when construed as equal outcomes of schooling, can be provided only by undermining family influence or by purposely depressing the achievement of educationally advantaged pupils. Whether either of these policies ought to be pursued is a moral question. They do appear however to be inconsistent with widely accepted values such as achievement, freedom, individuality, and work.

Some nations have been more willing than has the United States to take dramatic steps in breaking through the strength of the family in order to mold the next generation to some ideal model. There are several examples to suggest that it is possible to socialize children to a culture other than that of their parents. One example is the Israeli kibbutz in which young *sabras* learn values and norms that are somewhat different from those of their European forebears. This is accomplished by rearing children, including the very young, away from their families for most of each day under the guardianship of carefully selected socializing agents.[34] Another example is Nazi Germany in which school-age children learned values reportedly unlike those of their parents through formal socialization and closely monitored youth groups.

A third example is resocialization, or the acquisition of totally different values through brainwashing. This technique first came to the attention of the Western world with the release by North Korea of American prisoners who had voluntarily signed erroneous confessions of war crimes that they believed to be true at the time. Subsequent investigations of released European and American prisoners from mainland-Chinese prisons document brainwashing processes and attest to their effectiveness. The Chinese have been extremely successful in removing vestiges of their adult prisoners' original cultures and in socializing them to alien values and norms.[35]

These three examples, taken from very different societies, illustrate that it is possible to radically change the culture of a family across generations. In the Israeli example, parents willingly supported the socialization of children to a new culture because they believed it to be essential for survival in a pioneer environment. Whether or not parental support was present in the Nazi example is unimportant since state socializing agents had power to control most of the children's life-space through boarding schools and camps, and they had other potent sanctions at their disposal as well. The Chinese example took place entirely within a closed environment. Although resocialization of adults has generally been viewed as unlikely, with the possible exception of religious conversions, these efforts were successful because captors had absolute control over the experiences of their prisoners and employed strategies that are usually outside the limits of acceptability to the Western world. It seems clear, then, that the effects of family socialization can be substantially reduced.

The questions members of a society must ask are what socialization practices are consistent with its underlying values and whether the ideal of equal opportunity for all children to participate in the larger society has higher priority than the preservation of family subculture.

DEMOCRATIZATION OF HIGHER EDUCATION

Until recently, the cost of higher education has been a severely limiting factor on the amount of education received by children from low-income families. Aside from tuition, other expenses such as books, appropriate clothing, living accommodations, and the money students might have earned if they were employed, have made it difficult if not impossible for many motivated and able young adults to go to college. In addition, proportionately fewer lower-income than higher-income pupils are academically prepared for traditional college programs, and many are not able to meet traditional entrance criteria. In recent years, however, opportunities for less costly higher education and education with less stringent entrance requirements have greatly expanded. These developments now make college attendance a realistic option for many more people.

One example of expanding opportunity is the growing number of *two-year public community colleges* which admit applicants with significantly less educational preparation. Some do not require a high school diploma. These two-year colleges charge little or no tuition and are often designed for commuter students. Like elementary and secondary schools, community colleges engage in sorting and selecting, and provide different kinds of socialization. For students who want to fulfill requirements for entrance into traditional higher-educational institutions they provide a second chance, and for other students they offer various vocational programs. Upon completion of the community college course of study, students are usually allocated into either upper-division college programs or directly into the labor force, depending upon their scholastic record, their motivations and aspirations, and the resources that are available to them.[36]

Another example of expanded opportunity for higher education is the *open-admission policies* of some universities which allow high school graduates to enroll regardless of their demonstrated academic ability. While open admissions has existed in many land-grant colleges, it has only recently been adopted as a way of providing expanded opportunity for educationally disadvantaged students. The City University of New York adopted such a policy in 1969 whereupon the number of students in its entering class doubled that of the previous year.[37] In addition to allowing all graduates of New York City high schools to enroll, CUNY is providing remedial and tutorial courses to assist students who lack adequate academic preparation.

Even without open-admission policies, many institutions actively recruit students from subpopulations that have been underrepresented on their campuses. In order to encourage the entrance of minority students, some universities, including the most prestigious, have developed programs which sometimes include tuition remission and other financial aid, curricula tailored to the special interests and educational needs of minority students, and modification in traditional entrance requirements. Programs such as Upward Bound have actively encouraged high school pupils from low-income minority families to go to college by providing courses at local colleges during the summer and on occasional Saturdays. Upward Bound pupils are taught many of the skills assumed to be helpful in college and are tutored in subjects in which they are weak. In addition, they are given small stipends.[38]

Graduate schools are also attempting to provide fuller educational opportunity. For example, some professional schools have reserved places in their entering classes for minority students and, where necessary, have provided financial assistance and tutorial programs. Intense competition for the limited student places in professional schools has stimulated resentment among people who feel that it is unfair to exclude students who have higher traditional academic qualifications than do the minority students who, for whatever reason, are admitted. Many have questioned the legitimacy of minority quotas in tax-supported institutions and this issue is undergoing a legal test. In fact one lower court ruled that admission to a state-university law school on the basis of subpopulation membership is contrary to the Fourteenth Amendment of the Constitution. However, this decision was reversed by a higher court on appeal.[39]

Since there are vast differences in the quality and content of programs, statistics pertaining to years of education can sometimes be misleading. However the amount of education acquired by members of American minority groups does indeed reflect growing opportunities for higher education. For example, in 1970 the median number of school years completed by nonwhite adults between ages 25 and 29 was 12.2; the median for whites of comparable age was 12.6. The difference between them is considerably less than it was in 1950 when the median school attainment of nonwhites in the same age group was 8.7 years, and the median for whites was

12.2.[40] This decrease in difference between racial groups is due to the substantially higher educational attainment of the current generation of young nonwhite adults over that of their parents, which suggests that, for these groups at least, the opportunities for education have become almost equal to that of whites.

American institutions of higher education have, in fact, made substantial progress in the provision of equal educational opportunity. Although in most industrial nations postsecondary schooling systems are presently changing from elite to mass orientation, in the United States the transition is from mass education to universal access.[41] In a growing number of states, college applicants can easily find a place at least in a junior college, and, once enrolled, they can often transfer. Transfers from junior college, like college graduation, are based largely on academic performance.[42] Indeed equality of opportunity at higher levels of education begins long before college entrance. Aside from economic limitations and racial-ethnic discrimination which are both on the decline, socialization in families and schools determines more than any other factor a young person's capacity to benefit from both the democratization of higher education and its resultant opportunities in the larger society.

NOTES

[1] Talcott Parsons, "The School Class as a Social System: Some of Its Functions in American Society," *Harvard Educational Review*, 29, no. 4 (Fall 1959), 297–318.

[2] Kenneth A. Simon and W. Vance Grant, *Digest of Educational Statistics: 1971 Education*, Washington, D.C., U.S. Department of Health, Education, and Welfare, table 10, p. 9. This is a sizable increase in first-time college enrollments over 1959 when one-third of the eligible age group entered college.

[3] *Ibid.*, p. 8.

[4] Joseph A. Kahl, "Educational and Occupational Aspirations of 'Common Man' Boys," *Harvard Educational Review*, 23, no. 3 (Summer 1953), 186–203.

[5] Malcolm X and Alex Haley, *The Autobiography of Malcolm X*, New York, Grove Press, 1966, p. 36. First published 1965.

[6] There are many schools that fall into this category. For a listing of most degree-granting institutions in the U.S. and their entrance requirements see Alexander W. Astin, *Predicting Academic Performance in College: Selectivity Data for 2300 American Colleges*, New York, Free Press, 1971.

[7] Parsons, *op. cit.*, p. 299.

[8] Robert Rosenthal and Lenore Jacobson, *Pygmalion in the Classroom:*

Teacher Expectations and Pupils' Intellectual Development, New York, Holt, Rinehart & Winston, 1968, p. 176. This work has been subjected to reanalysis by other social scientists who point out some of its methodological limitations. Nevertheless, the "expectancy" effects in grades one and two remain. See, for example, Janet D. Elashoff and Richard E. Snow, eds., *Pygmalion Reconsidered: A Case Study in Statistical Inference*, Worthington, Ohio, Charles A. Jones, 1971.

[9] Robert S. Lynd and Helen M. Lynd, *Middletown: A Study in American Culture*, New York, Harcourt Brace Jovanovich, 1929; W. Lloyd Warner, Robert J. Havinghurst, and Martin B. Loeb, *Who Shall Be Educated?*, New York, Harper & Row, 1944; James S. Coleman, *et al.*, *Equality of Educational Opportunity*, Washington, D.C., U.S. Office of Education, 1966.

[10] On this last point see Coleman, *et al.*, *op. cit.*, pp. 273–275; George W. Mayeske, "Teacher Attributes and School Achievement," *Do Teachers Make a Difference?*, Washington, D.C., U.S. Office of Education, 1970, p. 108.

[11] Henry M. Levin, "The Case for Community Control of the Schools," James W. Guthrie and Edward Wynne, *New Models for American Education*, Englewood Cliffs, N.J., Prentice–Hall, 1971, pp. 143–145. See also Chap. 5 above.

[12] Simon and Grant, *op. cit.*, table 78, p. 59.

[13] "Financial Report, Los Angeles County School District, 1971–72," pp. 193–199.

[14] Serrano v. Priest, *Official California Supreme Court Reports*, 5, 3rd series (1971), 585. But see *San Antonio Independent School District* v. *Rodriguez* in which the U.S. Supreme Court opined that education is not a constitutionally protected issue, and therefore, the equal-protection clause of the Fourteenth Amendment does not apply to the question of school financing. *Supreme Court*, 93 (1973), 1278. However, Superior Court judge Bernard S. Jefferson ruled in April, 1974 that the California public school financing system "is invalid as a violation of the equal-protection-of-the-laws provision of the California Constitution." *Serrano* v. *Priest*, p. 106.

[15] David J. Armor, "School and Family Effects on Black and White Achievement: A Reexamination of the USOE Data," in F. Mosteller and D. P. Moynihan, eds., *On Equality of Educational Opportunity*, New York, Vintage, table 5, p. 192; table 14, p. 213.

[16] Coleman, *et al.*, *op. cit.*, p. 132.

[17] *Teachers and Students: Differences in Teacher Interaction with Mexican-American and Anglo Students*, Washington, D.C., U.S. Commission on Civil Rights, March 1973, p. 43.

[18] Simon and Grant, *op. cit.*, table 54, p. 41.

[19] Edward L. McDill, Edmund D. Meyers Jr., and Leo C. Rigsby, "Institutional Effects on the Academic Behavior of High School Students," *Sociology of Education*, 40, no. 3 (Summer 1967), 199.

[20] See, for example, *Brown* v. *Board of Education of Topeka, U.S.*

Official Reports, 347 (1954), p. 483. Commonly held American values are discussed more fully in chap 1. See also Robin M. Williams Jr., *American Society: A Sociological Interpretation*, 3rd ed., New York, Knopf, 1970, pp. 454–502.

[21] Because black families are poor in larger proportion than are white families, most predominantly black schools have low-income children. An exception is the Windsor Hills school in Los Angeles where 90 percent of the pupils come from middle- and high-income black families. In 1969, the mean I.Q. of its sixth-grade class was 115 points, which is considerably above the national mean. The mean reading achievement score was the same as the national norm. *Los Angeles Times*, 30 September 1969, part 2, p. 25. See also Thomas Sowell, "Black Excellence—The Case of Dunbar High School," *The Public Interest*, 35 (Spring 1974), pp. 3–21.

[22] Coleman, *et al.*, *op. cit.*, p. 302.

[23] David J. Armor, "The Evidence on Busing," *The Public Interest*, no. 28 (Summer 1972), 105–106.

[24] Thomas Pettigrew, "Adult Consequences of Racial Isolation and Desegregation in the Schools," *Racial Isolation in the Public Schools*, vol. 2, Washington, D.C., U.S. Commission on Civil Rights, 1967, pp. 211–241.

[25] Eric A. Hanushek, *Education and Race: An Analysis of the Educational Production Process*, Lexington, Mass., Heath, 1972, p. 111.

[26] For the relationship between ability grouping and classroom segregation see David L. Kirp, "Schools as Sorters: The Constitutional and Policy Implications of Student Classification," *University of Pennsylvania Law Review*, 121, no. 4 (April 1973), 704–797.

[27] Ralph H. Turner, "Sponsored and Contest Mobility and the School System," *American Sociological Review*, 25, no. 5 (December 1960), 855–867.

[28] Coleman, *et al.*, *op. cit.*, p. 20. See Table 6.1 above.

[29] Harvey A. Averch, *How Effective is Schooling? A Critical Review and Synthesis of Research Findings*, Santa Monica, Calif., Rand, 1972.

[30] These two views have sometimes been termed liberal and radical. Equality of output is most associated with the American political left whereas equality of input is associated with traditional liberalism. See Seymour Martin Lipset, "Social Mobility and Equal Opportunity," *The Public Interest*, no. 29 (Fall 1972), 90–108. For an early explication of these two conceptions of equality, see Martin Trow, "Two Problems in American Public Education," Howard S. Becker, ed., *Social Problems: A Modern Approach*, New York, Wiley, 1966, pp. 76–117.

[31] Simon and Grant, *op. cit.*, table 145, pp. 116–117.

[32] Averch, *op. cit.*, p. 125.

[33] Lipset, *op. cit.*, p. 26.

[34] Bruno Bettleheim, *Children of the Dream*, New York, Macmillan, 1969.

[35] Robert Jay Lifton, *Thought Reform and Psychology of Totalism: A Study of "Brainwashing" in China*. New York, Norton, 1961.

[36] For a sociological study of one community college see Burton R. Clark, *The Open Door College: A Case Study*, New York, McGraw–Hill, 1960.

[37] Martin Mayer, "Higher Education for All? The Case of Open Admissions," *Commentary*, 45, no. 2 (February 1973), 40. See also "Letters from Readers," *Commentary*, 45, no. 5 (May 1973), 4–24; John Valley, "Increasing the Options: Recent Developments in College and University Degree Programs," Princeton, N.J., Educational Testing Service, 1972.

[38] Walter I. Garms, "A Benefit-Cost Analysis of the Upward Bound Program," *The Journal of Human Resources*, 6, no. 2 (Spring 1971), 206–220.

[39] De Funess v. Odegaard, *Official Washington Supreme Court Reports*, 82, 2nd series, 1973, 11. The U.S. Supreme Court refused to rule on this case since the student involved was about to graduate from law school. The issue, then, must await further legal testing.

[40] Simon and Grant, *op. cit.*, p. 9.

[41] Martin Trow, *The Expansion and Transformation of Higher Education*, New York, General Learning Press, 1972, p. 1.

[42] Joseph Ben-David, *American Higher Education: Directions Old and New*, New York, McGraw–Hill, 1972, p. 3.

Bibliography

ALMOND, GABRIEL A., and SIDNEY VERBA. *The Civic Culture: Political Attitudes and Democracy in Five Nations.* Boston: Little, Brown, 1965.

ANDERSON, E. N., JR. "Correspondence: Political, Technical, and Theoretical Comments." *Harvard Educational Review, 39,* no. 3 (Summer 1969), 581–585.

ANDERSON, JAMES G., and WILLIAM H. JOHNSON "Stability and Change Among Three Generations of Mexican-Americans: Factors Affecting Achievement. *American Educational Research Journal, 8,* no. 2 (March 1971), 285–309.

ANDERSON, THEODORE, and MILDRED BOYER. *Bilingual Schooling in the United States.* Washington, D.C.; U. S. Office of Education, I and II, 1970.

ARGYRIS, CHRIS. "The Individual and Organization: Some Problems of Mutual Adjustment." *Administrative Science Quarterly, 2,* no. 1 (June 1957), 1–24.

ARMOR, DAVID J. "The Evidence on Busing." *The Public Interest,* no. 28 (Summer 1972), 105–106.

ARMOR, DAVID J. "School and Family Effects on Black and White Achievement: A Reexamination of the USOE Data." In F. Mosteller and D. P. Moynihan, eds. *On Equality of Educational Opportunity.* New York: Vintage Press, 1972, 168–184.

ARONFREED, JUSTIN. "The Concept of Internalization." in David A. Goslin, ed. *Handbook of Socialization Theory and Research.* Skokie, Ill.: Rand McNally, 1969, 263–323.

ASTIN, ALEXANDER W. *Predicting Academic Performance in College: Selectivity Data for 2300 American Colleges.* New York: Free Press, 1971.

AVERCH, HARVEY A. *How Effective is Schooling? A Critical Review and Synthesis of Research Finding.* Santa Monica, Calif.: Rand Corporation, 1972.

BAKAN, DAVID. "Adolescence in America: From Idea to Social Fact." In J. Kagan and R. Coles, eds. *Twelve to Sixteen: Early Adolescence.* New York: Norton, 1972, 73–89.

BALL, RICHARD A. "A Poverty Case: The Analgesic Subculture of the Southern Appalachians." *American Sociological Review, 33,* no. 6 (December 1968), 885–895.

BALL, SAMUEL, and GERRY ANN BOGATZ. *The First Year of Sesame Street: An Evaluation.* Princeton; Educational Testing Service, 1970.

BANDURA, ALBERT, and RICHARD H. WALTERS. *Social Learning and Personality Development.* New York: Holt, Rinehart & Winston, 1963.

BANFIELD, EDWARD C. *The Unheavenly City: The Nature and Future of Our Urban Crisis.* Boston: Little, Brown, 1968.

BANKS, OLIVE. *The Sociology of Education.* New York: Schocken, 1968.

BARON, GEORGE, and ASHER TROPP. "Teachers in England and America." In A. H. Halsey, Jean Floud, and C. Arnold Anderson, eds. *Education, Economy, and Society.* New York: Free Press 1961, 545–557.

BARRY, HERBERT, III; MARGARET K. BACON; and IRVIN L. CHILD. "A Cross-Cultural Survey of Some Sex Differences in Socialization." *Journal of Abnormal and Social Psychology, 55* (1957), 327–332.

BECKER, HOWARD S. "Social Class Variation in the Teacher-Pupil Relationship." *Journal of Educational Sociology, 25* (April 1952), 451–465.

BECKER, HOWARD S. "The Teacher in the Authority System of the Public School." *Journal of Educational Sociology, 27* (November 1953), 128–141.

BEN-DAVID, JOSEPH. *American Higher Education: Directions Old and New.* New York: McGraw-Hill, 1972.

BEREITER, CARL, and SIEGFRIED ENGELMANN. *Teaching Disadvantaged Children in the Preschool.* Englewood Cliffs, N. J.: Prentice-Hall, 1966.

BERELSON, BERNARD, and GARY A. STEINER. *Human Behavior: An Inventory of Scientific Findings.* New York: Harcourt Brace Jovanovich, 1964.

BERNARD, JESSIE. *American Community Behavior.* Rev. ed. New York: Holt, Rinehart & Winston, 1965.

BERNSTEIN, BASIL. "The Role of Speech in the Development and Transmission of Culture." In Gordon J. Klopf and William A. Hohman, eds. *Perspectives on Learning.* New York: Banks Street College of Education, 1967.

BERNSTEIN, BASIL. "Social Class and Linguistic Development: A Theory of Social Learning." In A. H. Halsey, J. Floud, and C. A. Anderson. *Education, Economy and Society.* New York: Free Press, 1961, 288–314.

BETTELHEIM, BRUNO. *Children of the Dream.* New York: Macmillan, 1969.

BIRDWHISTELL, RAY L. *Kinesics and Context: Essays on Body Motion Communication.* Philadelphia: University of Pennsylvania Press, 1970.

BLOOM, BENJAMIN. *Stability and Change in Human Characteristics.* New York: Wiley, 1964.

BLUMER, HERBERT. *Symbolic Interactionism: Perspective and Method.* Englewood Cliffs, N. J.: Prentice-Hall, 1969.

BRONFENBRENNER, URIE. "Socialization and Social Class Through Time and Space." In Eleanor E. Maccoby, *et al.*, eds. *Readings in Social Psychology.* 3rd ed. New York: Holt, Rinehart & Winston, 1958, 400–425.

CALLAHAN, RAYMOND C. *Education and the Cult of Efficiency.* Chicago: University of Chicago Press, 1962.

CAMPBELL, ERNEST G. "Adolescent Socialization." In David A Goslin, ed. *Handbook of Socialization Theory and Research.* New York: Rand McNally, 1969, 821–859.

CAPLOW, THEODORE. *Elementary Sociology.* Englewood Cliffs, N.J.: Prentice-Hall, 1971.

CAUGHEY, JOHN W.; JOHN HOPE FRANKLIN; and ERNEST R. MAY. *Land of the Free: A History of the United States.* New York: Benziger, 1966.

Center for the Study of Public Policy. *Educational Vouchers: A Report on Financing Elementary Education by Grants to Parents.* Cambridge, Massachusetts, 1970.

CHOMSKY, NOAM. *Aspects of the Theory of Syntax.* Cambridge, Mass.: Massachusetts Institute of Technology Press, 1964.

CLARK, BURTON R. *The Open Door College: A Case Study.* New York: McGraw-Hill, 1960.

COHEN, DAVID K. "Immigrants and the Schools." *Review of Educational Research,* 40, no. 1 (February 1970), 13–27.

COLEMAN, JAMES S. "Academic Achievement and the Structure of Competition." *Harvard Educational Review,* 29, no. 4 (Fall 1959), 330–351.

COLEMAN, JAMES S. *The Adolescent Society: The Social Life of the Teenager and its Impact on Education.* New York: Free Press, 1961.

COLEMAN, JAMES S. "New Incentives for Schools." In J. W. Guthrie and E. Wynne, eds. *New Models for American Education.* Englewood Cliffs, N.J.: Prentice-Hall, 1971, 72–90.

COLEMAN, JAMES S., *et al. Equality of Educational Opportunity.* Washington, D.C.: U. S. Office of Education, 1966.

COLLINS, RANDALL. "Functional and Conflict Theories of Educational Stratification." *American Sociological Review,* 36, no. 6 (December 1971), 1002–1019.

Commission on the Reorganization of Secondary Education. *Cardinal Principles of Secondary Education.* Washington, D.C.: National Education Association, 1918.

COOLEY, CHARLES HORTON. *Human Nature and the Social Order.* Rev. ed. New York: Scribner, 1922.

COOLEY, CHARLES HORTON. *Social Organization: A Study of the Larger Mind.* New York: Schocken, 1962, xv. First published in 1909.

CORWIN, RONALD G. *Militant Professionalism: A Study of Organizational Conflict in High Schools.* New York: Appleton, 1970.

CORWIN, RONALD G. *A Sociology of Education.* New York: Appleton, 1965.

COSER, LEWIS. *The Functions of Social Conflict.* New York: Free Press, 1956.

COTTRELL, LEONARD S., JR. "Interpersonal Interaction and the Development of the Self." In David A. Goslin, ed. *Handbook of Socialization Theory and Research.* Skokie, Ill.: Rand McNally, 1969, 543–570.

CREMIN, LAWRENCE A. *The Genius of American Education.* New York: Random House, 1965.

CUMMINGS, ELAINE, and DAVID M. SCHNEIDER. "Sibling Solidarity: A Property of American Kinship." *American Anthropologist, 63,* no. 3 (June 1961), 498–507.

DAHL, ROBERT A. *Modern Political Analysis.* Englewood Cliffs, N.J.: Prentice-Hall, 1963.

DAVIS, JAMES. "The Campus as a Frog Pond: An Application of the Theory of Relative Deprivation to Career Decisions of College Men." *American Journal of Sociology, 72,* no. 1 (July 1966), 17–31.

DEUTSCH, MARTIN. "Happenings on the Way Back to the Forum: Social Science, IQ, and Race Differences Revisited." *Harvard Educational Review, 39,* no. 3 (Summer 1969), 523–557.

DEWEY, JOHN. *Human Nature and Conduct.* New York: Holt, Rinehart & Winston, 1935.

DILLARD, J. L. *Black English: Its History and Usage in the United States.* New York: Random House, 1972.

DOMHOFF, G. WILLIAM. *Who Rules America?* Englewood Cliffs, N.J.: Prentice-Hall, 1967.

DREEBEN, ROBERT. "The Contribution of Schooling to the Learning of Norms." *Harvard Educational Review, 37,* no. 2 (Spring 1967), 211–237.

DREEBEN, ROBERT. *On What Is Learned In School.* Reading, Mass.: Addison-Wesley, 1968.

DUNCAN, BEVERLY, and OTIS DUDLEY DUNCAN. "Minorities and the Process of Stratification." *American Sociological Review, 33,* no. 3 (June 1968), 356–364.

DURKHEIM, EMILE. *Education and Sociology.* Translated by Sherwood D. Fox. New York: Free Press, 1956. First published 1922.

DYMOND, ROSLIND F. "A Scale for the Measurement of Empathic Ability." *Journal of Consulting Psychology, 13* (April 1949), 127–133.

EFFRAT, ANDREW; ROY E. FELDMAN; and HARVEY M. SAPOLSKY. "Inducing Poor Children to Learn." *The Public Interest, 15* (Spring 1969), 106–112.

ELASHOFF, JANET D., and RICHARD E. SNOW, eds. *Pygmalion Reconsidered: A Case Study in Statistical Inference.* Worthington, Ohio: Charles A. Jones, 1971.

ELDER, GLEN H. "Parental Power Legitimation and Its Effects on the Adolescent." *Sociometry, 26*, no. 1 (March 1963), 50–65.

ESPOSITO, DOMINICK. "Consequences of Ability Grouping: Ethnic and Socioeconomic Separation of Children." New York: Teachers College, Columbia University, 1971.

ETZIONI, AMITAI. *A Comparative Analysis of Complex Organizations: On Power, Involvement and Their Correlates.* New York: Free Press, 1961.

ETZIONI, AMITAI, ed. *The Semi-Professions and Their Organization: Teachers, Nurses, Social Workers.* New York: Free Press, 1969.

EVANS, FRANCIS B., and JAMES G. ANDERSON. "The Psychocultural Origins of Achievement and Achievement Motivation: The Mexican-American Family." *Sociology of Education, 46* (Fall 1973), 396–416.

FANTINI, MARIO D. *The Reform of Urban Schools.* Washington, D.C.: National Education Association, Center for the Study of Instruction, 1970.

FLACKS, RICHARD. *Youth and Social Change.* Chicago: Markham, 1971.

FREUD, SIGMUND. *Civilization and Its Discontents.* Translated by James Starchey. New York: Norton, 1962.

FURTH, HANS G. *Thinking Without Language: Psychological Implications of Deafness.* New York: Free Press, 1966.

GANS, HERBERT J. *The Urban Villagers: Group and Class in the Life of Italian Americans.* New York: Free Press, 1962.

GARMS, WALTER I. "A Benefit-Cost Analysis of the Upward Bound Program." *The Journal of Human Resources, 6*, no. 2 (Spring 1971), 206–220.

GERTH, HANS H., and C. WRIGHT MILLS. *From Max Weber: Essays in Sociology.* New York: Oxford University Press, 1946.

GETZELS, JACOB W., and PHILIP W. JACKSON. *Creativity and Intelligence: Explorations with Gifted Students.* New York: Wiley, 1962.

GINSBURG, HERBERT, and SYLVIA OPPER. *Piaget's Theory of Intellectual Development: An Introduction.* Englewood Cliffs, N.J.: Prentice-Hall, 1969.

GITTELL, MARILYN, et al. *School Boards and School Policy: An Evaluation of Decentralization in New York City.* New York: Praeger, 1973.

GLAZER, NATHAN, and DANIEL P. MOYNIHAN. *Beyond the Melting Pot: The Negroes, Puerto Ricans, Jews, Italians, and Irish of New York City.* Cambridge, Mass.: Massachusetts Institute of Technology Press, 1963.

GOLDBERG, MIRIAM; A. H. PASSOW; and J. JUSTMAN. *The Effects of Ability Groups.* New York: Teachers College, Columbia University, 1966.

GOODMAN, PAUL. *New Reformation: Notes of a Neolithic Conservative.* New York: Random House, 1972.

GORDON, C. WAYNE. "The Role of the Teacher in the Social Structure of the High School." *Journal of Educational Sociology, 29* (September 1955), 21–29.

GORDON, C. WAYNE. *The Social System of the High School.* New York: Free Press, 1957.

GORDON, C. WAYNE, and LETA MCKINNEY ADLER. *Dimensions of Teacher Leadership in Classroom Social Systems: Pupil Effects on Productivity, Morale, and Compliance.* Los Angeles: University of California, Department of Education, 1963.

GORDON, MILTON M. *Assimilation in American Life: The Role of Race, Religion, and National Origins.* New York: Oxford University Press, 1964.

GOULDNER, ALVIN W. "Organizational Analysis." In Robert K. Merton, et al., eds. *Sociology Today: Problems and Prospects.* New York: Basic Books, 1959, 400–428.

GREELEY, ANDREW M. *Why Can't They Be Like Us?* New York: Dutton, 1971.

GREEN, ARNOLD W. "The Middle Class Male Child and Neurosis." *American Sociological Review, 11* (February 1946), 31–41.

GREER, COLIN. *The Great School Legend: A Revisionist Interpretation of American Public School.* New York: Basic Books, 1972.

GROSS, NEAL, and ROBERT E. HERRIOT. *Staff Leadership in Public Schools.* New York: Wiley, 1965.

GRUBB, NORTON W., and MARVIN LAZERSON. "Vocational Education in American Schooling: Historical Perspectives." *Inequality in Education, 16* (March 1974), 5–18.

HAGEN, EVERETT E. *On the Theory of Social Change: How Economic Growth Begins.* Homewood, Ill.: Dorsey Press, 1962.

HALEY, JAY. "The Family of the Schizophrenic: A Model System." In G. Handel, ed. *The Psychosocial Interior of the Family.* Chicago: Aldine, 1967.

HALL, G. STANLEY. *Adolescence: Its Psychology and Its Relations to Physiology, Anthropology, Sociology, Sex, Crime, Religion and Education.* New York: Appleton, 1904.

HAMILTON, CHARLES V. "Race and Education: A Search for Legitimacy." *Harvard Educational Review, 38,* no. 4 (Fall 1968), 669–684.

HANUSHEK, ERIC A. *Education and Race: An Analysis of the Educational Production Process.* Lexington, Mass.: Heath, 1972.

HARBISON, FREDERICK, and CHARLES A. MEYERS. *Education, Manpower, and Economic Growth: Strategies of Human Resource Development.* New York: McGraw-Hill, 1964.

HARRINGTON, MICHAEL. *The Other America: Poverty in the United States.* New York: Macmillan, 1963.

HERBERG, WILL. *Protestant-Catholic-Jew: An Essay in American Religious Sociology.* Garden City: Doubleday, 1955.

HESS, ROBERT D., and VIRGINIA D. SHIPMAN. "Early Experience and the Socialization of Cognitive Modes in Children." *Child Development, 36,* no. 4 (December 1965), 869–886.

HESS, ROBERT D., and JUDITH V. TORNEY. *The Development of Political Attitudes in Children.* Garden City, N.J.: Doubleday, 1967.

HOBBES, THOMAS. *Leviathan*. New York: Dutton, 1950. First published in 1651.

HOLLINGSHEAD, AUGUST B. *Elmtown's Youth*. New York: Wiley, 1949.

HULL, C. L. *A Behavior System*. New Haven, Conn.: Yale University Press, 1952.

HUMMEL, RAYMOND C., and JOHN M. NAGLE. *Urban Education in America: Problems and Prospects*. New York: Oxford University Press, 1973.

HÚSEN, TORSTEN, ed. *International Study of Achievement in Mathematics*. New York: Wiley, 1967.

HYMAN, HERBERT. *Political Socialization: A Study in the Psychology of Political Behavior*. New York: Free Press, 1959.

ILLICH, IVAN. *Deschooling Society*. New York: Harper & Row, 1970.

JANOWITZ, MORRIS. *Institution Building in Urban Education*. Phoenix ed. Chicago: University of Chicago Press, 1969.

JEFFERSON, THOMAS. *Crusade Against Ignorance*. Gordon C. Lee, ed. New York: Teachers College, Columbia University, 1961.

JENCKS, CHRISTOPHER, *et al*. *Inequality: A Reassessment of the Effects of Family and Schooling in America*. New York: Basic Books, 1972.

JENSEN, ARTHUR R. "How Much Can We Boost IQ and Scholastic Achievement?" *Harvard Educational Review*, 39, no. 1 (Winter 1969), 1–123.

JOHNSON, HARRY M. *Sociology: A Systematic Introduction*. New York: Harcourt Brace Jovanovich, 1960.

KAGAN, JEROME S. "Inadequate Evidence and Illogical Conclusions." *Harvard Educational Review*, 39, no. 2 (Spring 1969), 274–277.

KAHL, JOSEPH A. "Educational and Occupational Aspirations of 'Common Man' Boys." *Harvard Educational Review*, 23, no. 3 (Summer 1953), 186–203.

KATZ, MICHAEL B. *Class, Bureaucracy and Schools: The Illusion of Educational Change in America*. New York: Praeger, 1971.

KATZ, MICHAEL B. "From Voluntarism to Bureaucracy in American Education." *Sociology of Education*, 44, no. 3 (Summer 1971), 297–332.

KELLER, SUSANNE. "The Social World of the Urban Slum Child: Some Early Findings." *American Journal of Orthopsychiatry*, 33, no. 5 (October 1963), 823–831.

KERR, NORMAN D. "The School Board as an Agency of Legitimation." *Sociology of Education*, 38 (Fall 1964), 34–59.

KIRP, DAVID L. "Schools as Sorters: The Constitutional and Policy Implications of Student Classification." *University of Pennsylvania Law Review*, 121, no. 4 (April 1973), 704–797.

KOHLBERG, LAWRENCE, and ROCHELLE MAYER. "Development as the Aim of Education." *Harvard Educational Review*, 42, no. 4 (November 1972), 449–496.

KOHN, MELVIN L. *Class and Conformity: A Study in Values*. Homewood, Ill.: Dorsey Press, 1969.

LABOV, WILLIAM. *Language of the Inner City*. Philadelphia: University of Pennsylvania Press, 1973.

LANGER, SUSANNE K. *Philosophy in a New Key: A Study in the Symbolism of Reason, Rite and Art.* 3rd ed. Cambridge, Mass.: Harvard University Press, 1969. First published in 1942.

LEACOCK, ELEANOR BURKE, ed. *The Culture of Poverty: A Critique.* New York: Simon & Schuster, 1971.

LENNENBERG, ERIC H. "The Capacity for Language Acquisition." In Jerry A. Fodor and Jerrold J. Katz. *Structure of Language: Readings in the Philosophy of Language.* Englewood Cliffs, N.J.: Prentice-Hall, 1964, 579–603.

LESSER, GERALD S. "Learning, Teaching and Television Production for Children: The Experience of Sesame Street." *Harvard Educational Review,* 42, no. 2 (May 1972), 232–272.

LESSER, GERALD S.; GORDON FIFER; and DONALD CLARK. *Mental Abilities of Children from Different Social Class and Cultural Groups.* Chicago: University of Chicago Press, 1965.

LEVIN, HENRY M. "The Case for Community Control of the Schools." In James W. Guthrie and Edward Wynne. *New Models for American Education.* Englewood Cliffs, N.J.: Prentice-Hall, 1971, 134–148.

LEWIS, OSCAR. *A Study of Slum Culture: Backgrounds for LA VIDA.* New York: Random House, 1968.

LIEBOW, ELLIOT. *Tally's Corner: A Study of Negro Street-Corner Men.* Boston: Little, Brown, 1967.

LIFTON, ROBERT JAY. *Thought Reform and Psychology of Totalism: A Study of "Brainwashing" in China.* New York: Norton, 1961.

LIGHT, RICHARD J., and PAUL V. SMITH. "Social Allocation Models of Intelligence: A Methodological Inquiry." *Harvard Educational Review,* 39, no. 3 (Summer 1969), 484–510.

LINTON, RALPH. *The Cultural Background of Personality.* New York: Appleton, 1945.

LIPSET, SEYMOUR MARTIN. "Social Mobility and Equal Opportunity." *The Public Interest,* no. 29 (Fall 1972), 90–108.

LIPSET, SEYMOUR MARTIN, and ALDO SOLARI. *Elites in Latin America.* New York: Oxford University Press, 1967.

LYND, ROBERT S., and HELEN M. LYND. *Middletown: A Study in American Culture.* New York: Harcourt Brace Jovanovich, 1929.

LYONS, JOHN. *Noam Chomsky.* Modern Masters Series. New York: Viking Press, 1970.

MCARTHUR, CHARLES. "Personality Differences Between Middle and Upper Classes." *Journal of Abnormal and Social Psychology,* 50, no. 2 (March 1955), 247–254.

MCCARTY, DONALD J., and CHARLES E. RAMSEY. *The School Managers: Power and Conflict in American Public Education.* Westport, Conn.: Greenwood, 1971.

MCDILL, EDWARD L.; EDMUND D. MEYERS, JR.; and LEO C. RIGSBY. "Institutional Effects on the Academic Behavior of High School Students." *Sociology of Education,* 40, no. 3 (Summer 1967), 181–199.

MCDILL, EDWARD L. *Structure and Process in Secondary Schools*. Baltimore: Johns Hopkins University Press, 1973.

MAYER, MARTIN. "Higher Education for All? The Case of Open Admissions." *Commentary*, 45, no. 2 (February 1973), 37–47.

MAYESKE, GEORGE W. "Teacher Attributes and School Achievement." *Do Teachers Make a Difference?* Washington, D.C.: U. S. Office of Education, 1970, 100–119.

MEAD, GEORGE HERBERT. *On Social Psychology*. Anselm Strauss, ed. Chicago: University of Chicago Press, 1964. First published in 1956 under title *The Social Psychology of George Herbert Mead*.

MEAD, MARGARET. "Socialization and Enculturation." *Current Anthropology*. 4, no. 2 (April 1963), 184–187.

MERTON, ROBERT K. *Social Theory and Social Structure*. Rev. ed. New York: Free Press, 1957.

MEYER, JOHN W. "High School Effects on College Intentions." *American Journal of Sociology*, 76, no. 1 (July 1970), 59–70.

MICHELSON, STEPHAN. "The Association of Teacher Resourceness with Children's Characteristics." *Do Teachers Make A Difference?* Washington, D.C.,: U. S. Office of Education, 1970, 120–168.

MILLER, DAN, and GUY E. SWANSON. *Changing American Parent*. New York: Wiley, 1958.

MILLS, C. WRIGHT. *The Power Elite*. New York: Oxford University Press, 1956.

MOELLER, GERALD H. "Bureaucracy and Teachers' Sense of Power." *School Review*, 72, no. 3 (Summer 1964), 137–157.

MOORE, WILBERT E. *Social Change*. Englewood Cliffs, N.J.: Prentice-Hall, 1963.

MULHERN, JAMES. *A History of Education*. New York: Ronald Press, 1946.

MURDOCK, GEORGE P. *Social Structure*. New York: Macmillan, 1949.

MYRDAL, GUNNAR. *An American Dilemma*. New York: Harper & Row, 1944.

NEILL, A. S. *Summerhill: A Radical Approach to Child Rearing*. New York: Hart, 1964. First published 1960.

NELSON, JOEL I. "High School Context and College Plans: The Impact of Social Structure on Aspirations." *American Sociological Review*, 37, no. 2 (April 1972), 143–148.

Panel on Youth of the President's Science Advisory Committee. *Youth: Transition to Adulthood*. Washington, D. C.: Office of Science and Technology, Executive Office of the President, 1973.

PARSONS, TALCOTT. "The School Class as a Social System: Some of Its Functions in American Society." *Harvard Educational Review*, 29, no. 4 (Fall 1959), 297–318.

PARSONS, TALCOTT. *Social Structure and Personality*. New York: Free Press, 1964.

PARSONS, TALCOTT. *The Social System*. New York: Free Press, 1951.

PARSONS, TALCOTT, and ROBERT F. BALES. "Theoretical Statement of the

Functional Prerequisites of a Social System." *Working Papers in the Theory of Action.* New York: Free Press, 1953.

PETTIGREW, THOMAS. "Adult Consequences of Racial Isolation and Desegregation in the Schools." In Racial Isolation in the Public Schools, 2. Washington, D.C.: U. S. Commission on Civil Rights, 1967, 211–241.

PIAGET, JEAN. *The Language and Thought of the Child.* Translated by Marjorie Gabin. London: Routledge & Kegan Paul, 1926.

PIAGET, JEAN. *The Moral Judgement of the Child.* Translated by M. Gabin. New York: Free Press, 1948. First published in English, 1932.

PIAGET, JEAN. *The Origins of Intelligence in Children.* Translated by Margaret Cook. New York: International University Press, 1952.

PRAGER, ARTHUR. *Rascals at Large.* Garden City, N.Y.: Doubleday, 1971.

REIMER, EVERETT. *School is Dead: Alternatives in Education.* Garden City, N.Y.: Doubleday, 1972.

RIESMAN, DAVID; NATHAN GLAZER; and ROUL DENNEY. *The Lonely Crowd.* New Haven: Yale University Press, 1950.

ROSEN, BERNARD. "The Achievement Syndrome: A Psychocultural Dimension of Social Stratification." *American Sociological Review,* 21, no. 2 (April 1956), 203–211.

ROSENTHAL, ROBERT, and LENORE JACOBSON. *Pygmalian in the Classroom: Teacher Expectations and Pupils' Intellectual Development.* New York: Holt, Rinehart & Winston, 1968.

ROUSSEAU, JEAN JACQUES. *Émile.* Translated by William H. Payne. New York: Appleton, 1918.

ST. JOHN, NANCY H. "Thirty-Six Teachers: Their Characteristics and Outcomes for Black and White Pupils." *American Educational Research Journal,* 8, no. 4 (November 1971), 635–648.

SAMUELS, JOANNA JENNY. *Bureaucracy of School Districts and Teacher Autonomy.* Doctoral dissertation, Los Angeles: University of California, 1966.

SAPIR, EDWARD. "The Status of Linguistics as a Science." *Language,* 5, 1929.

SCHEFFLER, ISRAEL. *The Language of Education.* Springfield, Ill.: Thomas, 1966.

SCHRAG, PETER. "Appalachia: Again the Forgotten Land." *Saturday Review* (January 27), 1968.

SCHULTZ, THEODORE W. "Investment in Human Capital." *The American Economic Review,* 51, no. 1 (March 1961), 1–17.

SCHWARTZ, AUDREY JAMES. "A Comparative Study of Values and Achievement: Mexican-American and Anglo Youth." *Sociology of Education,* 44, no. 4 (Fall 1971), 438–462.

SCHWARTZ, AUDREY JAMES. "The Culturally Advantaged: A Study of Japanese-American Pupils." *Sociology and Social Research,* 55, no. 3 (April 1971), 341–355.

SCHWARTZ, AUDREY JAMES. *Traditional Values and Contemporary Achieve-*

ment of Japanese-American Pupils. Los Angeles: Center for the Study of Evaluation, University of California, 1970.

SCHWARTZ, GARY, and DON MERTON. "The Language of Adolescents: An Anthropological Approach to the Youth Subculture." *American Sociological Review,* 72, no. 5 (March 1967), 453–468.

SEWELL, WILLIAM. "Some Recent Developments in Socialization Theory and Research." *The Annals of the American Academy of Political and Social Science,* 349 (September 1963), 163–181.

SHAYCROFT, MARION F. *The High School Years, Growth in Cognitive Skills.* Pittsburgh: University of Pittsburgh, 1967.

SHAYCROFT, MARION F., et al. *The Identification, Development and Utilization of Human Talents: Studies of a Complete Age Group—Age 15.* Pittsburgh: University of Pittsburgh, 1965.

SIMON, KENNETH A., and W. VANCE GRANT. *Digest of Educational Statistics: 1971 Edition.* Washington, D.C.: U. S. Department of Health, Education and Welfare, 1972.

SKARD, AASE GRUDA. "Maternal Deprivation: The Research and Its Implications." *Journal of Marriage and the Family,* 27 (1965), 333–343.

SKINNER, B. F. *Science and Human Behavior.* New York: Macmillan, 1953.

SLATER, PHILIP. "Parental Role Differentiation." *The American Journal of Sociology,* 67, no. 3 (November 1961), 296–308.

SMITH, MARSHALL S., and JOAN S. BISSELL. "Report Analysis: The Impact of Head Start." *Harvard Educational Review,* 40 no. 1 (February 1970), 51–104.

SOWELL, THOMAS. "Black Excellence—The Case of Dunbar High School." *The Public Interest,* 35 (Spring 1974), 3–21.

SPITZ, RENÉ A. "Hospitalism." In Rose L. Coser, ed. *The Family: Its Structure and Functions.* New York: St. Martin's Press, 1964.

STINCHCOMBE, ARTHUR L. *Rebellion in a High School.* Chicago: Quadrangle Books, 1964.

STODOLSKY, SUSAN S., and GERALD LESSER. "Learning Patterns in the Disadvantaged." *Harvard Educational Review,* 37, no. 4 (Fall 1967), 546–593.

STRODBECK, FRED L. "Family Integration, Values and Achievement." In David C. McClelland, et al., eds. *Talent and Society.* New York: Van Nostrand Reinhold, 1948, 135–194.

STRYKER, SHELDON. "Symbolic Interaction as an Approach to Family Research." *Marriage and Family Living,* 21, no. 2 (May 1959), 111–119.

SULLIVAN, HARRY STACK. *Conceptions of Modern Psychiatry.* New York: Norton, 1953.

Surgeon General's Scientific Advisory Committee on Television and Social Behavior. *Television and Growing Up: The Impact of Televised Violence.* Washington, D.C.: U. S. Public Health Service, 1972.

SUSSMAN, MARVIN B., ed. *Non-Traditional Family Forms in the 1970's.* Minneapolis: National Council on Family Relations, 1972.

THOMAS, WILLIAM I. *The Unadjusted Girl.* Boston: Little, Brown, 1927.

TOCQUEVILLE, ALEXIS DE. *Democracy in America: The Republic of the United States of America and Its Political Institutions.* Translated by Henry Reeves. New York: Schocken, 1961. First American publication in 1963.

TROW, MARTIN. *The Expansion and Transformation of Higher Education.* New York: General Learning Press, 1972.

TROW, MARTIN. "Two Problems in American Public Education." In Howard S. Becker, ed. *Social Problems: A Modern Approach.* New York: Wiley, 1966, 76–117.

TURNER, RALPH H. *Family Interaction.* New York: Wiley, 1970.

TURNER, RALPH H. *The Social Context of Ambition.* San Francisco: Chandler, 1964.

TURNER, RALPH H. "Sponsored and Contest Mobility and the School System." *American Sociological Review,* 25, no. 5 (December 1960), 855–867.

U. S. Commission on Civil Rights. *Teachers and Students: Differences in Teacher Interaction with Mexican-American and Anglo Students.* Washington, D.C., March 1973.

U.S. Department of Health, Education and Welfare. *Toward a Social Report.* Washington, D.C., 1969.

U. S. President's Committee for the White House Conference on Education: A Report to the President. New York: Greenwald, 1969.

VAIZEY, JOHN, and MICHAEL DEBEAUVAIS. "Economic Aspects of Educational Development." In A. H. Halsey, J. Floud, and C. A. Anderson, eds. *Education, Economy and Society.* New York: Free Press, 1961, 37–49.

VALENTINE, CHARLES A. *Culture and Poverty: Critique and Counterproposals.* Chicago: University of Chicago Press, 1968.

VALLEY, JOHN. "Increasing the Options: Recent Developments in College and University Degree Programs." Princeton: Educational Testing Service, 1972.

WALLER, WILLARD. *The Sociology of Teaching.* New York: Wiley, 1965. Originally published 1932.

WARNER, W. LLOYD; ROBERT J. HAVIGHURST; and MARTIN B. LOEB. *Who Shall Be Educated?* New York: Harper & Row, 1944.

WARNER, W. LLOYD, and PAUL S. LUNT. *The Social Life of a Modern Community.* New Haven, Conn.: Yale University Press, 1941.

WELLER, JACK E. *Yesterday's People: Life in Contemporary Appalachia.* Lexington, Ky.: University of Kentucky, 1965.

WELTER, RUSH. *Popular Education and Democratic Thought in America.* New York: Columbia University Press, 1962.

Westinghouse Learning Corporation. *The Impact of Head Start and Evaluation of the Effect of Head Start on Children's Cognitive and Affective Development.* Washington, D.C.: U. S. Office of Economic Opportunity, 1969.

WHORF, BENJAMIN LEE. *Language, Thought and Reality: Selected Writings of Benjamin Lee Whorf.* John B. Carroll ed. Cambridge, Mass.: Massachusetts Institute of Technology Press, 1956.

WILLIAMS, ROBIN M., JR. *American Society: A Sociological Interpretation,* 3rd ed. New York: Knopf, 1970.

WILLIAMS, ROBIN M., JR. "Individual and Group Values." *The Annals of the American Academy of Political and Social Science,* 371 (May 1967), 20–37.

WILLIAMS, ROBIN M., JR. *Strangers Next Door: Ethnic Relations in American Communities.* Englewood Cliffs, N.J.: Prentice-Hall, 1964.

WILSON, ALAN B. "Educational Consequences of Segregation in a California Community." In U. S. Commission on Civil Rights. *Racial Isolation in the Public Schools, Appendix.* Washington, D.C.: 1967, 165–206.

WILSON, ALAN B. "Sociological Perspectives on the Development of Academic Competence in Urban Areas." In A. H. Passow, ed. *Urban Education in the 1970's: Reflections and a Look Ahead.* New York: Teachers College Press, Columbia University, 1971, 120–140.

WILSON, ALAN B. "Social Stratum Differences and Sex Differences." Mimeographed. Berkeley, University of California, 1966.

WIRTH, ARTHUR G. *Education in the Technological Society.* Scranton, Pa.: Intext Educational Publishers, 1972.

WITKIN, HERMAN A. "Social Influence in the Development of Cognitive Style." In David A. Goslin, ed. *Handbook of Socialization Theory and Research.* Skokie, Ill.: Rand McNally, 1969, 687–706.

WRONG, DENNIS. "The Oversocialized Conception of Man in Modern Sociology." *American Sociological Review,* 26, no. 2 (April 1961), 183–193.

X, MALCOLM and ALEX HALEY. *The Autobiography of Malcolm X.* New York: Grove Press, 1966. First published in 1965.

Index

75 76 77 9 8 7 6 5 4 3 2 1